THE DEAFENING SILENCE

A Memoir

By
Rosemarie Manes

ISBN: 1-4107-3204-5 (e-book)
ISBN: 1-4107-3205-3 (Paperback)

Library of Congress Control Number: 2003091543

This book is printed on acid free paper.

Printed in the United States of America
Bloomington, IN

The Deafening Silence
Rosemarie Manes

1stBooks - rev. 06/10/03

TESTIMONIALS

The Deafening Silence is a riveting story, powerfully told. By crafting the plot from her child's viewpoint, Rosemarie Manes takes the reader by the hand and ushers them through this painful period in her young life and the lives of her family. She does not let go and I, as a reader, felt completely connected to Manes and her plight.

The minuscule details she incorporates, with regard to her day-to-day existence, seem almost overpowering. Yet, it is just this kind of drawing out of the storyline, that provides the strength, and depth it needs to stand as a uniquely told memoir.

She has constructed this story with such skill and passion that it extracts from the reader the very feelings she, as a child, felt while grappling with terrible family secrets. She could not stop living this story and I could not stop reading it. It made me cry. It made me think. It gave me hope. It works!

Nancy Baumgartner, Author – Journalist

Manes' story told simply, directly and with amazing detail, transported me back to my own similar circumstances of childhood and growing up. This moving book began my journey to acceptance of my own father's suicide.

Carole

ACKNOWLEDGMENTS

There are so many to acknowledge, but so little space. But especially:

Emily Hanlon, gifted novelist herself, who taught me to believe in myself as a writer.

Two very near and dear therapist friends, Betty Hughes and Kass Gunn, who gave me nonjudgmental support.

My sister, Josephine, who listened to the early pages with curiosity and love.

My daughter, Audrey, and her family, my son, John, and his family, have been my inspiration.

My husband, John, who listened to every rewrite and cheered me from the first to the last page.

You have helped me recall a child's wonder.
I am blessed.
Thank You God.

DEDICATION

This book is dedicated to my brothers and sisters — Ralph, Trudy, Grace, Christine (deceased), Patrick, George, John (deceased), Carmella, Josephine, Antoinette, and Anna.

Also, I dedicate this book to our mother whose love and tenacity kept the family together. Her example has taught me how to love.

Chapter 1

MY SKINNY ELEVEN-YEAR-OLD BODY is hiding behind the dining room doorway on this South Philadelphia cloudy Wednesday afternoon, May 11, 1955, and that's because I don't want Mommy and my oldest sister, Trudy, to know I'm watching. Trudy's got her head buried in Mommy's lap and she's crying in a way I never heard her cry before. Her crying's more like sobbing and wailing at the same time, it's coming from way down deep. Listening to her makes me feel sick to my stomach; it's reminding me of an Easter Saturday two years ago when I was making friends with a little lamb in a wooden cage in front of the butcher shop next door to my Daddy's produce store. For the life of me I couldn't understand why Daddy kept telling me not to get attached to that little lamb no matter how cute I thought she was. I ignored Daddy and kept feeding her lettuce leaves and petting her, too. I had just ran out of lettuce leaves when the butcher shop's cellar door opened and Joe, the butcher, came up from the cellar.

That little lamb started going, "Baaaaahhh! Baaaaahhh!"

I began to giggle cause I thought it was so cute, but when Joe reached into the cage and lifted that lamb to his chest, I stopped giggling. The tiny lamb started kicking like she was throwing a temper tantrum; when I looked into her bulging red eyes, I started crying cause I never knew any living thing could be that afraid. Then she started to scream and, as I looked at Joe, I wondered how it was that he could turn a deaf ear to the lamb's wailing. But he did. He just carried her down into the cellar and slowly closed the door over them.

The door being closed didn't stop that lamb's screams from reaching my ears, and the more she screamed, the louder she got. Her screams were so loud that they started hurting my bad ear, and only cause I was so scared, I went and stood next to my Daddy. He put his hand on my shoulder. Once he patted my head, I was finally able to admit to myself that the little lamb was going to slaughter. Even though I wanted to save her, I knew I couldn't. I felt so sick to my stomach. As I started rubbing my burning eyes, Daddy gave me a dollar and told me to go to the drugstore and buy him a pack of Lucky Strike cigarettes and buy myself a Mound's coconut candy bar, my absolute favorite candy. I put the dollar in my dress pocket, but before

1

I ran across Seventh Street, I listened once again for the screams of that baby lamb. All I heard was numbing silence coming out of the cellar of the butcher shop.

I just can't get that baby lamb outta my mind as I'm watching my Mom let Trudy cry and cry and cry some more. I don't ever remember my Mom letting any of us twelve kids cry like that. Now don't get me wrong, cause I have a very nice Mom who sometimes gives us hugs and tissues when we cry. But she never sits down with us and lets us carry on, especially when she's got cooking on the stove like she does right now.

I get scared, almost like the way I did listening to that lamb, as Mommy pushes Trudy's wavy hair behind her ears and, in a hushed tone, says, "Bella mia, what's wrong?"

Trudy says, and she's stammering like it's the hardest thing in the world to talk, "Yesterday when-when-when I-I-I was at work, I looked out the office window and s-saw Daddy sitting on the park bench. I-I-I-I went outside and sat with-with him."

"What did he say?"

Trudy whispers, "He said, 'I can't let them win! I just can't!' W-When I asked him what he was talking about, he turned his back towards me and rambled on j-just like I wasn't there. And he wouldn't s-say who he meant. But he was scared, Mom. Who? Who could he mean?"

Mom's eyes get big, but she doesn't answer. Then, she tries to put her arms around Trudy, but my eighteen-year-old sister won't let her.

Instead, Trudy stares at the ceiling, and screams out, "I shoulda told somebody!" She vomits a blood-curdling wail that vibrates against the dining room walls and without hardly knowing it, I'm sobbing, too. I try to stop crying these big tears that hurt so bad, but I can't. Not just cause Trudy's crying, but cause there's something terrible about what she said about my Daddy. I'm so scared, I don't even realize I've walked into the dining room and am standing by Grandma's sewing machine. I realize it when I see Trudy wipe her tears with Mom's apron. She creases her forehead, clears her throat, stands in her stocking feet and faces me.

Mom's looking at me, too, now, but she don't say anything. She just smooths her apron and walks into the kitchen.

I know no one's going to tell me anything unless I ask, so I yell, "What's wrong?"

2

Trudy, with her sad eyes on me, rubs her nose and says, "Daddy's in the hospital again."

"Why?"

"He hurt himself and they had to operate."

"What happened?"

"Daddy cut his chest twice near his heart and ate DDT."

"What's DDT?"

"It's poison."

"Poison! How could Daddy put poison in his own mouth?"

Trudy doesn't say anything, and I start shaking off the chills running through my body as I think, Huuuhh! I wonder if he put that poison right in his mouth straight out of the bottle. Maybe he used a spoon or something like that so he could put it all the way in the back of his throat so he couldn't taste how bad it was.

This is what I'm thinking, but out loud, I'm screaming, "Why would Daddy do such a thing to himself?"

As soon as those words come out of my mouth, I'm sorry I said them so loud, cause Trudy's darting her eyes like I gotta remember I'm not the only person in the house. But it's hard not to talk cause I have a hundred questions in my head. And the first one is how this don't make no sense. Mommy always says Daddy's very, very fussy when it comes to what he puts into his stomach. She even has to fix only certain foods in a certain way and only on certain days of the week. So how could my Daddy eat poison?

Moving closer to Trudy, I whisper, "Is he gonna be all right?"

"Mom says he's gonna be fine."

I think I should be relieved, but I'm not. Not any part of me moves, not even an inch, but inside my head thoughts are speeding like a racing car. I can't stop wondering how my own father could put a knife right near his own heart. And I think he couldn't. I bet somebody did it to him. I think it so clearly that for a minute I'm sure I said it out loud, but I can tell by Trudy's expression that I didn't say anything. She's looking, sad and scared, into the kitchen. I look, too. When I see Mommy, I get down on myself as I think, Trudy just told you Mommy said Daddy did this to himself. So just stop!

But I can't stop. My mind is trying to figure out what DDT poison looks like. Maybe it's soft and powdery just like the Borax Acid Mommy uses to kill ants. Which makes me start fidgeting with my fingers, and my mouth goes dry. If Daddy put something like that into

3

his mouth, I bet it burned going down and it musta tasted like a bunch of rotten eggs . . .

I get a cold feeling all over me like somebody just walked on my grave and after my body stops shaking, I run into the kitchen and, with my eyes glued on her floured hands, I watch as Mom flips a veal cutlet through the egg wash, then dredges it through the flour. Watching her brings me great comfort, but soon I tire and walk over to the sink, stand on my tiptoes and reach for a glass that's on the shelf. As I do, my foot kicks something hard. When I look, I can hardly believe I'm seeing a gray metal bucket under the sink. I can't see what's in it, but as I drink my water, I think if there's anything around our house that my Mom can't stand it's a bucket left in the kitchen. I put my empty glass in the sink, and bend down to get a closer look. There's something soaking in there, but it's hard to see cause the water's got this funny red color.

Just as my stomach starts feeling queasy, Trudy asks in a twitching voice that makes me look up, "Mom! When's Daddy coming home?"

Mom keeps looking at the veal cutlet she's dredging and she says like it's just about the worst thing I ever heard her say, "I think he's gonna be away for a long time this time. He needs to be somewhere where he can't hurt himself."

This time. That sick feeling in my stomach grows worse. It was only six months ago when Daddy was in the mental hospital and even though it was only for a few weeks, it seemed like forever cause I missed him so much. And now, if he's gonna be away for a very long time, I don't know how I'm gonna stand it.

I know Trudy feels just like me cause tears are running down her face just like they're running down mine. But Mom, she keeps dredging the veal cutlet and says, "Once he's doing better, I'm sure they'll let him come home on weekends." She reaches for one of the two brown shopping bags sitting on the chair next to her and empties some green leafy broccoli rabe onto the table. But she's not looking at the broccoli rabe. She's staring at the ceiling. I don't know why cause there's nothing up there. So I'm really relieved when she starts pulling at the green leaves of the broccoli rabe. "I'm sure he'll be home on weekends," she says.

I put a very big smile on my face and tell myself, "My Dad's gonna be just fine."

But I start worrying all over again when Trudy moans, "What if he doesn't make it?" But I stop worrying when I see Trudy laughing through her tears as she's saying, "Oh, he's gonna be all right. I'm just being silly."

Mom stops pulling those leaves off the stems, looks at Trudy and smiles, too. Then she faces the stove, places some veal cutlets in the hot frying pan and says, "Trudy, get the garlic ready."

Trudy reaches for the garlic that's on the counter top. She takes a few steps towards the white cabinet, the one with the red trim all around it, and as she opens the drawer, I watch her as she clangs around looking for the only knife that Mommy uses to cut garlic. Then, like she's thinking about something else, she stops making noise. I move the wooden kitchen chair out of my way and stand next to Trudy and watch as she stares at all those knives. Even though she don't say it, I know she's thinking about the knife that Daddy used on himself. Tears form at the corners of her eyes, and once her eyes give up those tears, she puts her arms around me, kisses my forehead and mumbles, "Uhh! I feel so cold. I need a hug."

My arms dangle by my sides as she squeezes me and I want to tell her, "I don't want anybody touching me right now." Instead, I say, "I gotta pee," and pull away. As I run through the dining room, I see my eight-year-old sister, Carmella, sitting on the bottom of the steps with her head resting on her lap.

I quietly place my hand on the banister and whisper, "Carmella."

She looks up at me with tearful eyes. She's got a scared look on her face and I know she's heard us talking about Daddy. I reach for her, but she pushes my hand out of the way, jumps up and runs down the two playroom steps. "Carmella!" I call, but she's running for the screen door and all's I can see is her long brown hair moving like a hurricane.

"Trudy!" I shout. "Carmella just ran out of the house crying her eyes out!" Seconds later I hear the screen door slam again, and I stop feeling so scared for Carmella. I know Trudy's running after her. She'll bring Carmella back home.

It was last summer when my oldest brother, Ralphie, went away to be in the Army. That's when I started sleeping in his bed, which is in the same room where my brother Patrick, who's one year older than I am; Georgie, who's ten and one year younger than I am; and my youngest brother, Johnny, who's eight-and-a-half, also sleep. We're all in the bedroom now trying to sleep. I don't know how long I've been lying on my bed. All I do know is I couldn't eat not one thing at dinner and I can't stop saying over and over in my head, How can my own Daddy put a knife in his chest and eat poison?

My body keeps twisting and turning and my stomach aches. When I can't take it anymore, I pull my knees all the way up to my chest, hold the covers tightly over my crying face and I think, I don't want my Daddy to die! But what if he does?

All this worry is making my head feel like it's gonna burst, and it only stops feeling this way when I remember what my fifth grade teacher, Sister Josephine, says. With her pretty white teeth showing, and with a kind look on her face, she begins, "If you do your best to be good and you want something that's really important, pray and God will answer your prayers."

Quietly, I take my pink rosary beads off the headboard. I don't want to be disturbing my brothers, but I can see they're still up. Johnny's hands are fooling around with Georgie's and I know there's no way Pat could be sleeping for the way the mattress is moving every which way. Then, I hear Pat saying something to the two of them, but I can barely make out what he's saying cause of my bad hearing in my left ear. It's been this way since I had chicken pox when our baby sister, Anna, was born about three years ago.

But then, it's like my loss of hearing isn't going to stand in the way of me listening when, clear as day, Pat screams, "Bucket!"

I make the sign of the cross, turn my back to my brothers, face the wall, and try with all my might to start saying the rosary, but it's the word "bucket" that's going around in my head. I keep seeing the bucket of red water under the sink, I know that's what Pat's talking about, but even though I know, I gotta hear it from Pat. Lifting my head, I whisper, cause I don't want any of my sisters who are sleeping in the next room to hear, "Pat, whatiya talking about?"

His hand gestures for me to leave him alone, but I call out, "Pat! Tell me about the bucket!"

He puts his hand to his mouth, and after he's done biting down on it, he shrieks, "Shut up!"

I bite down on my teeth and scream out, "Tell me about the bucket!"

He punches the mattress and screeches, "Eeeeeeeeeh!"

"Pat! Tell me what you know about the bucket!"

He gets this peculiar look on his face and blurts out, "Mom has Daddy's shirt soaking in it. It's the shirt he wore last night."

I gasp as it begins to make sense and I say half to me, half to Pat, "It's the shirt Daddy wore when he put a knife into his chest? It's Daddy's blood?"

No one answers me and after that none of us talk anymore. I cover my shoulders with my blanket and look out the window. After awhile I begin to pray, "Please dear God! Don't let my Daddy die! I promise I'll do anything, anything at all! Just let him live!" I wipe my eyes with my arms, then wind my rosary beads around my hands, and pray the whole five decades. I make another sign of the cross, but this time with the cross that's hanging from my rosary.

Turning on my back, I give myself a good body stretch, let out a comforting sigh and think, I bet if I go to seven o'clock Mass every morning, God will see how much I'm sacrificing by getting out of bed so early in the morning. Then, he'll take really good care of my Daddy. Yeah! That's exactly what I'm gonna do until Daddy's all better.

I cover my head with the white sheet, close my eyes and the last thing I remember is me biting down on my bottom lip.

Chapter 2

IT'S THE NEXT NIGHT, Thursday, May 12, and I'm standing in the middle of the beige tile kitchen floor looking at the huge mounds of dirty dishes piled high on the table. "Hardly anybody talked to each other at dinner tonight," I say. "All's I heard was a lot of clanking of forks and spoons and some chewing, but not much."

My soft-spoken, sixteen-year-old sister, Grace, doesn't answer me; neither does my silly fifteen-year-old sister, Chris. They're busy leaning their elbows on the white china closet counter as they search for a station on the radio that plays their kind of music. Me, I'm thinking the reason no one talked at dinner was because there was only twelve of us at the table and not the usual fourteen. The ones who were missing was Daddy and my oldest brother, Ralph, who's in the Army in Fort Dix, New Jersey. I don't miss Ralph not being here so much, but Daddy — well, to tell the truth, I've been thinking about him and what he did almost all day long. I hardly heard anything my teacher said. I keep on wondering why he did such an awful thing, but I can't come up with an answer. I guess no one can, which is why no one's talking about Daddy. But we're all thinking about him.

Then the most peculiar thing happens. The radio stops making staticky sounds and starts playing the song "This Old House." What's peculiar is that Daddy's been singing that song for months now. I look at Grace and Chris, but I don't think they realize that's Daddy's song. I don't say anything. I sing along and feel close to my Daddy. I miss him so much. I wish I could be with him. I'd take really good care of him. I know I would, because I already help Mommy take care of him. I bring his lunch to the grocery store, and when I'm there sometimes I sweep the floor or dust the cans on the shelves. And when I sit on the wooden stand that's outside his store, I hand Daddy brown paper bags so he can fill them for his customers. And when I'm home, I even iron his handkerchiefs on my ironing board. I can't wait till he's home again. I can help take really good care of him. I know I can.

I fight back the tears and think, Why? Why did my own father do such a horrible thing to himself? The good memories are gone. In their place, anger creeps like a snake and in my head, I shout, Why can't he just be all right? Why does he have to get sad and try to kill himself? Why can't he just be okay?

My anger makes me feel real bad. Cause I know Daddy's sick and can't help himself. With sudsy hands, I reach for some dirty glasses, sigh and think, I love him so much. I just wish he could be here right now.

I let out another sigh and that's when Grace asks, "Are you all right?"

She doesn't wait for me to answer cause she gets distracted by the song that's playing on the radio called "Rock Around the Clock." Chris throws her dish towel onto the back of the wooden chair as Grace tosses the broom against the wall. Then, they reach for each other and start jitter-bugging to the musical beats of the song. I don't bother to look at them anymore even though the kitchen floor is vibrating like jackhammers from the crazy way they're dancing.

But once I hear Chris screaming, "Ariba! Ariba!" I know that means she's going to start dancing like the gypsy lady on the album cover of Grandpop's opera album called "Carmen." And only cause I love when Chris dances like the gypsy lady, I toss my white-and-red-striped washcloth into the sudsy water, then turn and watch as Chris puts one arm in the air and shakes her head like a wild lady. She pushes her chestnut-brown hair away from her face, stands with one bare foot in front of the other and, once guitar music starts coming out of the radio, she begins swinging her hips to the rhythms.

"Ariba! Ariba!" she yells as the music grows louder and as the fiery rhythms of more guitars join in. Chris swirls and grinds her body to the earthy sounds. The pulsating beats of bongos fill the kitchen, and as her dancing grows wilder, I tell myself I wish I could dance the way Chris dances.

Her snapping fingers join with the clicking sounds of the castanets, and once the music fires up again, she reaches for an imagined flared skirt and her body begins to sway. She's making guttural sounds and I think she's lost in her dance, but once our eyes meet, she smiles, and I smile back.

I stop smiling when, out of the corner of my eye, I see Grace standing only a few feet from me, and I feel tension coming from her body. I look to where her eyes are staring and I get frozen, too. We're looking in a bucket that Mommy left under the sink and Daddy's white shirt is in it and it's popping like a blister out of the red water.

Grace takes a few steps towards the bucket, then presses her arm under her breasts and moans, "Uuuhhhhhh!"

I can't stand looking at that bucket, so I look at Chris and tell myself, I want to dance and be wild like Chris.

There's a pause in the music and, with just a humming sound coming out of the radio, lonely silence fills the room. The three of us, we don't look at each other as we stand like manikins staring at the bucket of bloody water. Then the music begins again, but the bongos and guitars play softer. Like nothing bad is happening. Chris starts swaying in her earthy movements; her eyes have a faraway look and a great calm comes over me. It's as if she's floating on air. I swallow hard as I listen to the bongo beats growing softer and more distant. The strumming guitar plays its quiet melody until the music stops and Chris, she does, too.

Not wanting this to end, I jump in the middle of the floor, shake my hips, but stop when Chris giggles and shakes her hips as she says, "You don't have enough meat on your hips to dance like this."

Grace rolls her eyes and remarks, "Why don't you stop acting stupid! It always gets you into trouble and especially with Daddy!"

"Yeah, I know all about it!" Chris screams. "Daddy thinks you're Miss Goody Two-Shoes, but I know better! You want Daddy to think you're quiet and sweet! But it's all an act, that's all it is!"

Grace puts her hand on her shaking hip and says, "But I'm the one who gets to work at Daddy's store. Why, I even get paid, while you have to stay home and help Mommy and you don't get a dime."

Chris picks up a wet dish towel that's hanging from the oven door, and in a quick movement, hits Grace hard on her rear end. Grace yelps and right away reaches for a dish towel, and then hits Chris really hard across the arm. There's lots of hitting and screaming, but the really big scream comes from me, when Grace accidently hits me in the eye with her very damp dish towel.

I yell, "That really hurt!"

Grace shrieks, "Please! Stop your screaming! You sound just like a fishwife."

Chris snaps, "Yeah, Roe! It pierces my eardrums when you yell like that!"

Their comments hurt my feelings and I don't know why, but I look in the direction of the bucket under the sink. All that red blood makes me shiver, and I want to look away, but I can't. With tears in my eyes I look over at my two big sisters and I see they're looking in the bucket too, but they don't say one word. My crying gets louder because I can't pretend no more. I cry because I'm scared for him. I cry because I really miss him. I cry because I hate this awful nightmare we're living. I cry because nobody's talking about it.

I grab Grace's towel and cover my face as I almost double over because of the gnawing pain in my gut. I can't even stop when I hear Mom's dragging footsteps coming from the stairs.

That's when Grace grabs my arm and with words as brittle as dry twigs, she demands, "Stop it right now!"

I look at Chris and her eyes tell me that my tears frighten her. Then Mom's standing in the kitchen doorway demanding, "What's all this yelling about? Will you girls get this kitchen cleaned up." She looks at me and asks, "Why is your eye all red?"

I want to tell her that Grace hit me with the wet dish towel so she knows I have a reason for crying, but before I can answer, she says, "On second thought, just finish washing the dishes."

I feel so embarrassed by my outburst, and only cause I'm choking on my own tears, I run past my sisters and run past Mom, too. I don't look her way, not at all, cause for the life of me I can't get myself to stop crying.

Chapter 3

IT'S NOONTIME ON THIS SUNNY FRIDAY, the 13th of May, and I'm running home from school down Moore Street cause I wantta spend time with my Mommy before everybody else comes home for lunch. I can't wait to tell Mommy my made-up prayer that came to me first thing this morning. I've been praying it ever since and it goes like this:

God above, around and in me. I hope that I can make you see. I'm one of twelve, and they really don't need me. But him, oh God, it's plain to see. He's needed here much more than me.

I keep running and praying until I open the front door of my house and once I'm in the dining room, I get all excited cause I see Blind Man Joe sitting next to Mommy on the beige couch with the sunken-in pillows. Joe lives three houses up from us and all us kids call him Blind Man Joe, cause like Joe told Daddy, he went blind when he was a soldier in the Second World War. The only thing he can see is light from dark and remembered images and no more than that.

I run over to Mommy and we give each other hugs and kisses, and when I look at Joe I feel all tickly inside. After I giggle, I say, "Hi, Joe."

"Joe's come to see how everybody's doing. Isn't that nice?" Mom asks.

I shake my head yes and say, "Uh-huh."

Joe's got his head tilted back as he drinks his last drop of coffee and to Joe, Mom says, "How about another cup?"

Joe answers, "No, I don't think so. I have to pick up Donna at school."

Mom looks at the kitchen clock and says, "You still have time."

Joe covers his cup with his hand and says, "No. I don't think so. But thanks anyway."

"Oh! So, you don't like my coffee anymore!"

Joe laughs. "No! You know that's not it."

Only because I know Joe likes me the best out of all the kids living on the block including my brother, John, who plays with Joe's daughter, Donna, and only because when Joe hears me coming, I see his eyes light up, and only cause I know Joe can't say "No" to me, I say, "Come on, Joe. Have another cup of coffee."

His mouth opens wide with a big smile. "Okay. I'll have another cup."

Mom sighs, then says, "You'll take it from Rosemary. You'll do anything for her."

Mom laughs, Joe laughs and I put a proud smile on my face.

"Rosemary!" Mom says. "You might as well be the one to get Joe another cup of coffee." Even though Mommy knows Joe can't see her, she still looks at him, smiles and says, "The next thing you'll be telling me is that it's the best cup of coffee you've ever had, and it'll only be because Rosemary got it for you."

Once I'm holding Joe's empty cup, I walk into the kitchen and I'm thinking that whenever Joe's around, I feel all warm and toasty inside. I start pouring Joe's coffee and remember how it was just a few weeks ago when I was playing hopscotch in the middle of the street. I heard Joe's white cane making "clunking" sounds on the sidewalks, and once I heard "clanging" sounds on our sidewalk cellar door, that's when I yelled, 'Hi, Joe!' I didn't stop yelling his name until Joe figured out where my voice was coming from. That's when he put his foggy blue eyes on me and in the nicest voice he can ever speak, he said, 'Hi, Rosemary.'

That's how it is between us. I don't know why, but it is.

When I walk back into the dining room, Mom and Joe are laughing. I walk over to him and whisper, "Joe," and place his cup of coffee in his hand.

Not wanting to miss one thing Mommy and Blind Man Joe are talking about, I lean against Grandmom's old Singer sewing machine that's only a few feet from Joe. But I come out of being so nosey when I hear cracking sounds coming from only a few inches away. My whole body gets tight when I see I just knocked over the rhododendron plant, the one us kids gave Mommy for Mother's Day with the money Daddy gave Trudy. As I catch it by one of its clusters of deep-pink flowers, I'm thinking, Whew! I'm glad I caught it before it got ruined cause I know Mommy would be very, very, very sad.

With both hands around the pot, I fix it upright in the soup dish Mommy put it in and the sweetest scent fills my nose, which makes me think of the beautiful flowers Joe grows, even though he can't see. And I think how Joe's being here feels almost like Daddy's home. I bet the real reason why he's here is because God didn't get the doctors to fix Daddy good enough so he could be home today.

13

Instead, God sent Joe who's as blind as they come. But somehow he still finds a way to raise his family. Why, he even has a wife who's blind and they have two small daughters and they're all doing just fine. Yeah, I think there's another thing God's trying to tell me, and that's even though Daddy might not be as good as he was before, he's still gonna come home and be our Daddy.

A few minutes pass, then I shuffle my feet and shake my head as I'm thinking, I bet the absolute real reason why Joe's here is because he sees things we can't see and he knows for sure that my Daddy's not gonna die. I bet, too, that maybe, just maybe, God talks to Joe and God told him that Daddy's not gonna die. I'm telling you! That's why he's really here!

"Snap! Snap! Snap!" are the sounds that take me out of my head and I look in Joe's direction. I put a grin on my face cause I see he's got his two large thumbs pulling at his black suspenders. He lets go of those suspenders, this time for good, and when they snap back onto his big chest, he starts laughing so loud that even though I don't know what he's laughing at, I laugh, too. I laugh some more when I look at Joe's big stomach cause it's moving up and down. I look at Joe's face and I laugh louder cause Joe's hair, that he don't have too much of except for some dark ones that's growing at the very top of his head, is flying around with the twisting and turning of his laughing head.

To Mommy, Joe says, "What did the doctors say?"

Mommy moans, "It's hard to find a doctor who'll talk to me. They all seem so busy."

"What about the nurses? Sometimes they know more than the doctors do anyway."

"I did speak to the head nurse and she says he's doing as well as can be expected."

My eyes squint and ask myself, What the hell's that supposed to mean? But I know it's a waste of time to ask Mom any questions cause I know she'll never ever tell me anything cause all's she ever does is treat me like I'm a little kid.

I'm glad when I notice the dimple next to Joe's mouth growing deeper, and that's when he turns his eyes towards the kitchen and asks, "Rosemary, what did you learn in school today?"

"You sound just like my father."

He turns his body towards me and inquires, "Did Sister teach anything new about Da Vinci or Raphael this morning? How about Egypt? Did you learn anything new about Egypt?"

I don't answer Joe cause I don't want to tell him that I've had a headache all day and I can't remember anything Sister taught today. My shoulders tighten as awkward silence passes between us, and I'm glad when it's broken by Joe's empty cup and saucer making nervous noises.

I reach for his cup and saucer and say, "I'll take it, Joe."

"Thanks." He gives his legs a good stretch, then places his big hand on top of Mom's. I'm purely amazed as to how he does that cause I don't understand for the life of me how it is that he knows where Mom's hands are. He whispers, "I've got to go. If I can do anything, just let me know."

I say, "Stay, Joe."

He hesitates, then says, "I really can't. If I'm late for Donna, she'll be scared."

He reaches for his white cane that's resting alongside of him, and once he stands my heart sinks just a little and I think, I wish Joe could live with us until Daddy comes home. I feel so safe with him here.

Mom nudges me and says, "Walk Joe to the door."

I whisper, "Joe," and once he rests his hand on my arm, with me walking in front of him, we walk slowly into the playroom. That's when I get an idea. Pulling on Joe's jacket I say, "Joe, do you wantta hear a prayer I made up just this morning? It's a prayer for my Daddy."

"Of course."

With my fingers fidgeting, I look up into Joe's empty eyes and whisper, "God above around and in me. I hope that I can make you see. I'm one of twelve and they really don't need me. But him, oh God, it's plain to see, he's needed here much more than me."

With great strength, he grabs my arm and bellows, "Rosemary! No! No! No! I don't like that prayer! The part where you ask God to take you, that's an awful thing to be praying for! Don't you ever pray that prayer again!!!!"

My eyes blink a lot cause it looks like black darts are coming out of Joe's eyes, and my body starts shaking like Carmella's rag doll. I wish I could tell him that I'm praying that prayer cause I can't stand how much I'm missing my Daddy and I want him home where he belongs.

But then maybe he understands, cause he gently pulls at my arm and in a calmer voice, he says, "Rosemary, God wants you to be thinking about all the wonderful things going on this time of year. Just look around. It's springtime and God's making everything come alive again. Why, it was just this morning I was listening to the baby birds chirping from their nests that's in the tree in the alleyway behind your house. That's when I went out into my back yard and smelled the beautiful flowers blooming in my garden and I felt the warm breezes on my face. I have to tell you, just thinking about it makes me feel so alive. Do you know how lucky you are that you can watch the bushes blooming, the trees growing? That's what should be floating around in your head, and let God and the doctors take care of your father. Before you know it, he'll be home."

He holds onto his cane with both hands, and then sends it flying through the air like a sword and I tell myself, He's trying to find the door without my help.

He takes a few clumsy steps, stands near the screen door and in a demanding voice, he says, "Listen! Do you hear the flock of birds flying overhead? They're coming home for the summer. Look! Look up! Are you looking?"

I hold the screen door open, take hold of Joe's arm and I let go only after he's standing on the sidewalk and all of a sudden he turns around and waves, even though he's late picking up Donna, and that makes me think of Mommy being alone in the kitchen. So I call, "Bye, Joe!" and hurry back to her.

Chapter 4

"I WANTTA GO SEE DADDY," I say to Mommy as I'm standing in front of her vanity table mirror combing one of my tangled-up ponytails on this late Saturday afternoon, May 14th. She's standing next to me putting coral lipstick on, and as she's putting the lid back on, she's mumbling something to herself that I can't understand.

Convinced that Mommy didn't hear me, I take a deep breath and whisper, "Mommy, I wantta go see Daddy, too."

She looks at me and says, "The hospital's no place for kids." Smiling, she adds, "What am I gonna do with you? You're such a worry wart. Your father's gonna be just fine."

She reaches for her black handbag that's lying across her bed, and that's when I say, "When Daddy was in the hospital for his stomach operation a few years ago, Chris, Pat and I walked right into that hospital and once I saw Daddy with a big smile on his face, that put a very big smile on my face. It didn't matter that after only a few minutes the nurse chased us. I wantta see for myself that my Daddy's okay."

I don't think Mommy even heard me cause just then my three-year-old sister, Anna, begins crying, and from the way she's sounding, well, I think she's hungry. Mommy must think so too; she tosses her handbag back on the bed and runs down the stairs faster than a heartbeat.

I pick up Mommy's lipstick and pulling the top off, I mumble, "I wantta go see my Daddy." I'm just about to put on some of Mommy's lipstick when I hear my big sister, Trudy coming.

"Where's Mom?" Trudy demands just as I put that lipstick tube back down on the vanity table. "The cab's here to take us to the hospital."

"Mommy just went downstairs."

She reaches for Mom's handbag, but stops when she pulls at the white chenille bedspread that's clinging to her flared black skirt. I rush towards her, tug at her white starched blouse and whisper, "I wantta go see Daddy, too."

Placing her hands on my shoulders, she says in a bossy tone, "You can't! The doctors and nurses won't let you in!"

"Why? He's my Daddy, too!"

I guess she understands how I'm feeling, cause suddenly, she sits on the bed and pulls me close to her. Kissing my forehead, she gently whispers, "They won't let kids in. And not only that, Daddy's gonna be home before you know it."

Trudy's got her eyes staring at my messed-up ponytails, and with no time passing between us, she smiles and says, "Get me the hairbrush. I wantta brush your hair."

I stretch myself to reach Mommy's hairbrush, hand it to Trudy and after I take out the silver-colored clips, I turn my back to her. She begins brushing and I fall into the comfort of her gentle touch and soothing voice as she counts, "One. Two. Three." Each time the bristles gently touch my shoulders I close my eyes and almost forget about how sick my Daddy is.

When she reaches thirty, she stops brushing and says, "Rosemary, Daddy's gonna be just fine. You've gotta believe that. Because if you don't, you can make yourself sick over this. You've got to stop worrying."

I don't answer, and she keeps brushing. Once she whispers, "Seventy-nine," I turn towards her and say, "But if I only could see him. I won't worry no more. I gotta see for myself."

She brushes my bangs and states, "He's gonna be just fine. You've got to believe that because it's true."

I keep my eyes looking at her calm face, and in my head, I'm thinking, Maybe she's right. Mommy and Blind Man Joe are saying Daddy's gonna be fine, too. Why can't I get it through my thick skull! Oh, just stop, yeah, old worry wart. He's gonna be just fine.

She gives me a kiss on my cheek and says, "Turn around and let me finish brushing your hair. Eighty, eighty-one, eighty-two . . ." She doesn't stop counting until she whispers, "One hundred." Then she hands me the brush and hugs me once more.

"I miss Daddy." I can't help myself blurting out. "Since Daddy's been in the hospital, it feels creepy around here and I feel scared all the time."

After she blinks away her tears, she says, "I know what you mean. Almost every night Daddy and Mommy checked up on us before they went to bed. And once I'd hear Daddy snoring, I'd feel safe in my own bed and then I'd fall into a deep sleep. Now, nobody comes in to check on us and not hearing Daddy snore, well, I'm having lots of trouble sleeping." She gets a faraway look in her eyes and, after a few seconds, she comes back with a sparkle in them and whispers, "I'm gonna tell Daddy you were asking for him."

"You will! You will! Tell Daddy I'm praying for him, too, and tell him I miss him so very, very much!"

"Under one condition. If you promise to stop worrying. He's gonna be just fine."

"I promise."

Trudy hugs me real tight and once she stands, I hand her Mommy's handbag. She runs down the steps and I rush out into the hallway and watch her until I hear her screaming for Mommy to hurry up.

My promise to Trudy lasts about as long as it takes her and Mommy to drive away in that cab. When my worrying comes back it's worse than ever cause now I'm angry, too. "What kinda people are they who work in these hospitals who say I can't see my own Daddy." I slam the toilet lid down, sit and look through the open bathroom door at the Sacred Heart of Jesus picture that's pasted on my sisters' bedroom wall and to Jesus, I cry, "I wantta look in his smiling eyes and I wantta yell as loud as I can that I love him so very, very much."

I rinse my hands and with a long face, I say, "It's only been four days since I seen him and already it feels like forever. And what if he dies and never comes back? That will be forever."

I dry my hands, sit on the toilet lid and whisper, "Sacred Heart of Jesus. My Mommy, my big sister, Trudy, and even Blind Man Joe are telling me that my Daddy's gonna be just fine. But I'm still having a hard time believing it. But if you give me a sign, then I'll believe it for sure. But what kinda sign could you give me? Hum!"

Before I can think of another idea, my brain feels like it's getting hit by a bolt of lightning, and I smile as I exclaim, "I know! The plant that Mommy got on Mother's Day." What I'm thinking is that if somebody don't start taking care of it soon, it's gonna die. So I tell Jesus that I'm gonna take care of it! And if it lives, then, sweet Jesus, I'll take it to mean that you're telling me that my Daddy's gonna be just fine. I know it's gonna live cause I'm gonna take very good care of it. That's it! That's the sign! Thank you! Thank you! Thank you so much, sweet Jesus!

I jump up and down and around in circles calling out, "Thank you, sweet Jesus! Thank you! Thank you! Thank you, sweet Jesus!"

I don't wait for Jesus to give me another idea cause coming from downstairs, I hear, "Roe, you better get down here right now!"

It's my sister Grace, so I hurry down cause with Mom and Trudy gone, she's in charge. Grace is sitting in a rocking chair between the kitchen and the dining room and not far from Mommy's plant. Taking a few sighing breaths, I point to the plant and announce, "I asked Jesus for a sign. And that's when he put the idea in my head that I should take care of the plant cause if it liv-"

Grace stops rocking and says, "Will you stop yapping about what you're gonna take care of. I'll tell you what you gotta take care of. You gotta take care of Anna until Mother comes back from the hospital."

"Why do I gotta watch Anna? You're bigger than I am."

Grace looks at me sideways. "Mother told me to tell you to watch Anna. And she told me to watch everybody and everything else. I can't do that and watch Anna, too."

"Oh! Isn't this just a piece of cake! I'm old enough to watch Anna, but I'm not old enough to see Daddy! Huh! I can't stand it no more. Everybody's acting like everything's just fine around here, when the truth of the matter is that things are just really awful. Yeah! I know what's going on! Just so everything looks good on the outside, it doesn't matter what's really going on inside! It's like Daddy being sick is a big secret that everybody knows! So what kinda stupid secret is that! I just can't stand it no more! Why, I think my head's gonna explode!"

Her eyes get big, then she says, "You better shut up or I'm telling Mother."

It's getting on my nerves the way she keeps calling Mommy 'Mother,' and so I shout, "I don't care what you do! All's I know is that the big rule around here is children should be seen doing and not ever heard from!"

Then just to annoy her more, I go into the playroom and find Anna sitting on the wooden bench. She's wrinkling the pages in her Cinderella coloring book as she's doing her best to turn each page and I think, Boy, you are so lucky. You have no idea what's going on. I sit next to her, reach for her chubby hand and recite, "Round ball, round ball, pull the chicken's hair. One slice, two slice, tickle under there."

20

She don't laugh when I tickle under her arm and when I gently touch her face, she pushes my hand away, looks down at her feet and in her tiny voice, she says, "Where Daddi? Where Daddi?"

A chill runs down my spine and I look into her panicked oval eyes and I think, No one is escaping this nightmare. Not even Anna.

She looks up at me and again, she says, "Where Daddi? Where Daddi?"

"Daddy's in the hospital," I say like it's no big deal. "But don't you worry cause he's gonna be home before you know it. Mommy and Trudy and Blind Man Joe all say Daddy's gonna be fine. So don't worry cause it's not gonna do you any good to worry." Then I say, "Come here. I want to show you something." Taking her hand, I lead her to Mommy's plant. Cuddling her in my arms, I whisper, "I know something the two of us can do. It's a wonderful idea that sweet Jesus gave me when I asked him to give me a sign. The idea is that if Mommy's plant does fine, then that means Daddy's doing fine, too. But somebody's gotta be taking care of this plant. That's where you and me come in. If we take really good care of it, it'll do much better than just fine. The brown stems will grow taller and they'll have more and more baby flowers, just like the way Mommy and Daddy keep having babies. But the absolutest bestest thing about Mommy's plant getting bigger is that it's gonna mean that Daddy's getting better. Until one day soon the plant is soooooooo big that it covers the whole sewing machine. And on that very day, Daddy will be walking through the front door with a big smile on his face and he'll be whistling to let us know he's home. And when he sees that plant and how beautiful it looks, he'll want to know who took such very good care of it, and we'll tell him it was you and me. And on that day we're gonna be the happiest little kids in the whole wide world."

She reaches for one of the pink flowers and whispers, "Take care Mommy's plant."

Anna giggles, I giggle, then we hug each other cheek to cheek and with my arms wrapped around her, I spin around and say, "I don't know the first thing about taking care of a plant. But if I ask Blind Man Joe, I bet he'll tell us cause he's got such a beautiful garden in the back of his house."

Before Anna's feet touch the linoleum floor, to Grace, I say, "I'm going over to Blind Man Joe's with Anna so's Joe can teach us how to take care of Mommy's plant. We won't take long."

I'm standing in front of Joe's green garden door with one hand holding Anna and the other hand holding the plant, and I'm singing my new made-up song,

Lucky, lucky, lucky me. Lucky I didn't go to the hospital.

Lucky I had to stay home. Lucky that Jesus gave me the sign.

Lucky that I got a friend like Blind Man Joe.

Lucky, lucky, lucky me.

"Who's that singing in front of my garden door?" says Blind Man Joe.

"It's me and my baby sister, Anna, Joe. We wantta talk to you about how to take care of Mommy's plant."

"Rosemary, I knew it was you. I was just fooling. Come on in."

I put Anna down, then clank open the door by its metal handle and say, "Hi, Joe. How does your garden grow?"

"It grows fine. How yours?"

I put Mommy's plant on the wooden table that's right in front of us.

"What do you have here? It smells like a rhododendron. What color are its flowers?"

"Deep pink and it's got some baby flowers on it, too."

I put my hands in his and I don't let go until his hands are touching Mommy's plant. He's got his eyes looking up to the sky as he touches the deep-green leaves, then he puts his finger into the dirt and says, "This plant needs some loving care. What you've got to do is . . ."

He sits himself down on the cement bench that's under the crossing of his climbing roses, and my eyes feel like they're bulging out of my head, and I look at Anna and see she's got her eyes on Joe, too. We wait for Blind Man Joe to say something.

After a few quiet moments that's only interrupted by a baby robin's piercing chirping, Joe continues, "Once you take this plant home, you've got to give it a glass of water. No more than that. Then, tomorrow, give it another glass of water. This plant needs lots of sunlight, too, so you have to put it in a place where there's lots of sun coming in. And another thing, you got to talk to the plant just like you do a friend. And like a friend you've got to ask how it's doing. Is it getting enough of whatever it needs and especially attention. The plant will answer you by how its leaves look and how its flowers bloom or don't bloom. I'm gonna give you some dry plant food that I want you to put in the soil before you water it. This plant is strong with deep roots. If you take care of it, your whole family will enjoy it for years to come."

A smile comes over me and I say, "Thank you, Joe. We're gonna take really good care of it. Right, Anna?"

Anna reaches for the plant and says, "Mommy's plant."

Whissshhh! Whissshhh! are the sounds that the gusty winds are making as they blow through the kitchen window screens. Clomp, clump, clog are the noises coming from the playroom and I tell myself it's my three brothers sounding like a pack of wild horses. They're running in to get out of the sudden rainstorm that's brewing outside. I hear lots of laughing, too, and it's telling me my brothers are drenched right through to the skin. I smile to myself cause their laughter, somehow, it's a great comfort to me.

Grace yells, "Pat, make sure that screen door's closed. We already have three flies in here."

Georgie and Johnny come running into the kitchen and stand next to the table and, in an excited tone, Georgie hollers, "Roe, are you gonna hypnotize those flies if they land on something?"

I laugh and say, "Yeah!" Then, I think to myself, As hard as my brothers try, they still can't hypnotize flies even though they do everything I do.

Pat, he's standing in the doorway drying his black hair with a white terrycloth towel and, once he lifts his head, he points and whispers, "Roe, one's right there on the table."

"Only if you promise not to kill it."

"Whatiya gonna do with it?"

"Put it outside where it belongs."

"Just hurry up!"

I'm feeling real proud that I can hypnotize flies and no one else in the family can. So I point my index finger right at that fly and say, "Bzzzzzzzzzzzzzzzzzzzzzzzzzzzzzzzzzzzzzzzzzzzzzzzzzzzzzzzzzzzzzzzz zzzzzzzzzzzzzzzzzzzzzzzzzzzzzzzzzzzzzzzzzzzzzzzzzzzzzzzzzzzzzzzz zzzzzzzzzzzzzzzzzzzzzzzzzzzzzzzzzzzzzzzzzzzzzzzzzzzzzzzzzzzzzz."

The fly don't budge and my finger, it gets closer to that fly and once it's almost on top of it, suddenly, I feel a very loud whack brush right past my arm. There's globs of blood and specks of black on the table and I see lots of blood on Pat's white towel, too.

After a few frozen seconds, I make two fists, and shout, "Why? Why did you kill it? You said you wouldn't kill it and you killed it anyway!"

He shrugs his shoulders, and screams back, "I always kill 'em. What's wrong with dat?"

"Don't any of you see what Pat's done! He's killed it! Don't you see, he lied to me!" I look at Pat and yell, "I can't believe you lied to me like that!"

Pat laughs. "What's the big deal? It's only a fly."

"But it was alive and now it's dead! And you killed it and I helped you kill it! I can't stand you!"

Grace says, "Rosemary, why are you so upset? It's only a fly."

"Don't you understand! It's dead! It was alive and flying around but because he lied to me, I hypnotized the fly and now it's dead!"

Grace gets up from her rocking chair, puts her arms around me and says, "Shhhh. It's all right. Everything's gonna be fine." Holding me against her chest, she rocks me and says, "Shhh. Shhh. You've got yourself all worked up. Shhh."

My face is squashed against her arm and I don't hear what she's saying cause my eyes are wide open staring at the bucket under the sink that has my Daddy's bloody shirt.

And after I come out of my frozen body, I scream, "Aaaahhhhhhhhh!"

Grace's arm shakes as she says, "Whhaaa, what's wrong?"

I point to the bucket, and sob, "There's a fly in the bucket. It was alive just a minute ago, and now it's dead, too."

Grace turns and looks in the bucket. Pat, Georgie and Johnny all turn and look in the bucket, too, and nobody moves, not a fraction of an inch.

Chapter 5

I WAKE UP TO THE SMELL OF BURNT TOAST and the sounds of "Sparky and Our Gang" singing on the kitchen radio: "If you go out in the woods today be sure not to go alone." The singing tells me it's 8:00 and I'm upset with myself because I missed the early Mass and didn't keep my promise to God. But then I feel a little better because I remember it's Sunday and I can go to the 10:30 Mass. That's when I'll tell God just how sorry I am for not following through on my promise to go to Mass first thing in the morning. But I sure hope he keeps his promise and lets my Daddy live.

I get shaken out of talking to myself about God when from behind me, I hear, "What is this?"

I give Chris a smile when I see her standing next to my bed saying, "You lazy bum. When are you gonna get outta bed?"

I laugh, too, then toss the sheet off my legs and jump up. I rub my eyes and say, "Chris. Do me a fava. Go over to the bureau and in the second draw, get me an undershirt?"

She makes lots of noise when she opens the stuck drawer and I get surprised when I see Pat's head pop up. I almost say "Hi" to Pat, but I don't cause I'm getting hit in the face with my undershirt. That's when Chris says, "Come on, Mom sent me up to get the two of you. She wants the both of you downstairs."

Downstairs reminds me of the kitchen, which reminds me of the bloody bucket. I gotta ask about it. I just gotta. But the thought of asking sends chills right into the marrow of my bones. So I tell myself to look away from her and, with my eyes staring at the carved tree at top of my brothers' bureau, I whisper, "Chris, why does Mommy have Daddy's white shirt soaking in the-?"

Pat blurts out, "I, I, uh, took the dead fly out of the bucket after you went to bed last night."

I give him a big smile, but inside I'm ashamed because of my angry outburst from last night and I keep watching him as he reaches for his brown trousers hanging on his bed post. After he zips them up, he jumps out of bed and I give him another big smile cause of the way his belt is dangling from his pants. It's reminding me of Daddy and I'm feeling comforted just watching Pat acting more like Daddy every day.

I come back to my crazy question and repeat, "Chris. Why does Mommy have Daddy's shirt soaking in the kitchen bucket?"

Chris looks out the window and after an uncomfortable silence, shrugs her shoulders and says, "I don't know."

I look at Pat and I see curiosity in his eyes; this gives me courage to say, "Chris, tell us what happened."

I tell myself not to cry and don't get hysterical, cause if I do, she'll close up like a clam. I look down at the linoleum floor that's imitating the look of a gray rug and in a pleading voice, I say, "Chris, Trudy said it was Mommy who found him, but whata . . ."

My voice falls off and I don't say another word. I look at Pat and I know from the intense look in his eyes, he wants to know, too.

Chris glances around for something to do and when she starts slowly closing the drawer, she puckers her lips like she's trying to find the right words. Once the drawer is closed, her eyes keep blinking like a signal light on a Navy ship and I wait as she pauses for a few more seconds, then comes and sits next to me. In a very soft manner of speaking that's not her usual way, she says, "After we all went to bed, Mom went to the store. She kept banging on the door and calling to him, 'Browny! Browny!' but he didn't answer. The full moon was shining through the store window and Mom, she was able to see Daddy's bloody footprints on the wooden floor and that's how she knew he was in there."

In a demanding voice, Pat asks, "What did Mommy do?"

"She ran across the street to Mrs. Gratz, the pharmacist. She let Mom use her phone. Mom called the cops and waited in front of Daddy's store until they came."

"Mommy was standing out there all alone and he wouldn't let her in? Is that what you're saying?"

I look at Chris and she looks at me and I know we're thinking the same thing which is, I hope Pat don't explode and start punching things.

"Did they have to break the door down to get in?" he shouts.

Chris says, "No. Once the cops came, Daddy let Mommy in first, then he let the cops in. Mom said when she saw Daddy with the full moon shining directly on him, she could see blood all over his white shirt."

I wantta cry, but I don't cause I know my tears will make Chris stop talking, so I listen as she says, "The cops took Daddy to the hospital."

"It don't make no sense to me," I say. "It just don't make no sense at all that Daddy could . . . could . . . could torture himself like that. I think somebody wan . . . wan . . . wanted Daddy dead."

Chris holds down her twitching eye and says, "Who would want Daddy dead? Everybody likes Daddy."

The tiny hairs on my arms start standing on end, and as I gently start stroking my one arm, I stare into space, and whisper, "There was this one day at Daddy's store, well, I got to tell you, just thinking about it makes my skin crawl. It started out like any other afternoon when I'd run home, get changed out of my school uniform, then hurry to Daddy's store. But this time it was different cause when I got there I couldn't find Daddy and I was very shocked cause I don't never remember a time when Daddy wasn't outside, leaning on his produce stand or inside, sitting on the counter, looking out the window. So I kept looking for him, first inside the store all the way into the back room and when I couldn't find him there, I went outside and stood on the top step looking down Seventh Street. But when I looked up Seventh Street towards center city, it was exactly at that very moment I saw Daddy and two men coming out the side door of the empty apartment above Daddy's store."

Pat interrupts by saying, "What they look like?"

I think for a minute, then say, "They were all dressed up in suits. One was wearing a gray suit and the other one was wearing a navy-blue one and their shoes were as shiny as brand new black cars."

Chris stares at Pat for a few seconds, then back at me and says, "Did they have briefcases?"

"No."

"Then they weren't detectives," Chris says. "Detectives always have briefcases." She uncrosses her legs and asks, "When did this happen?"

"It was still cold, but it was starting to feel like Easter."

"I wonder what they wanted?"

I lean towards her and after my tongue stops feeling like it can't move, I say, "The one in the blue suit looked right at Daddy and with a cocky look on his face, he said, 'Do you understand?' Then, in Italian, he demanded, 'Capisc!' Daddy stood in front of the produce

27

stand, and he mumbled something as he made open hand gestures, but that only made the man, the one in the gray suit, very furious at Daddy. Then that same man, he walked over to Daddy, shook his head no, and then whispered something into Daddy's ear as he backslapped one hand into the other and screamed, 'Capisc! Capisc!'

"He kept his mean eyes on Daddy, then started laughing like a devil. I covered my ears cause I couldn't stand listening, and once Daddy looked away from that man, that's when I saw fear on Daddy's face. I know that look was put there by that awful man, and right then and there I was wishing him to go away and never ever come back so he can't ever again be so mean and rotten to our father."

Chris has her staring eyes on me, and as for Pat, he's sitting on the edge of his bed and watching me as my nose crunches up. Then I continue, "I didn't budge an inch, but it was only a few seconds after those two men started walking towards center city that Daddy finally saw me. It's the first time in my life I got so scared of Daddy, cause in a voice that sounded like thunder, he screamed, 'Get on home, now!!'"

I stop talking, hide my wet eyes by looking out the window and then I whisper, "And ever since that day, whenever I'd go to Daddy's store, even louder than the first time, he'd yell, 'Get on home, now!'" I don't say anything else, but in my head, I'm thinking how awful it makes me feel that my Daddy won't let me stay with him at the store no more.

With a smirk look on his face, Pat states, "The first time, ain't that a joke. I can't tell you how many times Daddy yelled at me. So whatiya complaining about, Daddy's little girl!"

I wantta say, "You're always doing things Daddy tells you not to do, that's why you keep getting yelled at all the time." But I don't say anything cause I don't have the energy. I come back to what's in my head and I whisper, "That's when my own insides shook like they never ever did before cause it was the second time I saw that man, the one in the gray suit talking to Daddy."

Chris, she touches my shoulder and shrieks, "When was the first time?"

"The first time I saw that man was the night in November when Daddy came out of the hospital. Remember how we were all in the dining room and Daddy got us all laughing cause he was teasing each and every one of us. But we all got quiet when Mommy came in from the playroom and said, 'Browny. There's a man here to see you.'"

Chris's eyes light up as she says, "I remember that! I thought it was one of Daddy's friends!"

I shake my head no and say, "I was holding Daddy's hand when we walked into the playroom and when Daddy sat on the wooden bench, I still held his hand and sat down right next to him."

"Who was the man then?" Chris asks.

"I don't know. The man wouldn't sit even when Daddy asked him to. He stood in front of Daddy and kept his hard eyes on Daddy and made twitching sounds like he had something caught between his teeth. Once he stopped making those awful sounds, he walked over to Daddy and whispered in his ear."

"What did he whisper?" Pat says like he's ready to kill that man.

"How am I supposed to know!"

"You were sitting right next to Daddy and you couldn't hear?"

"What do you think, I got some kinda x-ray hearing!" I shout back. I'm doing my best to sound tough even though I know I ain't. What I am feeling is plenty of guilt cause I didn't hear one thing that man said and I'm thinking that if I did my best to hear him then maybe I coulda told somebody and Daddy wouldn't be where he is right now.

I come out of my head when Chris looks at Pat and says, "Stop it. The two of you."

I guess Pat realizes he's being too hard on me and looking at me with nice eyes, he asks, "Roe, did Daddy say anything to the man?"

I give him a smile and say, "No." But I get a flash of remembering what I forgot until right now, and in an excited voice, I add, "Once the man was done whispering, Daddy let go of my hand, but I still held onto his. His hand didn't feel all soft and warm and strong like it did before. It changed to feeling cold like a dead fish packed on ice. And Daddy, he didn't bother to walk that man to the door either. He just kept his eyes on him until that man closed the door behind him. And I remember how I thought just looking into Daddy's eyes, well, it looked like he had a bunch of dark clouds in both of them."

Then, with my eyes starting to squint, I also tilt my head to one side and blurt out, "I-I-I bet-bet-bet-bet it was the one w-wearing the gray suit. The one with the evil laugh w-who put a knife into Daddy's chest. And I bet it was the other one who-who-who wore the blue suit who held Daddy's arms. And it was the one in the gray suit who came to our o-o-own house who shoved that poison right down Daddy's throat! And another thing, now they got Daddy, I bet they're gonna come after all of us and hurt us and even kill some of us. I know it's gonna happen cause I can feel it in my bones!"

Chris giggles, "Oh brother! There you go again, making more out of things than they are. You're so dramatic. And one more thing, stop acting like you know more than Mommy does. She said that Daddy did this himself. So stop all this nonsense."

Pat laughs, Chris laughs too, then Pat laughs louder, then Chris points her bony finger at me and squeals, "What do you know? You're just a kid."

I give Chris all kinds of dirty looks and in my head I'm thinking, I hate that she says I'm just a kid. Kids can see and hear and sense when something ain't right, too.

Pat clears his throat and when I look at him, he's smiling big and I tell myself, That's how Daddy smiles at me when he wants me to feel better.

I don't wantta be mad no more so I tell myself, Maybe Chris is right. Mommy's saying Daddy did this to himself. I gotta believe it cause I know Mommy loves Daddy very, very, very much and if she thought anybody ever wanted to hurt him, she'd be doing something about it. Yeah, Chris is right. I'm just a kid making something out of what ain't.

I come out of my thinking when Pat gets my attention, cause he's giving out a loud sigh as he's pulling his striped polo shirt over his head. I reach for my white slip and as I start pulling it over my head, I start to cry, but I tell myself to stop. Once I push the tears away with my little finger, I say, "Chris, why does Daddy wantta die?"

She whispers, "Mom said that Dad said he was sorry for what he did. He really doesn't wantta die."

"How is he doing?"

"They're still trying to get the rest of the poison out of his system. Mom said that Dad said that he forgot to tell them he took the poison. He remembered after he came out of the operation. But Mommy said he's gonna be fine."

"Yeah! He forgot all right!" Pat bursts out. He scares me the way he's grinning as he says, "If you believe that I gotta bridge I wantta sell yeah." He elbows me out of his way by pushing me onto my bed and once I look up, I get a very big shock cause he's punching the wall and screaming, "I hate all of this! I hate it! I hate it!"

After a few good shots to the wall, he stops punching it and bends over holding his hand by the wrist and screaming, "Oooooouuuuuuuch!"

Chris's eyes get sharp as she yells, "Hey! Whatiya doing? You punched in the wall! Things aren't bad enough around here, you gotta make them worse acting like a big baby!"

He fights back his tears and yells, "Leave me the Christ alone!" He barrels out of the bedroom and once he's running down the stairs, he kicks the railing wall each step of the way as he howls, "This is shit for the birds!"

Chris yells, "Boy! You're in big trouble cause I'm telling Mom!"

Chris takes deep breaths and I do, too. The only other thing we do is stare at each other with big eyes until she says, "You better get washed and come downstairs for breakfast."

Once I hear Chris running down the steps, I go into the bathroom, throw some water on my face and after I brush my hair, I close the bathroom door and stand in my big sisters' bedroom. I look at the picture of the Sacred Heart of Jesus that's glued on their wall, and as I stare into sweet Jesus' kind eyes, I tell Jesus about those two awful men who came to see my Daddy. Then before I run down the stairs, I make the sign of the cross and thank sweet Jesus for not laughing at me, but mostly, for listening to me even if I am just a little kid.

Chapter 6

IT'S NOON TIME THIS SUNNY MONDAY, May 16th and I'm standing in the playroom saying "Hi" to Daddy's sister, Aunt Mary, and I'm wondering why she ain't laughing real loud and telling me to give her a big fat kiss right on her cheek. My baby sisters, Antoinette, age five, and Anna are both sitting in the navy-blue coach that's standing in the middle of the playroom floor, which means Mommy and Aunt Mary just came in from pushing the coach up and down Hoffman Street.

I keep my eyes on Aunt Mary again and I'm wondering why her mouth's all puckered up like she just ate a whole lemon. That's when I tell myself that the reason why she's here is because she's feeling real sad about my Daddy and she wants to be near my Mommy so they can help each other feel better. But then, a loud knocking comes from the screen door. I turn to see who's pounding on our door, and when I see it's a policeman standing on our step, I quiver all over and ask myself, What's he doing here?

The screen door squeaks as he lets himself in. He don't go any further and I know he feels awkward as hell cause everybody's staring at him wondering why he's here. He takes his blue hat off, but he don't say nothing. He just stands there with his hat in his hand and the only thing about him that's moving is his fingers that slide his blue hat round and round. And I guess maybe he's making Mommy just as nervous as he's making me, cause suddenly she reaches out for his hat, takes it from the policeman, and places it on the large, white window sill beside him. Still the policeman don't move or talk. Neither do Mommy or Aunt Mary. I look at his hat. It looks so blue on the white window sill. And the way the sunlight is spreading over it, it's making the blue look soft. But I don't think there's nothing soft about a policeman, and I wish he'd take his hat and go away. Because there's something awful about his being in the house. And I wonder if anyone's done anything wrong. I can't remember a policeman ever being in the house before. I look from his hat to his face to see if I can see anything there to explain why he's here. But there's nothing mean on his face that says he's come to arrest one of us.

All of a sudden, he leans against the window sill where his hat is sitting and takes a piece of folded yellow paper from his pocket. He's still not talking. And I think I ain't never known a policeman to be so quiet. It's like his quiet is making time stand still, like I'm walking on a road where there's no end in sight.

Mommy must feel tired of waiting, too, and tired of the cop's silence, cause she moves over to see what's on the paper he's holding.

When she does, his hand jerks out and he says without looking at Mommy, and in a tone of voice that makes him sound like he's in charge of the world, "I need you to sign this."

He gives her the paper without even unfolding it. Mommy's hands are shaking when she opens the paper, and I wonder why the cop didn't open it for her. I think he should have cause from the confused look on Mommy's face, it's pretty obvious that she knows whatever's on that paper ain't good. And I wantta run over and be next to Mommy, but Aunt Mary is there instead. She's taking out her glasses and leans over to read the paper with Mommy.

Then they both cry out, "Ohhhhhhh!"

But it's only Mommy's cry I hear. And her cry is like someone's cry that's trapped in a nightmare and can't wake up. Mommy's face gets all white. It's a color I ain't never seen on the face of anyone before and I know whatever's on that yellow piece of paper is about Daddy, and it's terrible. I wantta scream at the policeman to take his hat out of the sunlight and go away. I want him to never have come here. I want time to stop, like when I stare into outer space. I wantta run and hide so I don't ever know what's on that piece of paper. But I don't do any of those things. Instead, I stand where I am, watching Mommy and listening to her sobbing.

It's Aunt Mary who finally says, "You mean he died this morning?" She says it in a questioning way, but it's really like she's doing more of telling than she is of asking.

The policeman's head jerks up and he looks at Mom. Nervously, he asks, "Are you saying no one contacted you?"

Mommy looks like she don't understand, and she shakes her head like she don't understand, but at the same time she's looking for something. I guess the policeman knows what she wants, cause all of a sudden, he's holding out a pen. But Mommy don't see it until Aunt Mary takes it and just about pushes it into her hand.

"You have to sign there," Aunt Mary says.

The policeman says, "You gotta sign."

Nodding and sobbing, Mommy tries to sign, but her hand's shaking and the paper tears when she tries. So Aunt Mary takes the paper and smooths it out on the white window ledge and puts her arm around Mommy.

I watch and I know I'm not going to run away and hide. I know I have to see what's on that paper. So while Mommy's still signing, I walk as quiet as a mouse and read the words. It's just a few words, but they're the most loud, ugly, mean words I've ever seen.

Michael Pasquarello. Monday, May 16, 1955. Deceased 7:30 A.M.

I'm looking at those words and inside I feel like I'm drowning. Like maybe the words are going to cause a great flood. Or maybe it's my eyes that's full of tears, and I'm shaking and all I can hear is Mommy's sobbing that's so loud and coming from her gut way down deep inside. Or maybe they're coming from my gut. There's so much tears and sadness, and I hurt all over. I ain't never hurt so much.

"He was sitting in a rocking chair in the hallway and the nurse found him. The nurse said he looked like he was sleeping," the policeman says and this time his voice is soft, like maybe he's crying, too. But then I think the whole world must be crying for my Mommy and me and my family and my Daddy, too. And time slows down again. Until there is no time. Only my Mommy's sobbing, and the flood of scary feelings inside me. And I want someone to hold me. I want someone to stop me from shaking. But Mommy can't and Aunt Mary can't. Aunt Mary's standing with her face buried in her handkerchief. And I think maybe the policeman can do something, cause they're supposed to help people. But the softness I heard in his voice is gone. He's reaching for the yellow piece of paper that Mommy just signed. Then he grabs his pen out of Mommy's hand and takes his blue hat off the window sill. It's clear he don't want to be here. He's going just as fast as he can. He's leaving us alone.

Just as he opens the screen door with the hand that's still clutching the yellow paper, I hear footsteps on the front steps. Next minute, through the screen door comes the rest of the little kids home for lunch. Pat, Georgie, Johnny, Carmella and Josephine are hurrying in through the screen door and running past the policeman like they don't want to know he's there.

Pat comes in first, and besides my big brother Ralph, who's in the army, Pat's the oldest boy. I feel better seeing Pat cause he likes to take charge even though sometimes he's got the worst temper and tries to make Georgie, Johnny and me do things we don't wantta do. I wouldn't mind if he did that now, cause with the policeman leaving, someone's got to be in charge. Mommy can't. And Aunt Mary can't. And I don't want to. But it looks like maybe I'll have to, cause when my eyes meet Pat's, I can see he's real nervous. His eyes are darting all over, from me to the policeman to Mommy and back to me. He's looking to me for answers. But it's Georgie, who in a jittery way asks, "Roe, wha-what's going on?"

I look at Georgie and even though he's talking to me, he's looking at Mommy. He's so scared and worried for her. He'd give his eye teeth to protect and take care of Mommy. And when he looks away from Mommy and looks out the screen door, I see hurt around his eyes. I hope he don't get cocky with his mouth like he usually does when he's hurting. And I don't wantta tell him, because when I do, I know it's gonna shock him like he ain't never been shocked before. And I know if I tell him I'm gonna be telling all the kids and they're all gonna be shocked just like I was shocked when I read those horrible words. And I don't mean a little shocked, I mean unbelievably shocked like the soldiers who were shell-shocked when they came back from the Second World War. But I'm the only one who read the paper other than Mommy and Aunt Mary. I figure I'm the one who has to tell, because if I don't, who will? I look at Mommy and she can't talk because she's crying so much. I look at Aunt Mary and she's got her arms around Mommy and she's sobbing, too. I got to be the one to tell.

I say, "Daddy died this morning."

There's a gasp, lots of gasps, but no one says nothing. Instead, like I'm some kinda giant magnet, all the kids huddle around me. I know they wantta know details, but they can't ask any more than I can. We just stand together, touching without touching, breathing like we were all the same person. Mommy's sobbing makes me feel like we're standing on top of the tallest building in the world and we're right on the edge, waiting to fall-not on the ground below, but falling forever and ever.

Then Pat asks like he's so confused nothing's ever going to make sense to him again, "What happened?"

"On the yellow piece of paper that Mommy had to sign, it said Daddy died at seven-thirty A.M. The nurse found Daddy on the rocking chair."

Everybody's heads are down and mine is, too. I hear lots of crying and tears of tremendous sadness like I never heard before. And I feel so guilty because it was me who gave all the kids the bad news about Daddy dying. And I wish I could wave a magic wand the way the good witch in Cinderella does to make all the sorrow and deep painful anguish go away. But I can't, and it's making me feel like I want to die, too. Not the way Daddy died, but I wouldn't mind if a cloud came down from heaven and carried us all away to a wonderful place that's far away from here.

The groans and tears and sobs are driving me crazy and I can't take it no more. I reach for Pat's arm, but he pushes me away. I feel all alone and rejected and I cry from the bottom of my pit. I feel horribly naked. I feel like one of the naked manikins in Goodman's dress shop window. The one that's got no torso or arms. Like that manikin, I don't have the stomach for all this and I don't have arms to comfort myself or anyone else. I think about my three big sisters and I cry some more, because I just wish they were here with us right now. They could put their arms around me and tell me everything's gonna be all right even though I know it ain't gonna ever be all right.

I look up at Mommy and I feel so much sadness for her. She has her clenched hands against her eyes and her sobs pound in my chest. I hear Aunt Mary moaning in a shaky kind of voice. And I look over at Antoinette and Anna and they're crying, which only makes me cry more; they're too young to know Daddy's dead, but they're still so sad and scared like me. And Georgie, he looks up towards Mommy with the fear I know I'm feeling, and he's wiping tears away by rubbing his eyes. And right in the middle of all this crying and fear, I get this thought that he won't have eyes no more cause he's rubbing so hard.

Carmella's long hair's hanging over her face, and she's not talking non-stop like she usually does when she gets nervous and she ain't her usual antsy non-stop moving self, neither. Johnny, he's just crying and crying and crying. Josephine's head is still hanging low and the only way I know she's crying is cause I see her tears wet the floor. She's crying a lot. I put my arm on her shoulder and she shrugs it away. There ain't no point in trying to comfort her or anyone, cause the only way any of us can be comforted is if Daddy walked into the house right now saying we've all been living a horrible nightmare and he's fine and everything's gonna be all right. But that ain't never gonna happen. That's when something inside makes me stop crying. All of a sudden, I'm clenching my teeth and making two fists. I look around the playroom and see all the tears and hear everybody's pain. And I know why I'm not crying. It's cause there's an anger that's so big inside me, like the fierceness of hundreds of hurricanes and thousands of tornadoes all rolled up into one ferocious black savage storm.

I look at Mommy. Her two closed hands that's up against her mouth ain't letting her gut-wrenching whimpering escape. Her eyes are closed tight and she's fighting back her tears, even though they shoot out like bullets from a machine gun. But then I think that bullets kill people so her tears ain't like bullets. Her tears are more like an overflowing river that's running wild with deep currents crashing every which way. And in my head I yell at him, "I'm glad you're dead! I feel happy you're dead! I hope you burn in hell forever for what you've done to all of us!" I'm so angry that I don't even feel bad for saying something so mean about my Daddy, no matter that he just died and I love him and I hate him, too.

But I come out of myself when I see Mommy saying something to Aunt Mary. Then, Mommy gets the two babies and puts one on each hip and goes upstairs. Aunt Mary clears her voice, then with lots of sternness, she says, "Everybody in the kitchen! It's time for lunch!"

She sounds like she's mad at us, but I think she's mad at Daddy for killing himself.

Aunt Mary don't say nothing else; she keeps busy pouring milk from the glass quart bottles Mommy gets from the milk man. When she starts making bologna and cheese sandwiches, I decide I ain't helping her only cause I'm in no kind of mood to be helping anybody. The three boys, they sit across the table from us three girls, but even so, we don't talk and we don't look at each other, either. It bothers me how quiet it is in our kitchen; the only sound I'm hearing is the rustling of the sliced bread bag every time Aunt Mary puts her hand inside. Once she unwraps the bologna paper, that's when all of us watch as she slaps the bologna onto ten pieces of bread she's got sitting on Mommy's meat platter. But when she unwraps the sliced cheese, that's when Pat looks away and drinks his milk, and Georgie and Johnny, they do the same thing. But us three girls, we keep watching Aunt Mary, and I drink my milk real slow cause it's helping quiet my churning stomach. She puts mustard on every piece of bread that's gonna go on top of the sandwiches, and I decide I ain't eating nothing. The awful smell of the mustard is making me sick to my stomach.

Aunt Mary wiggles her way in between Pat and Georgie and, after she places the bologna sandwiches on the table, she says, "You better hurry up and eat your lunch. You don't wantta be late for school."

We look at each other and I know we're all thinking the same thing, but it's Pat who speaks. With a nervous laugh, he says, "Aunt Mary, we can't go back to school."

I say, "Yeah, Aunt Mary. We all need to be with each other. We need to be a family now."

Georgie bangs the table and yells, "We oughtta stay home where we belong! We need to be near our Mom, too."

Quiet falls between us and the only sound I hear is coming from the dining room. It's Josephine and she's making lots of creaky sounds rocking on her rocking chair and I think she's rocking so hard she's gonna make a hole in the floor and fall right down into our dark dungeon-like cellar.

Carmella, she don't say nothing either, but her large dark eyes look wild and I get scared cause I'm afraid she's gonna do something crazy, even though I don't know what that might be cause that ain't her way. But after she takes a bite out of her sandwich, she squishes it between her fingers, then throws it across the table yelling, "There's hardly any mustard! Mommy always puts lots of mustard on my sandwich!"

She flips the chair out from under her and runs out. After a few quiet seconds, I hear a banging sound coming from Johnny's direction and when I look I see he's kicking the table leg; he's kicking it so hard, he's making dents.

My eyes fill with tears and when he yells, "I'm not gonna go back to school and you can't make me!" I laugh cause I know the only reason why I didn't yell it first is cause he beat me to it.

Aunt Mary holds onto the dish towel that's hanging off her shoulder as she demands, "Listen! This isn't my idea. Your mother wants all of you to go back to school."

Johnny says, "I'm gonna go ask her right now."

She pulls the dish towel off her shoulder and says, "You stay right where you are. I'm telling you, your mother wants you all to go back to school."

I look across the table and I see Pat's got a sympathetic look in his eyes, "Pat, please don't say you'll go back to school! Please don't!" He's the oldest boy at home right now and if he says he's going back, then the rest of us are gonna have to go back, too. But we can't. We need each other right now. And not only that, Mommy needs us, too, even if she don't think she does.

I open my eyes and I see Pat's got his shadowy eyes on me, but he don't say nothing. I look at Johnny and I can tell he's thinking same as me cause he's staring at Pat with pleading in his eyes.

Leaning towards Pat, I state, "Remember when Grandpop died? It was Daddy who made us stay home. And . . ."

Pat don't let me finish. He jumps up and, even though he's looking at me with darting eyes, to Aunt Mary, he whispers, "All right, Aunt Mary. We'll go back to school."

I can't hardly believe what Pat just said. "Daddy definitely would never want us to go back to school now!" I scream. "We gotta be a family! We all need each other!"

Pat yells, "Shut up! You're gonna go to school. See, cause if you don't, I'm gonna punch your face in!"

I scream, "I'm telling Daddy!"

Pat laughs, then moans, "Huh! That's a joke!"

Aunt Mary stands near the table and she's got both hands waving in the air and she's saying something, but I don't know what she's saying.

Then, the tops of my arms go weak like they're dropping to the floor as I watch Pat hit Georgie in the back of the head. Then, he gestures to Johnny and screams, "Let's go!"

Chapter 7

PAT'S RACING UP HOFFMAN STREET with Georgie and Johnny trailing behind him. I don't see Carmella, but I have a strong grip on Josephine's arm cause she's fighting me every inch of the way. She's crying, too, and saying she wants to go home. But I don't let her go even though she's dragging her legs and twisting her skinny body towards home.

I yell, "Pat, slow down!"

He turns towards me, bites down on his hand, grunts like a bulldog and walks even faster. I get mad, but I don't say nothing to him. Georgie and Johnny look at me. Georgie's crying and he runs and catches up with Pat. Johnny starts to follow, but suddenly he stops and he waits for us to catch up to him.

Pat turns on Seventh Street and as soon as Johnny, Josephine and I turn onto Seventh Street, too, I yell, "Pat. Wait up!"

He don't. He and Georgie keep running up Mifflin Street, which surprises me at first. We always stay on Seventh Street, until we pass Daddy's store. That's when I realize that no way is Pat going anywhere near Daddy's store today, and I'm very relieved. One thing for sure, I don't need another thing reminding me of what my Daddy's done.

I think Josephine's thinking that, too, cause she's dropping her legs out from under her again. So I grab her by her arm and yell, "You're staying with me whether you like it or not! We gotta be good for Mommy! We can't be giving her any more grief than she already has! So stop acting like a wild lady!"

She quiets down some and her and Johnny and me, we catch up to Pat, and I get real excited when I see Carmella standing at the end of Mifflin Street. But once we get closer, I think my heart's gonna break cause she's standing there crying buckets full of tears. They're dripping on the front of her navy-blue uniform, and if she don't stop crying soon, the skirt of her uniform is going to be drenched front and back. I yell, "Wait up, Carmella!"

When I catch up to her, she whimpers, "I told Sister I was gonna bring apples in for class on Friday for the party! Now what am I gonna do? It's my turn and I ain't got nothing to bring in!"

I shake my head like I don't have a solution. Pat shakes his head and says, "We better keep walking."

I'm glad we're all together finally. Once we're on Siegel Street, we cross to the other side and we don't look at each other and nobody says anything until we cross McClellan Street. Then, in a whimper Josephine asks, "Did it hurt Daddy when he died?"

Pat mumbles, "It only hurt when he lived."

I stop cause Pat's words stab me right in my heart. After I wait for my chest to stop pounding, I whisper, "I can't believe what you just said."

Pat stops walking, and his eyes get soft cause he sees the hurt he just gave me. After a few seconds, we stop staring at each other cause we both feel Georgie's eyes on us. And when I look at Georgie, I get scared cause he don't budge an inch until he puts his hands in his pants pockets and with the power of a bulldozer, kicks a piece of glass clear across McClellan Street.

We start walking, again, but at a snail's pace. That's because Johnny's crying slows us down. Nobody says nothing until we're at the corner of Ninth and Moore Streets, then Johnny cries out, "If Daddy loved us, then why did he wantta leave us?"

Johnny's words brings up feelings inside of me and they're coming right outta my mouth. "Why did Daddy wantta die? No matter what was so terrible for him, he shoulda wanted to live for us. What's the point in having all us kids if he don't wantta be here to raise us?"

I feel how deep in my insides my ache goes; it scares me cause the deeper it goes, the hurter I get. It's like I'm looking into a pit that's all black and yucky inside and it goes on and on until forever. It's the ugliest and scankiest and humongoust murky hole there could ever be in the whole universe.

My body does a double shake when Georgie pulls a white-handled pocketknife Daddy gave him out of his pants pocket and screams, "I don't want this!" He opens the blade, bends down, and with a force as great as the devil's, he makes a fist around the handle and jabs the blade on the cement sidewalk. Every time he jabs, he yells, "I hate it! I hate it! I just hate it!"

Johnny and Josephine, they're crying a lot. But me, I'm scared because the way Georgie's jabbing the pavement is making me think that if Daddy wasn't already dead, Georgie would be killing him right here and now. I wantta run over and give Georgie a hug and tell him

41

not to be so angry because I'm afraid for him. But I don't because I know I'm furious at Daddy, too, the same way Georgie is even though I ain't showing it like he is.

"Stop your crap!" Pat yells. "You're scaring everybody!"

"Who cares what the hell you think!" Georgie shouts back, but he jumps up cause Pat is moving towards him. I'm glad when I see the blade fall onto the sidewalk. Georgie, he runs up Ninth to Pierce Street and without so much as looking to see where we are, he runs into school.

Sister Josephine says, "Take out your rosaries and let's pray for a special intention."

I'm sitting at my desk that's next to Sister's, and I take the cross attached to my pink rosary beads and make the sign of the cross. We start with the "Our Father" and once we start praying the third "Hail Mary," my eyes look to the crucifix hanging above the blackboard.

In my head, I scream to God, "I don't have a father now and it's all because of what he did to himself. You know what I wantta do. I wantta run down Seventh Street where my Daddy's store is, break the storefront windows and once I'm inside I wantta break everything to shreds and tear it piece by piece completely apart."

These new and strange feelings are scaring me so much that I think I'm gonna start crying, so to Jesus, I plead, "Please, Jesus! Please don't let me cry!"

And like maybe God tells Sister my prayer, cause suddenly she's standing by my desk and she's taking me by my hand. At first I don't want to go, but I give in cause I think I'm gonna cry. It's so nice that Sister's giving me this little bit of concern. Once out in the hallway, she whispers, "I'm so sorry to hear about your Dad."

I want to ask, "Who told you?" But I don't, and I don't cry either. I figure if I start, I ain't never ever gonna stop. I stand stiff like a tin soldier, look down at the floor and say, "Mommy said he was sorry for what he did. And if he had it to do over, he wouldn't do it." I choke as I hear myself say these words, then I feel my whole insides wanting to come out as I tell Sister, "I don't want him to burn in hell for what he did. Mommy said he went to confession before he died." I pause, then bite down on my bottom lip and whisper, "My Daddy had to be crazy for what he's done. You can't hold somebody who's crazy for what they do, can you?"

Sister takes me by my shoulders, looks me in the eyes and in a very direct fashion says, "Rosemary, your Dad went to confession and God's forgiven him."

Her words, they comfort me a little, but then, I think, I'm not so sure God has forgiven him. It just seems to me it takes more than saying you're sorry and a few prayers to forgive this sin.

"When I was your age, I lived on a farm and one day I came home from school and found out my Dad died . . ." Sister continues.

I'm taken by surprise because I didn't think Sister ever had anything bad happen to her. She's always as happy as a singing bird perched high up in a tree, but when I look into her deep, dark eyes, I know she knows exactly how I'm feeling, and I ain't ashamed no more about crying. I put my arms around her waist and bury my face into her black habit and cry. I feel her gentle, strong arms around me and I just cry and cry and cry, and when I catch my breath, I cry some more. It feels so wonderful not to have to be strong for nobody and just be the broken-hearted, scared little girl that I am. I cry so hard, I'm sobbing and choking on my tears. Then I cough into the air and I bury my head again in Sister's habit and cry some more.

After a few sobbing moments pass, I stop when I hear an almost-big-person footsteps coming up the school steps. It's one of the eighth grade safeties and once he's on the top step, he says, "The kindergarten nun wants you to send Rosemary. Her sister Josephine is sitting in her chair and hasn't moved. She didn't even move when Sister was asking the class to stand for prayers."

I don't wait for Sister to say, "It's okay," before I start running down the three flights of steps and once I open the kindergarten classroom door, I softly yell, "Josephine."

Josephine, she jumps out of her seat and when she nears me, she squeezes her arms around me. I feel so sad for her and it's like my heart has found another way to be broken because it's a horrible thing for me to feel one of my baby sisters' bodies trembling against mine. I wrap my arms around her, with me still holding her and with me still watching her cry, I think, I wish I could take her outside of school. I wish we could both go home.

Then, the almost next best thing happens. Sister Josephine is running towards us and Sister Ida, the kindergarten nun, comes out in the hallway. Right in front of us, they put their hands up to their

43

mouths talking one to the other, and Sister Josephine asks, "Rosemary, is there anything we can do?"

There's something so sad and understanding in her face. Her eyes looking at me with the most compassionate gaze and her eyes are so watery like maybe she's crying, too. I remember how she told me about her Dad dying and I know I can tell her what's in my heart. "Yes," I say in a soft voice. "I think all my brothers and sisters and I should go home where we belong."

Sister Josephine nods like she understands and like she thinks what I ask for is a really good idea. "Why don't you wait here until the others come. Then you can go home together."

I feel such relief and I say, "Thank you." I want to run over to Sister and give her a big hug and a kiss too, but I don't. I think it's better if I stay with Josephine and do my very best to take good care of her. I'm rubbing Josephine's back and I can see it's calming her cause she don't seem so scared no more.

We wait for what seems like forever, but pretty soon I see Pat hurrying down the hallway, and Georgie and Johnny are trailing behind him. Carmella finally comes and we all have smiles on our faces and it feels good to be with each other.

"What's going on?" Pat asks.

"I asked if we could all go home," I whisper.

He gets a relieved look on his face and don't say another word. Nobody says another word. I take Joe's hand; Pat, he walks between Georgie and Johnny, and Carmella walks near me.

It's my brothers who first turn the corner of Hoffman Street; us girls are trailing behind, and when I turn the corner, I tell my knees not to be so weak as I take baby steps with Carmella and Josephine. All of us are so silent, and I know I don't look up from the street even when we cross. We're just getting too close to our house.

I don't know if I even would have looked up if I didn't hear Johnny cry, "What's that?"

That's when I see him; he's standing on the front step of our house and pointing to the small flowers with a purple ribbon tied around them hanging from the door.

"I hate it," I tell myself. "Every single bit of it; I hate."

I look at Pat. He's biting down on his top lip and he's looking down the street like he don't even see Johnny, much less hear him. Georgie, he's standing next to Johnny, but he ain't talking neither, so

I say, "It's called a wreath and it's to let everybody know who passes by our house that somebody just died."

Scruffy silence falls between us again and the awful scents of the flowers fill my nostrils and with my eyes almost burning holes in it, I tell myself, That wreath is telling me that beyond a shadow of any doubt my Daddy's really dead.

I want to run away and never ever come back again. I want to go someplace where I can pretend everything's all right like the way it used to be before he died, but I know I can't. There's lots of looking at that wreath and it's like we're staring at it together and even though I don't know why, I get mad and that's when I say, "We gotta stop looking at this smelly wreath and run right past it right into the house!"

Johnny, he runs in first with Georgie running behind him and Pat, he lets go of the screen door and with his eyes down, too, he runs up the steps.

I tell myself, Pat's afraid of his scary feelings, that's why he didn't wait for us girls, and that's when I look at Carmella, who's slowly walking away, up Hoffman towards Sixth. Josephine's walking towards the Mattresas' steps, which just makes me madder. At the top of my lungs, I scream, "I ain't going in until you two go in first. So get back here right now and get in the house."

I can't believe how fast Carmella and Josephine listen to me, like they ain't never listened to me before. They turn around and run right by me into the house and I know I gotta follow. Once all six of us are in a huddle inside, we inch our way towards the playroom steps.

That's when we hear voices coming out of the dining room.

"Trudy!" we hear Mommy say. "What's got you so upset?"

"It's my fault Daddy killed himself!"

I get surprised cause Mommy's voice sounds stiff like a board when she says, "I don't ever want to hear you say your father killed himself."

There's weird silence, lots of weird silence. I look at the rest of us kids and I know we're all thinking Mommy ain't making no sense saying she don't want to hear that Daddy killed himself —cause that's what he did.

Just when I think I can't stand the ugly silence no more, my big sister, Grace, comes rushing past us into the dining room. She's waving a little blue book and yelling, "Mommy, how much money do you want me to take out of the bank?"

Mommy says, "I have to pay the undertaker because your father's life insurance policies won't pay even though your father's been paying the premiums for years."

"Why won't they give you the money?" Grace asks.

"Mr. Baldi, the undertaker, read the policies and said that since your father died the way he did, they're not going to pay."

In a perturbed voice, my sister Chris, who I didn't even know was there, demands, "What's wrong with those people anyway? Those greedy creeps. They'll do anything for money." Chris almost always says what's on her mind, and sometimes that's exactly what's on my mind, like now.

I'm standing in the doorway now and I can see Mommy ignoring Chris. She turns towards Grace and says, "Take it all out. The whole sixty-five hundred dollars. Put the money in your handbag and hold it close to you when you walk home. I want you to go right now." Then Mommy turns to me and says, "Rosemary, I want you to go with Grace to the bank." I look real fast at Mommy cause I'm surprised she even knows I'm standing here in the doorway, but I'm even more surprised she wants me to go. I look at her again to see if I can figure out why she wants me to go with Grace, then I feel happy cause I figure Mommy knows how much I need to be with one of my big sisters since I can't be with her.

I walk over to Grace and feel comforted by her soft fingers gently rubbing my palm. Once outside, she starts walking real fast up Broad Street to the bank. I can barely keep up, but I know I have to because she's holding my hand so tight, it hurts. But I don't say nothing cause she's crying, but not in the usual way. Her tears don't come out of her eyes. Instead it seems like she's swallowing them. I feel sad for her cause I know she don't find it easy to cry in front of anybody, but I wish she'd slow down cause my teeth keep banging each other as I try to keep up with her.

My voice is shaking and my words are choppy when I say, "Graaaace, my leeegs are toooo shororort. I can't keeep up."

"You have to. We got to get to the bank before it closes. We only have five minutes."

We're running now like there ain't no tomorrow, and I'm exaggerating the sounds of my voice by saying, "Whaaat if there's rooobberers in the bank? Whatiya goooonna dooo?"

Grace is easy to joke with, even now, and she says, "It's not what I'm going to do, it's what you're going to do. Mommy wanted you to come with me because if the robbers want the money, I'll throw you in front of them and run!"

"Ohhhhh, nooooo! If there are bank rooobbbers, I'm goooonna screaeaeaeam on the top of my luuuunnngs and my pooooowerful vooooice will shaaake them uuuuup and we'll have tiiimme to get awaaaay. And thaat's why Mooommy sent me with yoooou."

She laughs, and we keep hurrying. We don't talk till we get near the bank steps and she leans towards me and whispers, "Once we're in the bank I don't want you to say one word. And especially don't say anything about Daddy."

"Yu-Yu-Yu don't haaave to worrrry. I cannn't taaaalk, cause I caaan't catch my breeeath."

I giggle and we walk into the bank together. Grace walks over to the counter and I follow. She fills out a piece of paper and puts her signature on it. Then she goes to a teller's window and gives her the piece of paper. The teller checks her signature against another card that has Grace's and Daddy's signatures on it. The teller counts out $6,500 in large bills, puts it in an envelope and hands it to Grace. Grace puts the envelope in her handbag and once she motions for me to hold open the door, we leave.

I can't believe it's so easy getting all that money. I think maybe Grace feels that, too, cause we don't talk all the way home, but we hold hands as we walk and she's holding her handbag close to her heart. The touch of her hand against mine is so soft and warm and I squeeze her hand tight just to let her know I care about her a lot. She looks down at me and gives me a smile. The tip of her nose is all red and her eyes are, too. We walk fast to get home, but not as fast as when we walked to the bank.

Mommy, Trudy and Grace are sitting on the beige couch with the sunken-in pillows. Next to them, sitting on a kitchen chair is my oldest brother, Ralph; with his Army jacket and Army hat on the back of the chair and he's got a new stripe on his shirt sleeve. I can hardly believe how happy I am to see him. Even though he ain't Daddy, at least there's a man in the house.

I stand next to his tall legs and stare at him; when he looks my way, he smiles. It feels good to have all my scariness leave my body. Taking a deep breath, I lean on Grandmom's sewing machine that's nearby and look around. We're all here, all my brothers and sisters either sitting on kitchen chairs or sitting or standing on the dining room floor. I tell myself that it's gonna be okay, cause we're all together, a family, almost . . .

The house is so quiet. Not even the radio is on. And the radio is almost always on except when we're all sleeping. It's all thirteen of us, and it's more quiet than it is in the middle of the night. I ain't never heard all of us quiet like this. It's so quiet, I think I'd hear a pin drop if one did.

Chapter 8

THIS IS THE VERY FIRST MORNING in our house without our father being alive. Even though it feels very spooky around here, I still sit at the kitchen table with a hot bowl of Cream of Wheat cereal Mom just set down in front of me. I don't know what else to do. I stir the dab of melting butter Mom put on top of my cereal and, at the same time, I look at my sister Antoinette. She's wrapping her tiny fingers around her spoon. After she moistens her lips, she puts a spoonful of that creamy cereal into her mouth. I look over at Anna, who's sitting in her high chair with hot cereal in front of her, too. She's putting her spoon into her white bowl, and after she scoops up some of her cereal, she giggles, then plops the gooey cereal onto her tray. She giggles again, and that's when Antoinette starts giggling, too. I know Mommy doesn't see Anna playing with her food. I know she doesn't hear Antoinette or Anna laughing like two monkeys; if she did, she'd start feeding Anna whether Anna wanted her to or not.

Mom's sitting next to me and I watch as she puts both of her hands around Daddy's beige coffee cup, but she's not drinking coffee. She's drinking chamomile tea cause it's the only thing that calms her insides, she says. I just hate that she's drinking so much of it, cause I can't stand how it stinks. But I don't say anything and move away.

I keep stirring my cereal and watch as she gently blows into the cup. She takes a small sip, then blows again. Then another small sip and it's like she forgets there's any of us in the kitchen cause she moans, "How am I gonna get rid of it?"

I blow on my hot cereal, and I'm purely amazed at how much older Mom looks than she did even just a few days ago. Her graying chestnut hair seems to have more white in it, and some of the ends of her hair are sticking out every which way even though she's got her hair pulled back into two buns. And those dark circles around her tired eyes makes her look like a haggard old lady.

I guess her talking to herself should upset me more than her looking like a haggard old lady, but her talking to herself ain't nothing new, except for one thing. Before today, whenever she'd talk to herself she'd be happy or laughing or mad at somebody. But now, well, she ain't happy or mad. She's sad, and watching her is making me sad, too. I know I could just leave the kitchen and she wouldn't even care, but I care. I can't leave Mommy with her being like this.

All of a sudden she stands up and, turning from the table and us kids, she walks towards the back door. Her black shoes are making rubbing noises as she drags one foot in front of the other. I watch too, as her eyes fix a gaze out the screen door. By the way her short plump body is facing, I know she's looking in the direction of the green wooden fence Daddy had a man paint last year. That's telling me she's looking at the black compost bin that's in front of the fence.

She pushes the screen door open with her hip and before she steps down, she looks at me and says, "Keep an eye on the two babies."

The screen door slams behind her and that's when Antoinette runs into the playroom and Anna shakes her arms as she's yelling, "Ro Re! Ro Re! Dooowwnn! Dooowwnn!" As soon as her feet touch the floor, she runs into the playroom, too.

Even though I know I should be watching my sisters, I gotta find out what Mommy's doing. I stand near the screen door watching, till I hear someone else coming. It's Pat and Georgie. I don't whisper, cause I don't want Mommy to know I'm watching her. I tilt my head towards her to let my two brothers know they ought to be watching her, too.

That's when we hear Mommy say, "How am I gonna get rid of it?"

Pat motions with his eyes like he wants to know what she's talking about and I shrug my shoulders, "I don't know."

Mommy brushes some loose hairs away from her face and looks down at the ground. That's when I see what's there. Mommy's standing over the gray metal bucket that was under the sink yesterday, the one that's got my Daddy's bloody shirt soaking in it. I tap Pat's hand, point to the bucket and after his eyes stop being big, he gets Georgie's attention by pulling the sleeve of his navy-blue polo shirt. But Georgie, he breaks away from Pat and climbs on Mommy's wringer washing machine so he can get a better look out one of the kitchen windows.

Wisssh! Splassssh! Wisssh! I look back at Mommy and I can't believe it, but she's got her hands in the bucket. With her back bent over, she lifts Daddy's shirt out of the bloody water, then pushes it back in like she's washing it on a washboard. But I know she ain't using any washboard cause she got rid of her washboard last year.

She closes her eyes and after she's done making a few splashes with her hand, she goes into a natural up-and-down rhythm to the swishing of the wet shirt. It's like she's not here with us, and I'm glad to see she's somewhere else. But once her shoulders start drooping, she opens her eyes and drops Daddy's shirt into the bloody water. Again, she puts both hands in, then pulls them out. With bloody water streaming down her hands, she says, "This is the only thing I have left of you."

It's like I got something gnawing at me and it ain't because she's talking to my dead Dad, cause sometimes I hear Mommy talking to her dead Mom. What's gnawing at me is how I'm feeling forgotten by Mommy. In my head I yell, "Why's she thinking the only thing she's got left of him is in the bucket. After all, he's our Dad and all of us got some of him and some of her. The two of them made all of us."

I stare at Pat and I see Daddy's pudgy nose and Daddy's midnight eyes. I look at Georgie and I see Daddy's top thin lip and his faraway look on Georgie's face. I look at Johnny, who's now standing with Georgie on the washing machine lid, and I see Daddy's dark wavy hair. And I'm remembering how Johnny likes to joke around, and how he loves to laugh, too, just like Daddy. I turn towards Mommy again and I get scared cause I tell myself she's not remembering she's got all of us.

Then a comforting smile comes on her face, as she says, "How could I forget even for a second that we brought twelve children into the world."

Mommy shakes her head and, holding the bucket, she rushes over to the dented trash can in the yard. She pulls Daddy's shirt out of the bucket and, with all her might, wrings out the dripping, bloody water; without so much as giving it a second look, she drops the shirt into the metal trash can. Then she lifts the bucket by its handle, walks back to the compost bin, and pours the bloody water into the compost.

"Mommy hardly ever uses that bin. So why's she using it now?" Pat asks.

I'm remembering what Blind Man Joe told me when I asked why he had such a smelly thing like a big heap of dead things in his backyard. He told me that a compost is a most wonderful thing cause it takes what once was old or decaying and sometimes even dead and, in God's good time, it becomes something wonderful and life-giving.

Since I got Joe's words running around in my head, to Pat I say, "Something wonderful can come from Daddy's bloody water being put into the compost bin. It was Blind Man Joe who said, 'In God's good time anything you put in a compost can become something wonderful and life-giving to trees or flowers and things like that.'" Which reminds me of the plant I promised to take care of, the one us kids gave Mommy on Mother's Day. I go into the playroom and I think, I don't care if it's alive or dead, I'm putting that plant into the compost.

I rush past Pat into the playroom and from the way the hot sun is beating on it, I see the plant is dead. All its flowers turned brown with some still hanging on the plant while others are lying on the window sill. I stand on my toes and look at the soil and I get sadder cause it looks gray like ashes and not at all dark and rich-looking like when we gave the beautiful plant to Mommy. I put my feet down on the floor as I yell to myself, Don't you remember the idea that Jesus gave you which was to take very good care of this forgotten plant? Cause if it lived, that meant Jesus was telling you that Daddy would live, too. It was only three days ago that Blind Man Joe taught you how to take care of this plant and you didn't do any of it. And now look at it. It's dead. I rub my eyes cause tears are in them. Then, it's like I get hit by a brainstorm and I stop rubbing them. I tell myself the best place for this plant is in the compost bin where Mommy's putting Daddy's bloody water. I stand on my toes again and wrap my arms around it. Once I untangle one of the brittle stems that's caught in my hair, I hurry outside. I stand on the back yard step with only my right arm wrapped around Mommy's plant and I watch Mommy pouring the last of Daddy's bloody water into the bin. She places the empty bucket quietly and as if she's pleased with herself, she smiles and she brushes the tiny hairs away from her face. What with her staring so lovingly at the compost bin, it gives me courage to walk over and drop the dead plant into it.

Mom doesn't look the least surprised. In fact, she smiles and I smile back. I want to tell her what Blind Man Joe said about God and compost. Before I can, there's booming noises coming from the kitchen. I know it's Georgie and Johnny crashing into Mommy's wringer washing machine. From the stern look on Mommy's face, I know she knows, too. Fast like she always walks, she hurries to the kitchen. Me, I can't go inside just yet. I gotta take one more look at the compost bin. I feel greatly comforted knowing that my Mom poured my father's bloody water inside it. I guess it's cause I'm believing wholeheartedly what Blind Man Joe said about it being in God's good time that good can come from what's in compost.

Chapter 9

"HOW'D YOU MAKE OUT?" Chris asks.

Mommy starts fumbling through one of the shopping bags, the one that has a boy's black tie sticking out of it. Lying next to the tie is a shiny slip that's wrapped with black tissue paper and I tell myself it's a half-slip for one of my big sisters. I strain to see what else is in the bag, but all's I see is yucky darkness like in a bottomless pit and I pull back. But I start to smile when Mommy sounds absolutely happy as she says, "I'm so glad Aunt Mary and Uncle Nick came with me. I would have bought the most expensive coffin and that would have been very foolish. But I did buy your father a very nice one. Now let me see . . . oh, yes, it's dark brown with gold-looking handles running across it. I also bought a vault. Holy Cross cemetery has lots of streams underground and the vault will protect your father's coffin. Water won't be able to get in and nothing else will either."

I watch as she straightens her back, then puts her hands on her lap and her face looks suddenly sad as she goes on in a whisper, "Aunt Mary said it wasn't necessary to buy a suit for your father. She said they could throw a blanket over him. At first I agreed. I thought the blanket would make him look like he's sleeping. But at the last moment I changed my mind. I said, 'Mr. Baldi, I want the nicest suit you have.' He showed me a dark navy-blue suit and I told him that's the one I want." She turns towards Trudy and says, "Remind me to press off the new shirt the boys gave your father for his birthday last month."

"Can I iron it, Mom?" Trudy asks.

At first Mom seems taken aback, but after the wrinkles stop being between her eyes, she looks again at Trudy and says, "Okay, but go do it right now. It's in the pile of clean clothes on my bed."

Trudy jumps to her feet and says, "I'll make absolutely certain that Dad's shirt will look just perfect. I'm gonna use starch, but not too much starch because I know Daddy don't like a lot of starch on his shirt. I'll mix a little water in the blue starch so his shirt won't be so stiff. And I'll put the starch only on the end of the collar. That way it won't rub against his neck and make his neck go blotchy red." She runs out of the room and up the stairs and for a minute I feel a strange excitement. Like maybe she's gonna iron that shirt and Daddy's gonna put it on and come right downstairs himself and show us what a great job Trudy did. But that feeling don't last long.

Mom turns to Grace and says, "I want you and Trudy to bring the shirt to the funeral home. Your father always wore his shirts open at the collar and that's how I want his shirt to be worn. So you tell Mr. Baldi I said no tie and your father's shirt is to be left open at the collar."

Grace doesn't answer, but I know she's gonna do what Mommy wants her to do.

"And another thing," Mommy says, her tone still very serious. Her lips pucker and she places three of her fingers to her chin. "I bought a headstone. Uncle Nick said I shouldn't cause the stone won't be put down until the ground settles and that won't be for at least a year. But when I saw one stone in particular, I knew I had to buy it."

"What does it look like?" Grace asks.

"Oh!! It's so beautiful." Mommy's face lights up like she's bought Daddy the best present in the whole world. "It's a big stone that stands about five feet tall and on its front it has a side profile of Jesus with downcast eyes. He's wearing a crown of thorns on his head. I asked the stone cutter to cut into the stone below Jesus' face the short prayer, Lord Have Mercy."

Stillness fills the playroom like a hot August afternoon. But the quiet ends once Mom's body shudders and she cries, "The thoughts of your father being in his grave and no stone marking it. Oohh! I couldn't do that." Then she looks at Grace and says, "I also bought three plots at the cemetery."

Grace's eyes get bigger than two bread rolls, and she demands, "What did yea do that for?"

With uneasiness written all over Mom's red face, she sheepishly says, "Well, when I die I want to be buried with your father."

Grace looks at Chris, who's sitting next to her on the playroom steps. And Chris looks at Grace and the two of them look as shocked as I feel. It's terrible enough thinking about Daddy being dead and now Mommy's gone and bought something called a plot for herself. I don't know what a plot is, but for sure it's got to do with being dead.

"Mother!! Three plots had to cost alotta money!" Grace exclaims as she leans against the wall.

Mommy reaches for her handkerchief from the side pocket of her navy-blue dress and nods. "I know. Uncle Nick kept saying Mike won't want me doing this. And Aunt Mary kept saying I can't afford to be spending money like this. But I kept saying it's what I wantta do." Mom now stands and adds in a whisper, "It's the least I can do for your father."

Stone silence falls around us and I see Grace staring at Chris, with Chris staring at Grace and I know it's only cause they don't understand why Mommy's spent so much money buying these plots. And I can't stand not knowing what a plot is, so I ask, "What's a plot?"

Chris laughs, Mom laughs and Grace stumbles over her own words trying to find the nicest way to say it, but blurts out, "It's a hole in the ground!"

Before she can add anything, I shake my head like I finally know as I say, "And that's where the coffin with the vault will go." What I'm really thinking is that's where Daddy's gonna go, but I don't say that cause we're laughing and I don't want to be the cause of any of us crying. Mommy gives me one of her loving-me kind of looks, and it feels like I just got stroked with a gentle breeze.

"Who are the other plots for?" Chris asks with a giggle.

"The family."

Chris is laughing really loud as she says, "What are we gonna do? Lay on top of each other? It'll be pretty crowded in those three plots." Pointing at Grace, she yells, "It's where you're gonna go!"

"Oh no, my dear! It's where you're gonna go, feet first."

"No! No! No!" Mom interrupts and she's serious again. "Some of you will marry and have your own families. But some of you won't marry and will live at home. And if that happens, those who stay single, will be together with your father and me for all eternity. The three plots hold six coffins."

Chris starts laughing again and with giddiness in her words, she says, "And whichever one of us dies first is gonna haunt the ones that are still alive and scare them so bad that they'll wish they were dead."

Mommy laughs, Grace laughs and I laugh, too.

Grace gives Chris big eyes and says, "I plan on living for a really long time. So don't be coming around and trying to haunt me, cause I'm not going to pay you any mind."

"It'll be the other way around with you haunting me!"

We're all laughing so hard now, Mommy, too, that we don't notice Johnny come in. When we quiet some, he asks, "Do you know why they're building a fence around the cemetery?"

I say, "No! Why?"

"Because people are dying to get in."

Everybody's laughing like a bunch of circus clowns and Johnny, he's still laughing even though he's running up the steps cause he has to go to the bathroom. It's then that I hear a very gentle knock on the screen door. Mommy stands and goes to see who's there. She holds open the screen door and two colored ladies come in.

"Hi, Oda Mae," Chris calls.

One of the ladies, the heavyset one, tilts her head as if to say "Hi" to Chris.

I listen as Mom invites the two colored ladies to sit on two of the folding chairs that Baldi's funeral home lent us for Daddy's funeral. I don't ever remember colored people being in our house before.

It's Oda Mae who talks first by saying, "My sister, Carey, and I, we stopped what we was doing and came soon's we heard."

Nobody says another word until Mommy and the two ladies get done checking each other up and down, then Mommy says, "Do you want something cold to drink?"

Oda Mae says, "No. No. Thanks anyway."

Mommy sits on the bench again and, after she puts one foot in front of the other, she says, "How's your son doing?"

I give Oda Mae the once-over now and after I finish looking her up and down, I tell myself that I like her a lot. She's got big breasts, soft eyes, fat cheeks, smooth dark skin like a brown satin slip and hair that's as straight as an arrow and pulled back into a big bun. But what I like the most about Oda Mae is the gentleness I hear in her voice. "He's doing real good," she says as she answers Mom's question. "He just graduated from college and he's out looking for a job right now."

The other colored lady, the one called Carey, well, she don't say nothing. She's on the thin side and has a serious look on her face, like she don't smile very often. But then I think maybe she don't want to be here in white people's home, but only came cause her sister made her.

Oda Mae looks down to the floor and starts crying, "He was a good man! He was a good man!"

Mommy don't move and don't say one thing, but Oda Mae, she keeps crying, and now, she's rocking back and forth as she says, "Your husband made a difference in my boy's life. He always talked sense to him."

I look right at Chris, thinking maybe she knows what Oda Mae is talking about. And she does, cause she comes towards me and whispers, "Ya know how Daddy always wants our brothers to get a college degree cause he thinks the only way for a young man to get ahead in this world is by having a college degree?"

I shake my head. "Yes, I heard Daddy say that lots of times."

"So once Oda Mae's son started working for Daddy, Daddy preached to him like he was his own son telling him he has to get a college education cause that's the only way for a young man to get ahead in this world."

With a feeling of tremendous pride, I say, "That was really nice of Daddy."

Mommy and Oda Mae are talking to each other, but I don't pay it any mind cause my thoughts are all about how I'm feeling deeply touched by Oda Mae's kind expression of tremendous sorrow and genuine grief. I'm still thinking that when I suddenly look at the screen door and see Mother Colombina, the principal of our school, standing at the side with another nun that I never saw before.

Oda Mae and her sister, Carey, can see Mother Colombina from where they're sitting. They can see how Mother Colombina is staring at them with her cold blue eyes, and Oda Mae, with her eyes still on Mother Colombina, reaches for her big straw handbag that's next to her feet. "It's time to go," Oda Mae says real politely as she wraps her handbag under her arm.

Mommy, she's got a bewildering look on her face and I know that's because she don't understand why all of a sudden Oda Mae is in such a big hurry to leave. But I know why, and it's because Mother Colombina, she's looking at Oda Mae and her sister, Carey, like they're dirt under her feet.

Mommy, still with creases on her forehead, gets off the wooden bench, walks over to Oda Mae and says, "It was so nice of you to come."

Oda Mae gives Mommy a big hug, and Mommy's face gets a gleam on it like she's glad she's getting a hug cause she sure could use one. Mommy sighs and hugs Oda Mae, too. Then they walk arm in arm to the door. In a loud, almost happy voice Mommy says, "Your coming means so much to me. I can't thank you enough. You come back and visit again. You're always welcome in my home."

Mommy holds open the screen door and once Oda Mae pauses on the bottom step, that's when Mommy sees Mother Colombina. She reaches her hand out towards Mother Colombina and with a warm smile on her face, says, "Come on in."

Mother doesn't offer her hand back to Mommy. She's giving dirty looks to Oda Mae and Carey. Oda Mae ignores Mother, but not Carey. She stares back at Mother Colombina, who looks away as she hurries into the house like a dark shadow.

Mother Colombina usually barges into our house unannounced; she always thinks she has good advice to be giving my mother on how to raise us. I wonder why Mommy listens to her, because even though she's the principal of our school, she don't know how to talk nice to little kids and especially kids who are afraid of her like I am. Which reminds me of how she barged in one Sunday morning last November when Daddy was in the hospital. I overslept that rainy morning, so when she let herself in our house, I was still in the bathtub.

I jumped right out of that bathtub when I heard her heavy feet coming up the steps as she was yelling, "I just came from visiting your father and he sent me to find out who still needs to go to Mass."

I jumped out of the bathtub and ran stark naked into my older sisters' bedroom, then into the back bedroom where I hid under my bed to the farthest corner of the wall where the heating vent is. But my whole body started shivering cause there was a very damp chill in the house. I put my hands together and, with my eyes having to look up at the bottom of my black-and-white-striped mattress, I started praying, "Dear God, if you don't let Mother Colombina find me under the bed, I promise I will never ever miss the children's Mass on Sunday morning ever again."

I saw the hem of her black habit passing by my bed and that's when I felt my eyes rolling like spinning wheels. My body started shaking even worse than before, and I had to hold my mouth shut to stop my teeth from making chattering noises. I started saying thank you to God when I saw the hem of Mother's black habit moving in the direction of my older sisters' bedroom and I almost started breathing in a regular way. Until that old witch shouted, "Who took a bath and didn't let the water out of the tub? That's disgusting!"

I covered my ears, closed my eyes and started crying when again she yelled, "Who took a bath?"

My eyes opened wide as I heard my big sister, Trudy, take the blame for me. "I forgot to pull the plug."

"You're old enough to know better!"

I stop thinking about that Sunday morning as I see the meanness in Mother's blue eyes peering out of her thin-rimmed glasses, and she says, "I have to talk to you. Alone!"

Chris has gone upstairs by now. So Mommy turns and motions me to leave and I do. But I don't go far. Once I'm standing in the dining room vestibule, I leave the playroom door open just a little so I can see what's going on. That's when I hear Mother Colombina announce, "Since Michael killed himself, you can't have a Requiem Mass for him, and you can't have him buried on sacred ground at Holy Cross Cemetery."

Mommy's got a shocked look on her face, and after a few seconds pass, she yells, "But I already bought three plots at Holy Cross Cemetery."

"He killed himself and he's forbidden to be buried on holy ground!"

I can't believe it when I hear Mommy, who never does anything but listen to Mother Colombina, scream, "What do you know of my husband? You have no idea what kind of pressures this kind of man would have to be under for him to take his life and leave us like this. What do you really know of life? You sit there behind your convent walls, behind your black habit and hide behind a bunch of rules that have nothing to do with life and death."

I wait for Mother to answer, but Mommy's words leave her speechless. I can't believe what a good job Mommy's doing telling her off. But it gets even better when Mommy, her voice loud but proud, like no one's gonna push her around, adds, "As God is my judge, I will not allow you to sit in our home that my husband provided for us and mock his memory!"

I want to run into the playroom, point at Mother Colombina as I yell, And another thing, it's my Daddy who gave you all those fruits and vegetables for you and the other nuns in the convent. And all those times you pretended you wanted to pay, my Daddy never took your money, not once. And it was my Daddy who made Pat and

Georgie put all the produce in their wagon and take it to the convent so you didn't even have to carry all those filled-up bags.

I start punching the air with my fists as I listen to Mommy screaming like I ain't never heard her scream before. "Wait a second! I've already spoken to Father Fabrizi and the Requiem Mass is scheduled for Friday. Father agreed that my husband is to be buried at Holy Cross Cemetery. I have better things to do with my time now, like making supper for my family. So if you'll please excuse me . . ."

Mommy comes storming up the playroom steps and passes right by me. I tell myself she don't see me because she's got fiery love on her face and she's got lots of determination in her walk. She marches into the kitchen and it's then I hear the playroom screen door open. It's all I can do not to shout, You go away and don't ever come back! When I see Mother Colombina's black habit caught on the screen door, it's all I can do not to laugh as the other nun pulls it out before she lets herself out the door, too.

Chapter 10

"HE'S MY DADDY, TOO! How-how-how come I-I-I ain't allowed to go to my own Daddy's wake! And how-how-how come Rosemary's allowed to go? She's only a year older than I am!" Georgie's crying these words to Mommy, who's standing near the steps that's in between the dining room and the playroom.

As for me, I'm in the playroom sitting on the wooden bench feeling sorry for Georgie cause he's looking like a lost puppy. It's his dark eyes that are peeking out from under his arm that gets to me first. Then, it's the whimpering sound in his voice that touches my heart and I wish there was something in this world that I could do to make him feel better. But I know there isn't, so instead, I bite my bottom lip, then start shaking my head back and forth.

As for Mommy, she don't answer Georgie, but what I do hear is Mommy putting her one foot onto one of the steps as she yells, "You girls better hurry cause the limousine's gonna be here soon!"

Georgie, he follows Mommy into the dining room and he keeps whining, whimpering and screaming, but I stop listening to him cause I just can't take it no more. I start swaying my feet under the bench as my mind starts floating back to the last time I saw my Daddy alive. I'm picturing Mommy telling me to take Carmella and Josephine to the store and tell Daddy that supper's waiting. When he saw us walk into the store, he smiled, then laughed and opened the cash register. Waving his hand to us, he said, "Come here."

I went first, then Carmella, then Josephine. He handed us each a nickel and said, "Be good to your mother and take care of her."

We gave him a kiss on his cheek cause he asked us to and, right before we left, I said, "Mommy said to come home cause dinner's waiting."

He looked down at the faded wooden floor and never looked at us or said no other thing again. And I know just as sure as I know my own name that at that very moment he knew he wasn't coming home no more.

I stop thinking about the last time I saw my Dad when my three big sisters go flying through the playroom and right out the front door. I run after them and by the time I get to the door, Mamie, our next-door neighbor, is coming up the walk. She's coming to babysit

Georgie, Johnny, Carmella, Josephine, Antoinette and Anna while the rest of us go see Daddy at his wake. Soon as Mamie arrives, Mommy calls to Pat and the three of us go out to the limousine. And once Mommy sits on the back seat, I climb in and sit next to her.

I sit back as I look out the window and I get to feeling very sad again cause who I see looking out of the house is Georgie; he's got his one hand leaning on the sill and his face is drenched. He's crying out something, too, but I can't hear what he's saying. The pain in his face makes me cringe inside as I'm thinking, I'm only a year older than he is and I don't know why Mommy said I could go and he can't. It could very easily be me standing with him and crying my heart out with him.

As the limousine turns the corner, I sink into the black leather seat and with big tears in my eyes, I tell myself, I feel so sad for Georgie. I know more than anything he wants to see Daddy one more time and say good-bye to him just like I'm gonna do. I look up at Mommy and I feel sad for her too, and I look at Pat and my three big sisters and I feel sad for all of us and to myself, I think, Seems to me nobody's getting what they want except for Daddy.

I get really mad at Daddy all over again, and I stay being mad at him for about five or ten or maybe even fifteen minutes. But once the limousine man starts parking in front of Baldi's funeral home, I start feeling scared. I don't want to go into the place, but I gotta. I follow close behind Mommy. Once inside, it's so quiet. We all stand around a wooden table that's in the middle of the lobby and even though I can't see even one flower, I know for sure there's lots of them cause my stomach is doing flip-flops from the smell. I never smelled a flower that wasn't pretty, but those in the funeral home make me feel sick. I squeeze my belly like a lemon and quietly go sit on the gray love seat, the one that's tucked away in the corner in front of the big brown window that's covered with a see-through white curtain.

I look out at the room and I see gold-colored lamps with honey-colored light streaming from them. I see large paintings of waterfalls and trees and big rocks hanging on two of the walls. There's beige wallpaper with lots of white flower designs running through it, and next to the five or so green chairs leaning against the walls I see tiny wooden tables with little candy dishes on them, but there's no candy in them. And I don't know why, but I start rocking back and forth until Grace sits next to me. She wraps her arms around me and tells me to place my head on her lap. Once I do, I smile cause it feels so good to have her put her hand gently on my forehead. The way she's stroking my hair is making my insides calm down, and I tell myself that this ain't so bad, after all.

But the mood, it gets broken when I hear a powerful voice coming from the next room, the room where my Daddy is. It's Trudy and she's screaming, "Daddy! Daddy! Who's gonna walk me down the aisle when I get married?"

Very hot tears fall from my eyes and I start getting off the love seat. "Where do you think you're going? You stay right here!" Grace grabs my arm.

I want to say, I wantta go and help Trudy, but Grace looks so mad, I think it's best if I just stay put. I sit back on the love seat and start crying bigger tears, cause all's I'm hearing is Trudy screaming, "How could you do this to us?"

Grace grabs hold of my chin and makes me look into her eyes. "Shh!!! Stop!!!" she whispers. "You know what Mr. Baldi says about Italian funerals!!"

"No. What did he say?"

"Italian people are too emotional. He doesn't want us getting carried away and start yelling like the way Trudy's doing right now. Why, he even said he doesn't want a big mess with some of us fainting all over the place."

Grace and me look up and see Chris, who's standing a few steps away. With a silly smirk on her face, she asks, "Did Mr. Baldi say that in his broken English?"

She holds her fingers together the way some old Italian men do when they have themselves all excited, and with her chin tucked in, too, she hunches her shoulders, and with fire in her eyes, she says, "Did he say, 'Ye know whata de say 'bouta Etalian funerals. Tu, tu tu mucha crrrrrry!!!'"

I laugh, Chris laughs, but Grace looks straight ahead like she don't want to hear or see anything.

I hide my laughing mouth behind my hand until my laughter turns to tears when again, I hear Trudy screaming, "Where are you! Daddy! Daddy! Who's gonna walk me down the aisle when I get married?"

Trudy's wails fill the room like black smoke and I see some ladies crying into their handkerchiefs and I hear some men clearing their throats and shuffling their feet. I cry and I cry and I cry some more, and when I look at Chris, I see she's crying, too; watching her somehow makes me cry even more. I look out at all the people, some I know and some I don't and none of them wants to look at us. It's like maybe they think they'll catch suicide if they do.

"Daddy! Daddy! I only want you to walk me down the aisle when I get married, but you won't be here to do ttthhhaaaatt cause of what the hell you did to yourself!"

Silence falls like black rain, and I'm glad it gets broken by Mommy's cousin, Polly. She's standing next to Chris and after she holds Chris' hand, she whispers, "Your sister's in a lot of pain. She's already realizing how much she's missing your father. That's what's tormenting her. I know cause I lost my father at a young age, too." She gives Chris a kiss on her cheek, then she leans towards Grace and kisses her. She puts her arm around me and I kiss her, too.

Trudy's moans sound like the wind in trees as she calls out, "I shoulda told somebody that Daddy came to see me at work the day he killed himself!! I shoulda told somebody!!"

I stare into the empty space in front of me and, with my frostbitten heart barely beating, I mull over in my mind the fact that I didn't tell anybody about those two awful men coming to see Daddy. Maybe if I did, he wouldn't be in the next room lying in a coffin.

Polly lets go of my hand and to Chris, she says, "Will you walk with me into the viewing room?" Chris takes Polly's hand and I watch as she keeps whispering in Chris's ear as they walk through the viewing room's darkened doorway.

Cold eyes are on me now and when I look, I see Aunt Ruth, one of Daddy's sisters, who's standing next to her grown-up daughter, Teresa, and she's whispering something into Teresa's ear. Then Teresa slithers like a snake over to us and sits on the love seat right next to Grace. Her face tightens as she whispers, "Trudy's putting on a big show trying to get everybody to feel sorry for her. But all's she's doing is getting everybody upset."

I look at Teresa and throw her one of my meanest looks ever as I'm thinking that I'm not allowed to talk back to grown-ups, but what about when they talk mean like Teresa's doing? I keep my sharp eyes on Teresa, who's crossing one leg over the other, and I'm getting madder and madder. How'd she know what it's like to lose a father? How'd she know what it's like to have her father die the way my

Daddy did? How'd she know what it's like to feel guilty the way Trudy feels guilty? She don't know nothing.

Teresa, she fixes her frigid eyes straight ahead like she don't see nothing. She don't even move when Trudy begins wailing again. I hear her fists, too, punching over and over again something very hard, like metal. I close my eyes as I tell myself, I think she's punching Daddy's coffin.

"Daddy! Daddy! I said who's gonna walk me down the aisle when I get married? You always had an answer for me!! Always! Always! Always! Answer mmmeee!!"

My head is aching so bad. I ain't never heard Trudy being this angry at Daddy before. What's making her blood boil hotter than hell is how hard it is for her to be arguing with somebody who don't answer her back. And I think nothing more can go on to upset me. And just as I got myself convinced of it, I see someone running like a wild stallion out of the viewing room towards the front door. It's my brother Pat, and my oldest brother, Ralph, the one who just got leave from the Army. I watch as Ralph's black trouser legs are moving faster than a runaway train; he's doing his best to catch up with Pat and once he does, he grabs Pat, first by his shoulder, then by his white collar.

Ralph's looking hard at Pat, but Pat don't see him. He's got a blank stare on his face and his body is frozen. Still I can see all his pain and grief in that blank stare and the way his mouth is drooping like he'll never be able to make sense out of anything ever again. I know that's what he's feeling cause I'm feeling it, too. Now Pat's pulling and pushing his body as far away from Ralph as possible. That's when Ralph opens the door and motions with his head for Pat to go first.

"Are you all right?" Grace whispers as she pats my head.

I shake my head yes even though it ain't true. I got my hands holding each of my elbows and I'm squeezing them against the fiery pain in my belly.

"I gotta go see Daddy, Grace," I say. "It's the only reason I came to this awful place. To see him one more time."

"I'll go with you."

"I gotta go alone."

I'm surprised she don't argue with me, but she don't, and I get up and go through those doors to where I know my Daddy is lying dead in the shirt with the open collar that Trudy ironed and the dark suit Mommy picked out for him.

My feet are on the hardwood floor and I'm looking down at the faded brown rug. "Sweet Jesus! Sweet Jesus! Please help me to look!" But all I see is the beautiful bouquets surrounding my father's coffin. There's one white lily that stands taller than the rest, and I know I'll never smell flowers again without thinking of this moment.

"Look," I whisper. "You gotta look now!" And I do.

I see my father lying in the coffin and I close my eyes. I take a deep breath, force my eyes open, and this time I can't take my eyes off him. I see in his face familiar things like his strength, his gentleness, and sadness is coming over me like the biggest wave in the ocean. Until, it's like a miracle-instead of crashing, the wave is bringing me memories that even make me smile. Memories of just a few weeks ago when Pat and I brought Daddy his usual breakfast of a cup of coffee and two pieces of toast up to his bedroom.

He was lying down, then, too, but there was so much life in him. First I giggled, then Pat giggled and Daddy smiled and said, "Buon giorno, Rosa Maria, buon giorno, Pasquale." He didn't move. He just waited until one of us answered.

It was Pat first, then me who said, "Buon giorno, Papa."

Just as fast as the memory came, it was gone. Cause I can't take that the life of my Daddy is gone. But it's strange cause I'm not afraid to look at him now. I think he's so handsome in his navy-blue suit and white shirt. Just like Mommy ordered, he's not wearing a tie and his top button is left open. He's wearing his black corrective shoe, too, his shoe that I put on hundreds of times to see just how awful it was to be crippled, the shoe that Georgie polished over and over. And I keep looking. My knees start to feeling weak, so I lean on the empty chair in front of me. After I take a deep sigh, I look at Daddy's curly graying hair and I'm reminded of the hundreds, maybe thousands of times I brushed his hair while waiting for Mommy to finish cooking supper. I'd brush it every which way, and when I was finished, he'd run his fingers through his hair and tell me what a great job I did.

My heart's beating with the love I have for him, but my throat goes dry and I tell myself to stop looking. Seeing him lying in his coffin hurts so bad, but I can't help myself, so I keep looking. I stare at his lifeless eyes, his pasty coloring that's not anything like his usual olive complexion. I look at his long thin fingers and I remember how I held onto those fingers when we went walking together. I weep in silence, but I keep looking.

In my mind's eye I see the night he came home from the hospital six months ago. As he walked through the door, I reached for his hand and kissed it; he smiled as he reached for my hand and I didn't let go of him, not until it was my bedtime and he gave me a kiss. My heart was beating with so much joy then but now, my heart is broken glass. But I keep looking.

I press my thin body against the wall to keep my heart from racing. I have the strangest sensation-it's like I can see his chest moving. I stand on my toes and scream to myself, "My Daddy's alive! My Daddy's alive!" But I know it's only my eyes playing tricks on me. I pinch my arm and instead of waking up from this horrible nightmare, my hurting arm tells me I'm living a nightmare. His eyes will never look at me again. His lips will never kiss me again. His arms and legs will never move again and his voice is forever silent. Then I think I hear Trudy screaming again, but I know it's me. I'm screaming, not out loud like she did, but inside. What happened to your heart, Daddy, that you could leave us like this?

I wait, almost as if he'll answer me. But he don't. Words are lost on him. Dead is dead! Dead is especially dead when it's by your own hand. I don't bother with people who don't want to be bothered with me, even if it is my own father.

I bite down on my bottom lip and the sharp pain of it brings me back to what's around me. That's when I see Pat standing against the opposite wall only a few feet away from me. Watching him scares me cause he don't blink; he keeps that hard stare on Daddy, the one that makes him look like he's lost in his head.

Thinking Pat ain't never coming back to us, I call, "Pat! Pat!"

He don't answer. He keeps those staring eyes on Daddy. I look around for Ralph. He's on the other side of the coffin and he's bending down towards someone. I stretch to see Trudy, and I know there ain't no point in telling Ralph how scared I am for Pat. He's got his hands filled trying to comfort Trudy.

Just as I turn back to Pat, Chris walks into the viewing room and stands on the left side of me. "Are you all right?"

I pull at her to lean towards me. Once she does, I whisper, "I gotta go so bad. Where's the bathroom?"

She holds onto my shoulder and says, "Come on."

Soapy bubbles form on our hands as we stand in front of the bathroom sinks and that's when Chris looks at me in the mirror, giggles and asks, "You know what they say about dead bodies, don't you?"

I look at her in the mirror, too and say, "No. What do they say?"

With a silly look on her face, she says, "Sometimes bodies sit up on their own and they can even belch and guess what else they do, they can even fart."

"Yeah! Right away." I smile, thinking how good it is to be with Chris, who's always able to find something light no matter how dark thing are.

As she dries her hands on the circular white towel hanging from a wall unit, she says, "But I tell you, it's true."

I shake my head like I don't believe her and, after I dry my hands, I use Chris's comb on my two ponytails and say, "Pat's scaring me. He's just staring at Daddy and he don't say one word. And even when I called to him, he didn't answer me. I was gonna tell Ralph, but when I looked for him, he was with Trudy trying to comfort her."

Chris is putting her hairpins in her mouth, but it's like her eyes are speaking cause I can tell by looking at the fierce look in them that she's thinking hard about Pat. She takes the last hairpin out of her mouth and as she pins it into her hair, she whispers, "Let's go get him."

She rushes out of the bathroom and when I catch up to her, she's already got her hand on Pat's shoulder. I stand next to her and she puts her other hand on my shoulder and says, "Let's get outta here."

Pat don't budge. Chris clears her throat and says in a voice that sounds exactly like she knows what she's talking about, "It ain't good the way you keep staring at Daddy. Let's get the hell out of here right now!"

Pat's eyes blink like he's thinking over what she just said. After a few seconds, he nods like he agrees. And if I had to guess what's going on in his head, I'd say he's glad that Chris is showing him the way to come back to us. But that's the way it is between Chris and Pat.

Once Chris, Pat and I are sitting on the couch in the small parlor that's farthest away from the viewing room, Chris asks, "Do you wantta hear a joke? I got some new ones."

I say, "Yeah."

"Okay, here goes. There was a baseball game and there were two doubles, two triples, and one home run, but not a man scored. Do you know why?"

"Naaaah."

"It was a girls' game!" She tilts her head and lets out a roaring laugh.

I laugh out loud, too, and when I look at Pat, I'm glad he's smiling, even if it's just a little. I say, "Chris, tell us another joke."

"Okay. Sister Mary said, 'What do you think of the Taft-Hartley Bill?' The sixth grade boy says, 'You oughtta pay the damn thing.'"

I start laughing, but Chris cries, "Wait! There's more! Sister gave him a zero. He took the grade home and told his Mom it was Outstanding."

Pat laughs really loud and that makes me feel very good. But me feeling good doesn't last long and that's cause Aunt Nettie, Daddy's youngest sister, is watching us. "It's a disgrace the way the three of you are carrying on at your own father's wake. Is this how you're gonna be tomorrow at his funeral? I hope not!"

She keeps looking at us until she's outta the room. After a few seconds of absolute silence between us we look at each other. We can't hold it in anymore, and without making no noises, we keep laughing.

Chapter 11

TODAY IS MY DADDY'S FUNERAL, and as usual nobody tells me nothing except to put on my navy-blue dress and go and wait in the playroom. So I'm wearing my navy-blue dress, the one with the pretty beige lace collar that matches the lace veil I'm holding. It's the veil I'm gonna wear when I go to my Daddy's Requiem Mass. Pat's in the playroom, too. He's wearing his navy-blue school pants and one of his long-sleeve white shirts with his new black tie. I like the way he looks, that is until I see he's wearing a black armband. But I don't have time to think about that. The screen door opens and Uncle Nick, Daddy's brother, comes in. I'm just about to smile at Uncle Nick like I always do, but I see he's wearing a black armband, too and I get to feeling sad all over again cause of how I keep getting reminded that my father isn't ever gonna be with us no more. Instead I just say, "Hi."

Pat says, "Hi," too.

Uncle Nick acts like he doesn't hear us, which is very unusual. He rushes over to the playroom steps and in a voice that's as nice as can be, he says, "Ramona, do you want me to take them over now?"

I don't hear Mommy's answer because it sounds like a pack of wild horses running down the stairs. Then Georgie and Johnny race into the playroom. I look at Uncle Nick, who's still standing near the playroom steps, and I see he's got a determined look in his dark eyes, and that look's telling me we gotta go with him. But then it's like Uncle Nick just remembered something, and he walks into the dining room. I'm glad cause I got something to ask Pat. "What are we supposed to do when we get to church?" I whisper.

"Are we supposed to wait for Mommy before we go into church?" Johnny asks.

"Well, I'm telling you one thing," Georgie says. "I'm not going to wait for everybody else to go into church before me. It's our father's funeral Mass, ya know!"

Pat throws dirty looks at Georgie as he yells, "You're gonna do whatever we're told to do or else you know what's good for you!"

Georgie, well, he's got cockiness coming out of his eyes. Pat starts making two fists. I stand in between them the way Mommy does when it looks like they're going to go at it, and I don't stop until

Uncle Nick rushes into the playroom. He goes right to the screen door and, looking at us like we're supposed to know what to do next, he says in a perturbed voice, "What are you waiting for? Come on!"

Georgie, Johnny and I sit in the back seat of Uncle Nick's station wagon and Pat sits up front where Aunt Myra usually sits.

We drive for about seven or maybe fifteen blocks; then Uncle Nick pulls over to the sidewalk and when I look out the car window, my eyes do a double-take. He's not parking in front of the church, and where he's parking sure ain't where I want to be. I can't believe we're in front of Aunt Mary's house. I don't bother to ask what's going on, cause I know I won't get a straight answer.

We all go inside and I sit on my favorite love seat sofa that's right next to Aunt Mary's fake fireplace. I look around her house, and a calm comes over me cause I'm enjoying once again just how beautiful her home is. She has Oriental rugs in her parlor and dining room, there's crystal lamps sitting on leather-top tables, and she even has a television. But the thing I love the most in Aunt Mary's house is the Grandfather clock that's standing next to the vestibule door. I love the way it ticks so loud every second, and I especially love the chiming sounds it makes every hour. But even though my eyes enjoy what I see, the rest of me ain't happy cause I can't relax when I'm sitting in Aunt Mary's house. She's usually saying, "Watch this and watch that and then watch this again and then watch that again."

With all the watching I gotta do, I don't have any time to have fun, but a sniffling sound brings me back to the moment. I look at my brothers, who are sitting near me. None of them are sniffling. The sound comes again and I look over at Uncle Nick. He's leaning against the banister, and he's got a dazed look on his face that's streaked with tears. I don't never remember him crying before in my whole life. Not even when he says he don't want to talk about what it was like being a soldier in the Pacific Ocean during the Second World War.

I guess Pat's real nervous seeing Uncle Nick cry. He starts twiddling his thumbs and says to Uncle Nick without looking at Uncle Nick, "We could have walked to church by ourselves and saved you a trip. What time is our father's Mass anyway? I don't wantta be late."

Uncle Nick takes his hand off the banister and with big eyes, he says, "Didn't anybody tell you? You're all staying here until we come back from the cemetery."

I bite down on my teeth, sink into the love seat and say, "Nobody told us nothing!"

Johnny yells, "It's our father's Mass! We should go!"

I scream, "I wantta go!"

Georgie hits the arm of the love seat and cries, "Don't tell me I can't go again! He's my Daddy! I should be there!"

"Hey! Don't take this out on me," Uncle Nick says like he's as confused as we are. "I'm only following your mother's orders."

I see tears in Pat's eyes, but I know he ain't gonna say nothing cause he don't want to go against what Mommy wants, even if it hurts him real bad. I give up, too, cause I know it's a losing battle trying to get big people to hear how sad and sick we feel way down deep inside. So I just sit back on the love seat and stare at nervous Uncle Nick. I stop watching him when I hear Aunt Mary walking down the stairs. Once she's on the last step, she looks at me, then at my brothers, and that's when I think she's gonna say something, but she don't say nothing. After she looks down at her black heels like she needs to make sure she's standing on her Oriental rug, she turns to us again and puts a mean look on her face. "I put my figurines on the mantle so you can't break them. I paid two hundred fifty dollars for each one of them, and I paid hundreds more for my crystal lamps. So don't any of you be touching any of my things!" She walks towards the vestibule door, turns to look in the mirror that's hanging above the tiny wood leather-top table; she pins her black hat to her graying hair, and with her dark eyes piercing like darts as she looks directly at me and demands, "I mean it! Don't break any of my things!" She clears her throat, then says, "My friend, Ester, is in the kitchen preparing food for when everyone comes back from Holy Cross Cemetery. She's gonna keep an eye on you. So you better be good."

I wantta say we don't need her to keep an eye on us cause our Mommy and Daddy taught us how to be good. But I don't-I know Mommy would be plenty mad if I did.

Aunt Mary turns off her mean voice and in a nice one, says, "Ester may need your help, so give her a hand. I told her to let you unfold the chairs, set the table or anything she needs you to do."

As soon as Aunt Mary and Uncle Nick are gone, Pat walks over to the mantle and touches the figurine of a lady that don't have her breasts covered. I stand next to Pat and touch the folds of the lady's long skirt. Georgie and Johnny stand next to me and Georgie touches the figurine of the muscular man who's carrying the world on his shoulders. I stare at this very strong man, and wonder why his skin got painted white and gold. I'm almost gonna say something, but I change my mind.

Johnny starts giggling as he touches the arm of the man. "His muscle's as hard as a rock."

Georgie smiles. Pat don't say nothing. I laugh.

A few more moments pass, and I stop touching the lady figurine and sit on the Oriental rug. Looking up at Pat, I whisper, "How come we ain't allowed to go to Daddy's funeral? Us not being allowed to go makes me feel like we don't matter. It's like we don't even exist."

Pat stops touching the lady figurine and when Georgie and Johnny see Pat, they stop, too. When Pat sits next to me on the floor, they do too, and we sit in a circle on Aunt Mary's Oriental rug.

"I wonder what everybody's doing right now in church?" I say.

I know Pat ain't got the answer, but I keep looking at him anyway.

With hurt in the sound of his voice, Johnny says, "We belong at church."

"Johnny's right," I say, even though I know it was Mommy's decision to send us here. "It should be us at church cause we're his kids."

We're all looking at Pat, hoping he's gonna agree.

Johnny says over and over again, "We gotta be there! It's for our Dad!"

Johnny's words keep ringing in our ears, until Pat nods, "Yes," then says, "Yeah, I think we should be there, too."

"Let's go! Right now!" Johnny starts to stand.

Pat gestures for me to stop him. I grab Johnny's arm and Pat says, "We just can't leave. We gotta say something to Aunt Mary's friend."

Johnny says, "What are we gonna say?"

"I don't know. But you come with me into the kitchen and I'll think of something."

I sit back on the floor and I stop staring into space when I hear Pat running back towards us saying, "Let's go!"

Georgie stands and asks, "What did you tell her?"

"I said we were bored and if she didn't need us for anything would it be all right if we went for a walk?" Pat's giggling as he swings open the vestibule door and when he looks at me, he says, "She said it was okay with her. But she don't want us to go too far."

Pat, Georgie, Johnny and me, we're standing in front of the live chicken store that's right across the street from St. Nick's Church where my Daddy's Requiem Mass is going on. I'm out of breath from running to keep up with my three brothers. Pat's leading like always, and he decided to run almost all the seven blocks from Aunt Mary's house to St. Nick's Church. It's Georgie who, pointing towards the church, exclaims, "There's Blind Man Joe walking down the church steps. We must really be late."

With annoyance in his tone, Pat asks, "What makes you say that?"

"Blind Man Joe always leaves before Mass is over cause that way he don't have to fight the crowd," I say.

Like what I just said is being ignored, Georgie runs across the street; Pat goes after him, Georgie reaches Joe first, but Pat catches up and together, they take hold of Joe's arm, one on each side. They walk Joe across Ninth Street and I feel real proud of my brothers cause I think they're remembering how Daddy says that when we see Joe crossing streets, we got to be his eyes for him.

Once Joe's standing on the pavement only a few feet away from me, I say, "Hi, Joe."

"Hi, Rosemary." He rolls his head back and forth pretending he's looking for somebody, then he asks, "Where's the little guy?"

Johnny's eyes light up. "I'm right here."

Joe puts his white-and-red cane on one arm, then stretches his hand out into the open space. Johnny touches Joe's hand, and that's when Joe reaches for Johnny's head, shakes his hand through Johnny's hair and says, "My daughter should have your curls."

Then Joe gives out a big smile as he makes two fists pretending he's boxing with Johnny and Johnny, he makes two fists, too, and starts bobbing and weaving in between Joe's pretended punches. I smile when I see Pat smiling and I hear Georgie giggling and I think how nice it is to have a friend like Blind Man Joe.

After Joe and Johnny stop play fighting, Joe puts a serious look on his face and says, "Why aren't all of you in church?"

Pat stares at me and to Joe he says, "Our uncle said that our Mommy said we weren't allowed to go. But we came anyway cause it's for our Dad."

Joe rubs his nose with a white handkerchief he just pulled out of his pants pocket and says, "Yeah! This is where you gotta be. I think

75

it's a really good idea you coming to church." Joe puts his handkerchief back in his pants pocket and, once his hand is free, he clutches Pat's arm, then pauses. His face gets lots of wrinkles on it, especially his forehead, and it's like he's trying to figure out how to say what he wants to say next. But once all those wrinkles leave his face, he says, "I just don't know what to say. I'm so sorry."

I almost start crying, but don't because of the soothing way Joe talks. It brings a calm like a rippling wave over me and when I look at my brothers, I see they're just as touched as I am; they ain't looking at each other and all three of them have their heads down.

But the silence and tender moment is gone when Joe says, "You better get yourselves into church now."

Like Joe's a sergeant in the Army, Pat does just what Joe says. He starts running across the street and once he's in the middle of the street, he looks at us, squints his eyes and yells, "Move it!"

Georgie and Johnny start running after him; a part of me wants to run with them but another part of me wants to stay behind and watch Joe. His face and neck is turning red and his voice starts making throaty sounds like a gorilla as he growls, "Damn you, Mike!" He bangs his cane on the cement ground, then he bangs his feet on the ground, too, as he grumbles, "Didn't you stop to think about your twelve children?"

I know Joe don't know I'm here or he never woulda said what he just said. Even so I can't stand being near him no more. Like a scared kitten I run away, but the big difference between me and that kitten is that when she runs she don't trip on the curb, but I do.

But before I can scream, "Ouch!" Joe yells, "Rosemary! Is that you?"

I'm too scared to answer cause Joe's monstrous voice is something I don't ever remember hearing before; I get even more scared when he takes two steps towards me and with his stocky body casting a big shadow over me, he yells, "Rosemary!"

My heart, it's skipping lots of beats and only after I catch my breath, and just above a whisper, I say, "It's me, Joe."

He screams, "It's not right to sneak up on me like that!"

"I'm sorry."

He puts out his hands in a kind gesture and, since I know Joe wants me to put my hand in his, I do. I feel the softness of his touch and my anxious feeling is greatly relieved. Once again I feel safe with

Joe and when he speaks, his caring tone is back. "Is everything okay with you?"

"I'm okay, Joe. I just skinned my knee."

"I didn't scare you, did I?"

"No. You didn't."

But Blind Man Joe did scare me and even though I ain't afraid no more, I'm confused by the way he changed from being nice to being mad to being nice.

He still has a hold of my hand, and as I stand, he motions his head towards church and says, "You better hurry up."

After he lets go, I run across Ninth Street and catch up with my three brothers, who are standing on the top church step. I turn and take one last look at Blind Man Joe. With the bottom of his cane tapping the cement pavement, I watch as his step falters. Once he's standing on both legs, he pushes forward and turns onto Peirce Street before his cane does. I tell myself that I'm being weird being afraid of someone I love like Blind Man Joe.

Chapter 12

THE SMELL OF THE BURNING CANDLES mixed in with the smell of candles that burned days ago lingers in the darkened vestibule of the church where the four of us stand, almost in a circle. I make the sign of the cross as I look at the large black crucifix of Jesus, but I turn quietly away only because the sight of blood coming out of Jesus' side is reminding me of my Daddy's blood. But what I see next scares me even more: At the farthest wall in the vestibule there's statues of tortured souls being swallowed up by hell's fire. They got pure agony all over their faces, begging God for mercy in their uplifted arms. All around them are devils with horns on their heads and pitchforks in their hands. They're real ugly and they're laughing like they're having the time of their lives poking some of those tormented souls with their pitchforks. I can't believe I ain't never seen this horrible sculpture even though I passed by hundreds of times. I wish I wasn't looking now. Cause I can't stop looking as a sick feeling comes over me. My own Daddy can't be in hell right now with all those tortured souls. He can't.

"Put your veil on your head," Pat whispers. Even though he's whispering, I jump at being brought out of my horrible thoughts. When I turn to Pat, he's looking past me into those fires of hell. Instead of being scared, he's fuming mad at what he sees. Then he says, "Let's go inside."

I put a black bobby pin through my beige veil, then open the side vestibule door very slowly. I don't want this very old and very heavy door making creaking sounds. I slip in first, then Pat, Georgie, and Johnny follow. I can barely see the priest who's standing in front of Daddy's coffin and at first I think it's because there's hardly any lights on. But then I tell myself, It's because my eyes are burning cause of all the hot tears that's in them.. I blink away the tears and stare at my father's closed coffin that's draped in black with a cross of the crucified Jesus lying on it. I tell myself that I can't stand that his coffin is closed cause I'm never going to see my father ever again.

I swallow my tears when Johnny whispers, "How come the church is not all lit up the way it was for Grandpop's Requiem Mass?"

"Yeah, and who's that priest?" Pat grumbles. "Where's Father Fabrizi? He's the one who says the Requiem Masses. Who the hell's that priest anyway?"

I shrug my shoulders, "I never saw him before."

"And there ain't no flowers on the altar and they only got one candle lit," Pat says, still trying to sound angry, but what he's sounding is hurt. "When Grandpop died, there were lots of flowers and there were lots of candles, too. I remember cause I hate the smell of burning candles."

Johnny murmurs, "How come there ain't no organ music?"

"And how come there ain't nobody singing like there was when Grandpop died?" Georgie says more loudly than any of us.

"Shhhhhhh! You're talking too loud!"

Johnny shrugs, then whispers, "How come our neighbors ain't here? And where's Daddy's friends? How come none of Daddy's customers ain't here?"

It feels like a light bulb is going off in my head and to Pat, I whisper, "The reason why there ain't no singers, no organ player, no neighbors, no friends, no Father Fabrizi is because our father killed himself. That's why!"

Georgie looks shocked out of his mind and Johnny, he starts crying. And me, I'm thinking about Blind Man Joe, and how he left earlier. But I tell myself he wouldn't be mad at Daddy. Not Blind Man Joe. He only left cause he always leaves early.

"They ain't doing right by Daddy," Pat whispers.

I nod, "It's like our whole world is saying Daddy's got to be punished for what he did. But who's really being punished is Mommy and all us kids."

That's when the priest whose name we don't know stands in front of Daddy's coffin, shakes the smoking incense holder as he prays, "Kyrie eleison. Christe eleison. Kyrie eleison. Christe eleison."

I make the sign of the cross and that's when Pat mumbles, "What's it mean?"

"It means, God have mercy. Christ have mercy. God have mercy. Christ have mercy."

Georgie and Johnny make the sign of the cross, too, but Pat, he don't. The priest keeps walking around Daddy's coffin as he keeps shaking the incense holder. He keeps saying more prayers, but in Latin so I don't understand. That's when I start looking for Mommy.

She's sitting at the end of the pew next to Daddy's coffin. I wonder why she ain't kneeling like everybody else, and I wonder why she don't got her hands in a praying position like almost everybody else, and I get really scared cause Mommy don't say one Amen with everyone else . . .

It's when the Amens stop that I hear my big sister, Trudy, wailing. When I look to find her, I can't see her cause she's kneeling like everyone else, but I hear her vibrating sobs bouncing off the church's high ceiling and making the church sound more like an echo chamber than a church.

Johnny's still crying, Georgie, he keeps blinking his eyes and Pat, even though his eyes are watery, he won't let go of any of those tears and he tries to act tough in a nice way as he says, "I hope Trudy's gonna be all right."

I try to stop listening to Trudy cause her wailing is making my stomach twist in a knot and I don't know if any of us are going to be all right ever again. I want to say something to Pat, anything so I don't feel so alone and scared and when I look at him, I get surprised cause he's looking at me, too. We keep looking at each other, but we don't say nothing. We both know we don't need words to say just how disgusted and sad we're feeling.

That's when the priest starts talking in English. He's standing in front of Daddy's coffin and with his hands folded in prayer, he says, "Let Us Pray."

Almighty and most merciful Father.
You know the weakness of our nature.
Bow down Your ear in pity to Your servants, upon
whom You have laid the heavy burden of sorrow.
Take out of our hearts the spirit of rebellion,
and teach them to see Your good and gracious
purpose working in all the trials which
You send upon them. Grant that they may not
languish in fruitless and unavailing grief, nor
sorrow as those who have no hope, but through
their tears look meekly up to You, the God of
all consolation. Through Christ our Lord, Amen.

Soon as that priest we don't know says Amen, Pat pulls open the door and slips back into the vestibule. Me, Johnny and Georgie follow.

"What's that prayer got to do with Daddy?" Pat demands as he kicks the marble wall. He reaches towards the wooden table that's got about thirty or fifty missals, hands me one and mumbles, "Pick out a nice prayer for Daddy. We're all gonna stand near the Blessed Mother statue and pray for Daddy's soul."

I'm afraid I might not find a prayer that suits Pat, but that doesn't stop me from opening the missal to where a holy card is between two pages. My eyes get big and my heart gets happy cause it's a prayer that I remember Father Fabrizi saying at Grandpop's Requiem Mass. So with a smile on my face, I look at Pat, who's standing next to Georgie, who's standing next to Johnny; still holding the missal in both hands, I stand between Pat and Johnny, clear my throat and pray:

The Lord is my shepherd: I shall not want. He maketh me to lie down in green pastures: he leadeth me beside the still waters. He restoreth my soul: he leadeth me in the paths of righteousness for his name's sake. Yea, though I walk through the valley of the shadow of death, I will fear no evil: for thou art with me: thy rod and thy staff they comfort me. Thou preparest a table before me in the presence of mine enemies: thou anointest my head with oil; my cup runneth over. Surely goodness and mercy shall follow me all the days of my life: and I will dwell in the house of the Lord forever.

As soon as I close the missal, I feel Pat's hand on my shoulder. I can tell by his gentle touch that he's comforted by the beautiful prayer, and I am, too. Then Pat walks over to the vestibule door again and peeks into church. When he does, I walk over to the missal table, and before I place the holy card back into the missal, I notice on the front of the holy card a picture of St. Jude, the saint of hopeless causes. I kiss St. Jude's picture and in my head, I pray, "Please St. Jude. Help my Mommy and us. And please help my Daddy, too, if you can."

Just as I put the holy card back into the missal, I hear Trudy screaming a blood-curdling scream. I rush over to the vestibule door and see she's standing now, screaming and looking like she's pulling her hair out of her head. Then she starts climbing over Mom to get herself out of that pew. I can tell Pat is very, very scared cause he starts running towards the back of the church. He holds open the main church door and calls, "We gotta get outta here! Trudy's running here!"

I start to run, but not so fast I can't dip my fingers in the holy water font, but it's not until I run down the church steps that I make the sign of the cross with the holy water that's left on my fingertips. Once we're all down on the sidewalk, Johnny says, "What do we do now?"

Even though we ain't in church no more, Pat whispers, "Let's run across the street and stand in the chicken store."

"Do you think the chicken store man will let us?" I ask. "We don't buy our chickens from him."

"He ain't gonna say nothing."

Even though I'm crossing Ninth Street, I don't look to see if cars are coming-I have my eyes on the church doors worrying if Trudy's going to come running, crying and screaming. But once I'm on the other side of the street, I stop worrying cause the church doors stay shut like a bank vault.

"Let's go in," Pat says as he walks into the chicken store.

Right off the chicken store man says, "Can I help you?"

Pat points towards the church and in a quiet voice says, "Our Daddy's Requiem Mass is going on and would it be all right if we stand here and watch?"

"How come you're not in church?'

"We came out ahead of everybody so we can see better."

The chicken store man looks at us one at a time like he's trying to figure us out, and I guess he figures we're all right cause he says, "Okay. But just don't be causing any trouble, otherwise, you'll have to go."

The four of us stand next to the window facing the church, but right away our attention gets turned to someone walking into the chicken store: it's Fat Lady Concetta, one of Daddy's customers. She's fatter than the fattest pig I've ever seen, and the way she puffs up her thin blonde hair trying to make it look like she's got more of it than she does, well, I got to tell you, it just makes me shake my head back and forth as I laugh real loud inside me.

She looks at me with her cold blue eyes and screeches, "Ain't you one of Mike's kids?"

"Yeah, I am."

With cutting eyes, she looks at my three brothers, then she looks at the chicken store man and with her index finger going in circles near her right temple, she says, "Their father went loco and killed himself. The whole family's crazy."

The chicken store man is blinking his eyelids like he's having a hard time believing what he just heard. He stumbles over his words, stuttering, "W-w-why are you saying something so-so hateful?" And it's like he gains composure over himself cause he stops stuttering and demands, "What the hell's wrong with you?"

Fat Lady Concetta puts her hand on her fat hip and says, "Well, it's the truth, ain't it?"

The chicken store man shakes his head like his head's trying to shake off what Fat Lady Concetta's saying. Then he starts rambling in Yiddish. I don't understand what he's saying except for one word which is, "Oy vey."

That's what the Jewish store owners on Seventh Street, where my Daddy's store is, say when they give up on somebody.

Fat Lady Concetta's got an evil look like she wants to say more mean things, but she don't. Instead she walks over to the cages where the live chickens are and all the hens start screaming. Which is a lot of noise cause those cages are stacked to the ceiling. Fat Lady Concetta points to the chicken she wants and the chicken store man pulls the hen out of the cage by her two legs. With that chicken squawking, he walks to the back room and closes the door behind him.

"She's got some nerve saying what she said about our father," I say to my brothers. "Daddy's got two books of people who owe him money and she's in both books with lots of pages of money she owes."

Looking right at Fat Lady Concetta, Pat yells, "I wonder if she's gonna pay for her chicken?"

She looks at Pat and me with dirty looks, but she don't say nothing. But Johnny's hurt really bad by what she just said about our Daddy. I watch as he puts his hands in his pants pockets and, with his head down, starts crying.

I put my hand gently on his shoulder and, in the kind of voice Mommy uses when she wants to make Johnny feel better, I whisper, "Don't cry, Johnny. It'll be okay."

"Why she gotta say our Daddy's crazy?"

"Like Daddy says, some people are just plain igorant!" I say real loud. "And some people like kicking you right in the face when they think you're down and out."

Just then the chicken store man comes back and gives Fat Lady Concetta a brown bag with a dead chicken in it. We all look to see if she's going to pay, and she does. That's when Pat points to a sign on the wall that says, "No Credit."

I laugh, Pat laughs, Georgie laughs, but Johnny's still trying to stop crying.

Fat Lady Concetta picks up her brown bag and waddles out of the store.

"Just look at her!" Pat whispers. "She's disgusting. Where her two watermelons hang down in front of her, her filthy dress is worn so thin. Ugh!" Then he takes Johnny by his shoulder and says, "Look at her! How could you take what she's got to say seriously?"

"She looks like she's got two shelves coming out of her backside," I say. "I bet each cheek could balance a glass of water."

Pat giggles, I laugh and Johnny laughs, too, but I know he's only pretending cause of how his dark eyes got tears coming out of them. Georgie's already outside and racing down the steps after Fat Lady Concetta. When he's real close, he holds his fingers to his nose and shouts, "Don't you ever take a bath?"

Pat howls. "Daddy told me she got stuck in the bathtub because she's so fat. They had to call the fire engines to get her out."

Fat Lady Concetta don't say nothing. She crosses the street and once she's on the other side, Georgie hollers, "Is that the Goodyear blimp that just passed by? You fat-ass bitch!"

I get scared wondering if the chicken store man's going to do something about Georgie cursing, but when I look at him sitting behind the counter with a grin on his face, I get happy cause I think he's only pretending to be reading his Jewish newspaper.

"Roe, look," Pat nudges me. I turn to see the main church doors opening. Georgie sees it too, cause he comes running back inside the chicken store and we all stand and watch as Daddy's coffin is placed at the top of the church steps. Then the six pallbearers lift the coffin into the air and as they start carrying it down the first of the seven church steps, Pat takes the words right out of my mouth when he says, "I hope they don't drop him."

No one says nothing. We're just watching and trying not to think about Daddy being in the brown box. Then Pat says, his eyes still on Daddy's wobbling coffin, "Daddy's teasing and laughing is gonna be hard to not have around me no more. I really like Daddy."

I'm surprised hearing Pat saying that. It was just the other day when he was punching his bedroom wall cause of how mad he was at Daddy, and it was just last night at Daddy's viewing that Pat made me so scared.

The church side vestibule doors open, I see Mommy. She's wearing a black hat with a black veil covering most of her face, but I still can see her eyes, and they're as red as sunburn and her face is puffy, just like sunburn, too. She can't come down the church steps by herself. So Mommy's cousin, Leonard, is holding her arm.

Pat's hands are squeezed into fists; he stares out the window. "I always liked Daddy a lot until now."

Georgie moves away from Pat and stands near the screen door. I know why. He's afraid Pat's going to take his being mad out on him. "Fungol!" Pat shouts. "Fuck him!"

"Where have you been? It's getting late! Everybody's gonna be here soon!" Aunt Mary's friend, Ester, is yelling at us.

We don't answer and I can tell by the deep crease between her eyes and the big pile of dishes she has in her hands that she don't have any time to make us tell her we've just come back from our father's Requiem Mass. Instead, she looks me as she's placing the dishes on the table and says, "I need you to set the table." She looks at Pat and says, "Get your brothers to help you open the folding chairs and put them wherever you find room."

Once we finish doing what she asked us to do, we sit in the parlor on the Oriental rug. After we settle down, Georgie says, "We got to be very quiet. That way we show respect for Daddy."

We don't say nothing for what seems like a very long time, but the silence between us gets broken once the vestibule door opens and sunlight and people come pouring into Aunt Mary's house. I get all excited when I see Mommy. Her eyes ain't red no more, and I get a sense of relief all through me. I stand and yell, "Mommy! Mommy!"

She don't hear; instead, she walks into the dining room and sits on one of the folding chairs near the mahogany table. I want to go and take care of her, but there are so many grown-ups around her, and besides I agree with Georgie when he said we have to be quiet to show respect for Daddy. I sit on the love seat next to Pat and watch all the food being eaten, and all the drinks being drunk. I hear the jokes being told and I listen to the voices getting louder; some of the laughter getting meaner, and my feelings start to get hurt cause I'm thinking my Daddy's funeral is turning into a big party.

I lean towards Pat and whisper, "It's very nice of Aunt Mary having everybody come back to her house, but I wantta go home."

I wonder if Uncle Nick heard me cause only after a few seconds of me talking to Pat, he comes over and says, "It's time to go home. Go find your two brothers."

I go into the dining room, find Georgie and Johnny sitting together on the same phone chair, and whisper the good news in their ears.

Together, they jump out of the phone seat and as soon as we get done saying "Good-bye" to some of our relatives, we rush to the open door and stand next to Pat, who's leaning against it. We don't talk, but I can tell Johnny's as anxious as I am to get out of here; he's got his head down, his hands in his pockets and he's shuffling his feet. Georgie keeps looking out the front door. I think he's pretending he's outside and not in here where it sounds like a big party. Pat's got his eyes on the floor, and if I had to guess what's on his mind I'd say he feels like he don't fit in. If he had his way, he'd run home. But he won't and that's cause he don't want to upset Mommy.

When Mommy finally comes, she stands in the parlor only a few feet away from us, but she don't look at us. I can tell by that anxious look on her face she wants to go home, too. After a few quiet moments of us listening to all the screaming sounds coming from inside Aunt Mary's house, Uncle Nick finally comes. That's when Mommy nudges Pat on his shoulder. Rushing towards Georgie, Johnny and me, she says, "Let's go home."

Even with all thirteen of us at home, the house ain't the same. There's lots of darkness coming from inside the kitchen and the dining room, and the playroom, too. Georgie's sitting on the wooden bench and I say to him, "Ain't it weird to see our house so dark? Ain't it even weirder than anything not hearing any sounds coming out of all the walls in our house?"

At first he don't answer, but after his body stops shaking, he says, "This is the time Daddy used to come home for supper."

I sit real close to Georgie cause my heart just dropped to the floor remembering how Daddy used to come walking down the street whistling so loud that we could hear him all the way up the block or he'd be coming in the house singing a song he just made up or he'd be coming in yelling, "Yyyyyyoooooooooo!"

I open my mouth to say something, but since no words come my way, after a few seconds, I leave Georgie and stand on the playroom steps as I hold onto the banister. I look into the kitchen and see Ralph emptying a large brown shopping bag onto the kitchen table. Trudy and Grace are sitting at the kitchen table. Trudy puts her hands into the brown bag and I'm surprised when she pulls out lots of white and brown envelopes. I know most of those envelopes mean that Daddy got Mass cards, and I'm glad for that cause I think Daddy's gonna need all the prayers he can get.

Once all the cards are out of the bag, Ralph sits at the table, too. The three of them watch as Mommy rinses the coffee pot. Quietly, Ralph takes the lids off two of the white boxes of thank-you cards and Ralph says, "We better get started."

Mom don't say nothing. She don't ask to see the Mass cards. She's counting each spoonful of coffee grinds that she's placing into the coffeepot basket; once she counts up to five, she tosses the spoon into the sink and places the coffeepot on the stove. I think how she must be doing what she did when Daddy was home, when he and Mommy sat in the kitchen after supper and drank coffee.

I hear mutterings coming from the playroom. I turn and see Chris sitting on the beige couch with the sunken in pillows. "How come you ain't helping them write out those thank-you cards?" I ask Chris.

She rolls her eyes, then crosses her legs. "Yeah! Right away. I'm just gonna rush right in and help them write out those stupid thank-you cards. Ya know, it's not even ten hours since Daddy's been buried. Writing thank-you cards sure is the thing to do when you don't want to talk about what you don't wantta talk about."

Chris keeps staring at me and I keep staring at her and the lonely look in her eyes is only reminding me of the lonely way I'm feeling. I say, "It don't make no sense that we're all finally together with nobody rushing around to do this thing or that and there ain't no talking about the way Daddy died." The deafening silence I hear ringing in my ears is killing me and I can't take it no more, so to Chris, I say, "I'm really tired. I'm going to bed." Before I climb the steps, I look once more in the kitchen. Mommy's lowering the flame under the coffeepot and I breathe in the coffee's wonderful aroma. I look at Ralph, who's writing a thank-you note. I squint at Trudy, who's reading a Mass card. Out of the corner of my eye, I watch as Grace starts opening one of the brown envelopes. I listen to the sounds coming out of the playroom and when I look, I see Pat and Georgie tossing a baseball. Suddenly I wantta go running through the house screaming on the top of my lungs, "Why did Daddy kill himself? Do you know why Daddy killed himself? I wantta know why my Daddy killed himself! I can't believe that my Daddy killed himself!"

I wantta run and run and scream and scream all through the house. I wantta run and run and scream and scream up and down Hoffman Street. I wantta run and run and scream and scream up and down Seventh Street where my Daddy's store is. I wantta run and run and scream and scream until I fall down because I can't run and scream no more.

Instead, I climb the stairs, walk into my bedroom, take off my dress, and with only my slip on, I climb into bed and immediately tell myself to fall asleep and I do.

Chapter 13

IT'S A CLOUDY MONDAY MORNING around 7:15; I'm in the playroom waiting for Carmella and Josephine cause it's my job to take them to school. I'm standing next to the wooden bench looking through the window at the white clouds, and what I'm thinking is I didn't think nothing worse could happen to me after my Daddy killed himself. Boy, was I wrong. The day after my Daddy's funeral, when I went outside to play, none of the kids on Hoffman Street would look at me. They pretended they didn't even hear me when I said, "Hi." I'm beginning to feel like one of those ten lepers in the Bible who nobody goes near cause they're afraid they're gonna catch leopards, too. And even some of the big people in our neighborhood are treating me and my family like we don't even exist.

There's Vincent, who lives two doors away from us. When Mommy smiled at him, he looked down at his pavement and didn't even say, "Hi!"

There's Becky, who lives right above Rosenberg's deli. Yesterday morning I was in the street spinning Pat's spin top and Becky threw a small bag of trash right out her third-story window and it landed right next to me. I got so mad cause she couldn't help but have seen me. So I picked up that bag right by its string and threw it into the Rosenbergs' back yard. Then I went and told Mr. Rosenberg I smelled garbage coming from his back yard. There's even business people on Seventh Street, where Daddy's store is, who must be saying mean things to my Mommy. She didn't say so, but when she came back home from shopping, she sat at the kitchen table and cried. And Mary and Rita, the two old Italian ladies who live on our block, got bossy with Mommy and told her she's got to wear black all the time, even though she's got young kids to raise.

I don't think nobody likes us no more and them not liking us, well, it's making me not like anybody either. The only people I like in my neighborhood is my Mom and my brothers and sisters. I don't even like my Daddy no more cause if it wasn't for him killing himself we wouldn't be in this big trouble. But I gotta stop thinking about all this ugly stuff. I'm sick and tired of feeling so miserable all the time. So I run to the playroom steps, look at the red-faced kitchen clock.

It's already 7:25 and I yell, "Carmella! Josephine! Hurry up! I don't wantta be late for school!" I can't wait to be back in school with my school friends. None of them is gonna treat me the way the kids on Hoffman Street are doing.

"Stand still so I can put your school sweater on." It's Mommy and she's tugging on my arm so she can straighten my sweater sleeves that got twisted in my blouse sleeves.

"Josephine wants to walk to school by herself. I told her she's got to hold your hand and that's all there is to it."

I nod my head yes to let Mommy know I hear her. I watch as her pudgy fingers pull at the bottom of my sweater, and once she's done fussing over me, I look into her adoring eyes that's looking into my starving ones and I got to tell you I feel all warm inside like a flower ready to bloom again.

I don't think any morning in school ever went slower. I can't pay attention to nothing Sister Josephine says, except when she rings the bell on her desk and says, "It's time for recess."

Even though Carole, my best friend, is sitting across the room near the window, and even though I want to, I still don't yell to her cause I know Sister don't like us to. Instead, I stand and call just above a whisper, "Carole! Carole! Do you want to play hangman?"

She stands, but she don't really look at me and she mumbles like she's scared or maybe embarrassed, "I'ma-I'ma playing with Angela."

I sit down cause I can't believe Carole ain't gonna play with me, but after I get over being shocked, I get back on my feet and look for Anita. Her head's resting on her desk and she's drawing with a piece of charcoal, which is something she never ever does during recess. "Anita! Anita! You wantta play hangman on the blackboard?" I call.

She don't answer, and only cause I can't stand how lonely I'm feeling, I tell myself, It's your imagination that Anita don't want to play with you.

After a few moments of arguing with myself, I look in the direction of the coat closet, near where Nicholas sits. Our eyes meet right off, but when I call to him, he takes his eyes off me faster than a speeding bullet.

I gotta sit down again and, after I catch my breath, I stare at Paul, who's sitting next to me. I watch as his long eyelashes go up and down three or four times, then he gets up and goes over to the blackboard and starts drawing. I sink further into my seat and the arguing inside my head continues. One part of me wants to believe it's just my imagination that nobody wants to play with me. But there's another part of me that's saying I'm just plain stupid if I think anybody's gonna play with me ever again.

My brain feels all mixed up like when Mommy mixes eggs, sugar and flour, but, of course, with one very big difference. When Mommy mixes all that together, it always looks creamy yellow and smells so wonderful, too. But if I could see what's all mixed up in my head, well, I think it would look more like Johnny's mud pies, all sludgy black and slimy and stinking to the high heavens, too.

I'm standing in front of school at Ninth and Pierce waiting for Carmella and Josephine to come so we can go home for lunch. My best friend, Carole, is running across Ninth Street and I yell, "Carole! Carole! Why aren't you waiting here with me like you usually do so we can walk home together?"

She don't stop until she's standing near the trolley tracks; she turns and cries, "My Mommy says I ain't allowed to play with you no more."

Blood's rushing to my head like a river running wild, and I'm afraid to ask cause of the awful thing she might say about me, but I know I gotta ask. "What did I do?"

She's trying to wipe away tears that keep coming. "It's not what you did. It's the way your Daddy died."

I don't know what to say. I hardly know what words come out of my mouth. I'm just so angry at Carole, cause we've been best friends since second grade. Suddenly I'm shouting, "Whenever you came to my Daddy's store he always gave you lettuce leaves and carrots and celery for your pet rabbit. Don't that matter to you?"

Without answering, she starts running. That's when I start crying. I don't understand how Carole could do this to me. We've been friends so long. I remember in fourth grade when she was crying and crying. And even though I was chilled to the bone from the windy and damp day, I sat with her on a cold marble step and listened. She told me how her Mommy made rabbit stew out of her pet rabbit, Snoopy.

91

She kept crying and crying, and after I got over being shocked by what her Mommy did, I gave her some of my tissues and put my arm around her shoulder and just waited while she cried. And even though I knew she was upset, I still got curious; so I asked if she ate supper that night. And even when she screamed at me that she didn't, I waited until she put her head down on her lap before I laughed.

"Where's Carole?" It's Josephine, come out of school finally.

"She don't want to walk home with me no more."

"If she don't want to walk home with us, she don't have to," Carmella says.

I'm so upset, I didn't even see her.

"The three of us can walk home together," Josephine says.

I take her hand and once we cross Pierce Street and stand near the fish store, I reach for Carmella's hand. I'm really surprised cause she's reaching for my hand, too.

I'm sitting at the kitchen table where there's lots of gibber jabber and once Mommy walks into the dining room to get something out of the refrigerator, I whisper to Pat, "Nobody in school wants to play with me, and when I asked Carole why she ain't walking home with me, she said her Mommy said she ain't allowed to play with me no more cause of how our Daddy died. How was school for you?"

He looks at me with lost eyes and don't say nothing. I know that's cause he don't want to tell me what's going on with him, so I say, "I'm telling Mommy what happened in school."

He puts his hand on top of my hand and squeezes hard. "Don't tell Mommy what Carole told you if you know what's good for you!"

Mommy's back in the kitchen now. She's standing at the stove. Pat's still got his angry eyes on me and, as I slowly pull my hand away, I say, "Mommy, nobody in school played with me at recess."

She turns away from the stove and almost starts saying something as she waves her wooden spoon. But with a change-of-mind look on her face, she turns back to the stove and from the way her arms are shaking, I can tell she's stirring all those macaroni and meatballs that she put into that very hot frying pan. Usually I just love macaroni and meatballs, but right now I don't care. There's so much quiet in the house, and I wish Mommy would put on the radio and we'd be listening to Kate Smith singing "When The Moon Comes Over The Mountain." But the only noise I hear is Mommy putting macaroni in

Georgie's and Carmella's dishes. Standing next to me, she starts putting some macaroni and a big meatball in my dish. Without looking at me, she says, "Wasn't it last year when one of your classmates' father died? What's her name?"

"Theresa."

She says, "That's right. You came home from school and said you felt funny being near her because you didn't know what to say."

Mommy puts some macaroni and two meatballs in Pat's dish, then she looks at me and says, "That's what's going on. Just give them a few days and things will be back to normal."

"But I didn't turn my back on her or run away from her and neither did anybody else."

"That was last year and this is this year. Give them a few days."

After lunch, I go upstairs to the bathroom and start talking to the Sacred Heart of Jesus, whose picture is hanging on the wall in my big sisters' bedroom. I tell Jesus how none of my friends are playing with me and ask if he could please make my friends play with me again, the sooner the better.

It's Saturday morning, just twelve days after Daddy died. I'm sitting on Mamie's white marble steps with Carmella. If Carmella ever takes her hand out of the pink pull-string bag Mommy gave us to hold our jacks, we're gonna play. Georgie and Johnny are in the street writing numbers in large connecting boxes that Pat's drawing with chalk on both sides of the street.

"Georgie, you gotta draw the skull better than this!" Pat yells. Pat erases the skull with the sole of his shoe and Georgie walks towards the center of the street and starts drawing a new skull.

"They're gonna play dead box," I whisper to Carmella.

"Where's everyone?" Carmella asks.

I look around and wonder why I didn't notice that we're the only ones out this morning. Usually on a Saturday, there's lots of kids screaming and running; girls jumping rope or playing hopscotch; and boys hitting half-balls or racing on street skates. I don't hear windows opening and front doors slamming, and I don't see water hoses or hear crying babies.

"Where's everybody?" I call to my brothers.

My brothers stop writing with the chalk and, after Pat stands and looks at the house directly across the street, which is where my friend

Kathy lives, he says, "Where's Kathy's brothers, Anthony and Raymond? They always play with us on Saturday mornings."

Georgie's sitting in the middle of the street with his knees up to his chin and he says, "Hell! There's over fifty of us kids who live on the block and everybody comes out on Saturday mornings. Where are they?"

"Toni and Rita always play jacks and ball with us on Saturday mornings," Carmella says, finally taking the little brown ball out of the jacks bag.

As for Johnny, even though he's writing the number six with his fat piece of chalk, he's yelling, "Where are some of the men who wash their cars on Saturday mornings? I always talk to them."

"And none of the ladies are outside cleaning the front steps and pavements," I say.

"Mommy's not out cleaning either," Carmella says.

Pat's looking up the block; after he drops his chalk onto the black street, he rushes towards Carmella and me. I move my legs so he can sit on the bottom step next to me. Once Georgie and Johnny see Pat sitting on the step, they put their chalk in their pants pockets and come and sit with us, too.

Pat rubs his nose the same way Daddy used to. "It don't make one bit of sense that nobody's out here."

"It looks like a ghost town," Georgie says.

"What's going on?" Johnny asks.

I cross my legs and rest my elbow on my knee. "I know what's going on. Nobody's outside for the same reason why the kids at school don't play with me anymore. That's cause Daddy killed himself."

Pat gets a faraway look in his eyes and says, "Yeah! When Georgie and me wanted to play soccer in the school yard, like we always did before Daddy died, the other kids wouldn't let us. I got so mad at everybody that when that ball came near me, I kicked it so hard that it flew right out of that school yard."

We start to laugh, but a loud growl makes us look in the direction of Blind Man Joe's house. There's Joe with a great big German Shepherd.

"Look it!" Pat calls. "Blind Man Joe's got a Seeing Eye dog!"

It's my mouth that drops open as I exclaim, "Will you look at how big that dog is!"

Blind Man Joe's got both of his hands holding onto a black hand bar that's attached to two ropes that's attached to his dog. I get scared when I see Joe almost tripping down his steps cause the dog's moving faster than Joe wants to. Once they're on the pavement, the dog almost runs into the street. Luckily, Joe gives that dog a good yank, and the dog stops. That's when all of us kids run over. Once I'm standing near Joe, I say, "Hi, Joe. I like your new dog."

Pat's down on the pavement holding his hand up to the dog's nose, but it's Johnny who pets the dog's black coat that's streaked with beige as he says, "Nice dog. What's his name?"

Joe pulls at the harness so hard, the dog goes up on its hind legs, and in a snappy tone, Joe says, "Nobody can come near me while I'm training my dog. Do you know what German Shepherds are like? Do you know they can attack, maybe even kill you? You kids gotta stay away from him. I still don't have him under my control." Joe pulls at the dog's harness again. This time the dog walks as slow as molasses. Once Joe and the dog pass by us, the dog starts barking and running in the street again. Joe gets mad and yells something to that huge dog, but none of us hear it cause of how loud the dog is barking. Once Joe and his dog pass the fire hydrant, my brothers run back and start chalking up the street again. Carmella and I, we go and sit on Mamie's steps again, and finally we start playing a game of jacks.

Sometimes I think the only good thing about this summer is that my brothers let me play with them almost all the time, even when they play games girls don't usually play. I know it's cause no one else on the block plays with them, just like no one plays with me. Funny thing, I don't even miss those stupid kids anymore, but I sure do miss Blind Man Joe. Seems like he spends all his time training that dog of his. He's so busy he don't hardly have time to say hi to me anymore. I guess it's a good thing, Joe having a dog to help him get around, but I wish he didn't have one that needs so much training.

It's one day in July that I come up with words to a made-up song that I think Joe will really like. He always loves to hear me sing, especially my made-up songs. So I run over to his door and, after I knock a few times, I wait for Joe to come. I hear the door creak before I see it opening, but once I do, I get all excited cause Joe's standing there.

"Who is it?"

"It's me, Joe. I came to sing my new made-up song."

The door swings wide open and Joe's Seeing Eye dog is standing next to him. "I can't listen to your song right now. I have to take care of my dog. Another time."

"What's the dog's name?"

"I don't have time to talk. The dog's too difficult. Another time." He closes the door behind him.

I sit on Joe's step thinking how whenever I want to talk to Joe, he says he don't have time for me cause he's got to train that dog. Then cause I can't think of one good reason for me to be outside on this sunny day, I go home.

A few days later, I'm standing on our front steps looking up the street and I see Joe outside his house with his dog. Instead of Joe yanking and pulling at the dog, he's patting the dog's head as he's giving him a dog biscuit. I sigh a relief, thinking that Joe's finally got that dog under his control. So now he's got to have time for me.

I tiptoe up to Joe and, when I'm standing right behind him, I say, "Boooohhh!"

I laugh, but Joe, he gets mad and shouts, "Rosemary, I don't like when you sneak up on me. It's not right."

"I'm sorry, Joe. I just wanted to surprise you. That's all."

He puts his one hand on the top step, then with the other, he reaches for the dog's harness and to the dog, he says, "Let's go!"

I nearly choke on my words as I say, "You gonna be with that dog forever? How come you never talk to me no more? You're making me feel like you don't like me. Nobody likes me. I always thought you were my friend."

Joe takes a deep breath and as he yanks the dog's harness, he says, "Halt." He sits on the white step and tells me to sit next to him, and I do. He don't talk right away. First he wipes his wet forehead with his white handkerchief, then he coughs into it. Finally he whispers, "Sometimes things happen and people who really like each other like we do can't spend time together."

"I don't know what you're talking about. Since we both like each other, then what's the problem?"

Even though he's got a blank look in his eyes, I still can see his nervous smile by his twitching chin. "I gotta live here and my kids gotta grow up here, too. I don't want to hurt you, but I have to protect my family. We can't be friends anymore."

My face feels like it's on fire and I feel like I'm gonna explode. The next thing I know, I'm standing in front of him and with one hand on my hip and the other hand pointing in Joe's face, I scream, "I don't want to be friends with you either! The only reason why I was nice to you was cause my father told me I had to cause you're blind. And anyway, I don't need you for a friend. Mommy said that Pat and me are going to Atlantic City tomorrow and I'm gonna spend the rest of the summer at my Aunt Myra and Uncle Nick's house. So who needs you anyway?"

I start to leave, but Joe reaches for my arm and says, "Rosemary! Sit next to me and calm down."

I wave my hands in his face like I'm shooing away pesky mosquitos and as I feel my veins popping out of my temples, I scream, "Calm down! You want me to calm down after what you just said to me! I'm glad I don't have to be nice to you no more!"

Hot tears start coming down my eyes and, even though I never was glad about it before, I'm glad that Joe's blind cause I don't want him to see me crying. But I wish he could see how I'm sticking my tongue out at him as at the top of my lungs, I'm screaming, "Na! Na! Na! Na! Na!" I start running towards my house cause I want to tell my Mom what Joe just said to me.

"Rosemary! Come back here," Joe calls.

I keep running and after the screen door slams behind me, I sit on the floor in the farthest corner of the playroom thinking, What's the sense in telling Mommy? She ain't gonna hear me cause she never hears anything I say anyway. No point in telling Trudy cause she's crying all the time. It'll be a joke trying to tell Grace cause all she's ever doing is staring straight ahead. And Chris, well, it'd be really hard getting her to sit long enough to hear me cause she's always running around the house pretending she's cleaning when she ought to be eating or sleeping. So what's the use in telling anyone.

I put my knees up to my chin and after a few moments of rocking back and forth to myself, I whisper, "Daddy always told me to be nice to Joe cause he's blind. And now, when I need Joe to be my friend, he's only being mean. I just don't understand why he's gotta be so mean to me."

I start to get a little ascared cause I'm realizing there aren't any tears coming out of my eyes, and I stop rocking. Then after a few still seconds pass, I tell myself the reason why my eyes ain't wet is cause I'm all shriveled up inside like a dried-up wishing well. And I start rocking again.

Chapter 14

THE SUMMER SURE HASN'T gotten any better. Pat and I were supposed to stay at Uncle Nick and Aunt Myra's house in Atlantic City, but after only four weeks, Pat got an appendicitis and we had to come home. The kids on Hoffman Street still won't play with us, and Mommy had her hair cut real short, and she bought some very ugly furniture for the playroom so it don't even look like a playroom no more. There's a scatter rug made of mucky greens with disgusting brown threads running through it, and a couch that's covered with the same mucky green. And in the corner where my brothers used to put their stick bats and half-balls, there's a new television. And then there's Chris. Even though we've been away for only a few weeks, she changed more than I thought a person could change.

First time I saw her was the day Uncle Nick brought me home. I hardly got a chance to say hello to Mommy. I guess she was worried about Pat, him being in the hospital with an appendicitis, but I felt really sad that she left as soon as I got home.

"Hi, Roe! Long time no see!" Chris shrieks as she stands in the doorway with each hand holding onto the dining room door frame. I don't answer her cause I'm staring at her jet-black hair and her bright-red lipstick. I do a double-take when I look at her clothes. She's wearing a pair of black-and-white-striped pedal pushers with a bright-red sleeveless blouse that's tied in a knot in the front of her waist.

"What did you do to your hair?" I gasp.

She turns around so I can see more of her, and after her back is to me, she runs towards the kitchen. I run after her. I open the refrigerator door, pour some milk in a big glass and sit down at the table with Chris. I can't keep myself from staring. "Why did you dye your hair? Why are you wearing bright-red lipstick?"

She puts her legs on the chair that's next to her, turns her nose up towards the ceiling, moistens her lips and in a Marilyn Monroe voice says, "I always wanted black hair. It's called blue-black. It's the blackest of all blacks. And I just love the color of my lips." She puts her hand to her hair as if she's puffing it up. "Don't you think so, too?"

"Uuhh! Ohhh! You're in big trouble with Mommy."

Rosemarie Manes

She laughs, "Mommy knows and she didn't say nothing about it."

That makes me mad and I shout, "I don't like your black hair and I don't like your red lipstick either!"

She laughs again and says, "I'm grown up now and I can dye my hair and wear red lipstick if I want. Why, I even have a boyfriend."

I shake my head back and forth. "Uun-uhhh! You don't have a boyfriend. Mommy won't let you."

"Oh yes I do! And we go out almost every night and he even has a car."

What she's saying sounds strange to me and is making me scared. "Where's Trudy and Grace?"

"Trudy's out and Grace is in the bathtub getting ready to go out."

"Where did Trudy go and where is Grace going?"

"I don't know."

"They ain't allowed out unless they got somewhere to go."

"Not no more."

I throw her a dirty look as I say, "You seem happy about that."

"It's fine by me. Anyway," she says, standing up, "you're just a kid who ought to mind her own business!"

I put my hands flat on the table and yell, "Don't nobody know that Pat's in the hospital getting an operation?" Then I remember about my oldest brother, Ralph, being let go from the Army cause Daddy died, so I demand, "And where's Ralph?"

Chris's eyebrows arch real high and after a few strained seconds, she announces, "Mommy wants us to buy hoagies."

"We never eat store-bought hoagies!" I kneel on my chair and see there's nothing cooking on the stove. I rush over to the oven, but there's nothing there either. Slamming the oven door, I scream, "How come Mommy didn't make something I like since I just come home from being away!"

"Hey! You better stop slamming things!"

I wave my finger at her and cry, "If Daddy was here you wouldn't be dyeing your hair and wearing no red lipstick! If Daddy was here you wouldn't be having no boyfriend either! If Daddy was here Trudy and Grace wouldn't be allowed to go out unless Daddy knew where they were going!" I stop yelling cause I'm choking on my own tears, but once I clear my throat, I shriek, "And another thing, if Daddy was here the playroom wouldn't have all that ugly furniture in it!"

100

I sit on the chair that's next to the stove and start crying all over again as I say, "If Daddy was here Mommy would have given me a big smile and a kiss when I came in the house. If Daddy was only here!"

Chris places her hand on my shoulder and asks in a voice that's like the big sister I love so much, "What's wrong?"

"Nothing."

"Yes, there is. I know you, Roe. I know when you're upset."

I bury my face into her hand and whisper, "Mommy didn't even hug me when I put my arms out to give her a hug. She didn't tickle me under my chin or say anything at all to me."

Chris pulls over a chair and sits beside me. She reaches for a paper napkin and wipes the red lipstick off her lips. Then, she puts her arms around me, kisses my forehead and says, "Mommy wouldn't hurt you for anything. It's just that she has so much on her mind. Hey, I got an idea. You want to go for a ride in my boyfriend's car?"

I wipe my tears away with my fingers. "Yeah! When?"

"Let me ask my boyfriend, Coughdrop, when is a good time for him."

"He must be nice if you think he's gonna take me for a ride in his car. What's he look like? How many times have you gone out with him? Do you let him kiss you? How did he get a name like Coughdrop?"

"I can't believe all the questions you're asking me!" She giggles. "But we can talk about my boyfriend later. Right now we have to go to the hoagie shop."

I watch as she walks over to the white cabinet and after she opens the side door, she lifts the silver coffee canister lid and takes out a $5 bill. Once we're walking into the old playroom, I ask, "Why is the playroom turned into a parlor?"

"Mommy's cousin, Leonard, works for a company that makes televisions and he got Mommy a good deal."

"Why didn't she leave it the way it was? She could have just put the television in the playroom."

"I can't bring my boyfriend into the playroom to watch television? What's he going to sit on, the bench?"

"Oh! So it was you who convinced Mommy to get rid of our playroom."

"It wasn't only me. Trudy and Grace talked Mommy into doing it, too."

"Who picked out all this ugly stuff?"

As Chris opens the screen door she laughingly says, "Don't be looking at me. It was Mommy!"

Once outside, I walk a step behind Chris as we start walking down Hoffman Street, and then I ask, "How are the neighbors?"

"The hell with all of them."

"What about Blind Man Joe?"

"If he's sitting out on his front steps and hears our screen door opening, he reaches for his dog's harness and runs into the house." After a few quiet moments, Chris laughs as she says, "Guess what? Mommy wants me to go to St. Peter's commercial school in September and once I graduate in June, I'm going to get a clerical job so I can help out."

"But Daddy wants the boys to go to college and he wants us girls to finish high school."

"What good is any of that gonna do us now? Mommy needs money so if I can finish school sooner, why not."

I can't believe what Chris just said, but then I think it's just more things that keep changing in our house since Daddy killed himself. But I don't want to be thinking about that and I don't want to talk about anything that's going to make me feel sad. Giggling, I ask, "How did your boyfriend get a name like Coughdrop?"

She giggles, too and says, "It's a nickname. I have no idea how he got it."

"When he takes me out for a drive in his car I'm gonna ask."

She laughs louder than before and says, "You better not ask him any such thing cause I'll be so embarrassed."

We don't stop talking and giggling about Chris and her boyfriend until we're only a few stores away from the hoagie shop. And once we step inside, my mouth starts watering cause the delicious smells of salami, cheeses, tomatoes, lettuce, olive oil and just-baked rolls is being blown out of the very large fan that's in the hoagie shop wall.

"What kind can we get?" I ask.

"Any kind you want, seeing how this is a kind of a coming-home celebration."

"You think maybe when Pat gets out of the hospital, we can bring him here?"

"Sure, now go on and order. My favorite is the one that's got everything on it. You want that, too?"

"I don't like mayonnaise."

"Okay," she smiles. "Tell the man you don't want any mayonnaise." She pulls me towards her and kisses my head. I think what a great big sister Chris is.

"Okay," I say.

Chapter 15

IT'S THE END OF SEPTEMBER and it's almost dark. Pat, Georgie, Johnny and I are standing outside of Daddy's store, in front of his wooden produce stand, and we're scared cause we know we gotta go inside. Mommy said so. Right after supper she told us that we had to go with her to Daddy's store so we can all carry home some of the canned goods that are sitting on the shelves. She said it's the first time she's been back to the store since the night Daddy stabbed himself, and the reason she's going back is she's putting the store up for sale. Then she said as soon as she finds another house we're moving. I never thought I'd be glad about us moving away from here, but since nobody talks to me anyway, well, it seems like a very good idea.

So the four of us are leaning on Daddy's produce stand waiting for Mommy, Grace and Chris to arrive. I get tired of waiting and look into Daddy's big store window. But I don't look long. It's too dark and spooky inside. Instead I look at Daddy's door window and the picture I'd seen hundreds of times of a little girl wearing a navy-blue dress; she's holding a very large navy- blue umbrella over her head and, in her other arm, she's holding an open box of Morton salt that's pouring out all over the place. I can tell she don't know it's pouring salt cause she's got a big smile on her face, and I tell myself it's good she don't know-that way she can still be happy.

The other thing that catches my eye is what's written right above her umbrella, which says, "When it rains it pours." And at this very same moment, in my head, I say, "Ain't that the truth."

I get distracted when I hear Mommy jingling Daddy's store keys. I watch as she walks up the three brown steps and after the door opens, she turns and says, "Come on!"

I wait for my brothers and sisters to go in first, then after I stop biting down on my bottom lip, I walk up those brown steps. Once I'm on the top one, I hold onto the side of the brown door frame and only let go once I've plastered myself against the wooden counter where Daddy keeps his very, very large brown bags.

I keep my eyes glued on Mommy as she walks further into the store. Once she reaches the boxes of macaroni, she turns towards my big sisters, points towards the canned vegetables and soups and says, "Get some bags."

Chris heads towards me cause I'm standing near the bags. She bends down and reaches for the very, very large ones. She grunts and groans as she tries to pick them up, and I feel her breathing as she folds a few of the bags to one side. Suddenly she lets go of them like those bags are on fire. She looks right at me and whispers, "Daddy's machete knife is in between the bags and it's got blood on it. Anda-anda there's even blood on some of the bags."

I move away from the counter, too, and I get surprised when I bump into Grace as she's saying, "Shh! Don't get Mom upset. Put the bags down over it!"

Keeping as far away as she can, Chris starts flipping the bags, one at time, over the knife. Once the breeze from the flapping bags stops, I look at Mom and I'm happy to say she's got her back to us. So I put a big smile on my face as I look at Grace and Chris.

After a few seconds of us staring at each other, I look down at the wooden floor. That's when my heart nearly stops. Right in front of my feet are Daddy's bloody footprints that are dried into the wood. Right away, I look up at the carved-out beige ceiling and the only thing that makes me stop looking at the ceiling is Mommy calling, "Rosemary! Bring the boys' wagon here!"

I don't move cause Grace is rushing by me, and as she stands in front of Daddy's register, I know what's got her attention is the two black books next to the register. After she starts thumbing through a few pages, she starts making twitching sounds and blurts out, "There's names of people who owe Daddy lots of money!"

Mommy looks like she don't have time to be worrying about who owes what to Daddy. "Put the books down," she says to Grace. "Start taking some of these cans off the shelves."

I rush over to the soda water bottles, the ones that are against the wall, cause that's where the wooden wagon is, and I start pulling it towards Mom. But I get frozen when I notice that the side door that leads up to the empty apartment on the second floor is slightly open. I tell myself that even though Daddy told me I wasn't allowed to go up there, and even though my brothers never wanted to go up there again, and even though it always scared me to go up there by myself, I gotta go anyway.

I put the handle of the wagon down, but before I move towards the steps, I look at Mom; she's stretching to reach for something on the top shelf near the macaroni, and that's when I slowly walk up the first step. After only a second or two of my eyes staring up the darkened stairway, I pull away from the doorway cause of the smells of stale stogies and musty cigarettes that fill the stairwell. There's also the smells of stagnant beer and rancid wine. I rub my nose cause all that puts the fear of bad men in me, which makes me remember how Daddy had card games up in that apartment, card games that sometimes lasted all weekend. A chill runs through me like somebody just walked on my grave.

"Rosemary! Will you hurry up with that wagon!"

I come down from the step real quick and start pulling that wagon toward Mommy. I watch as her eyes look all around the store. They're wet eyes now and I watch as she folds her arms and starts walking towards the back of the store. Grace is following behind Mommy and saying, "I can't believe all those people still owe Daddy all that money!" But Mommy's not listening. She's looking to see what she wants to take home with us. Chris is looking really nervous, and I know it's cause she wishes she wasn't the one to find Daddy's blood. Pat's running ahead of Mommy towards the back room and Georgie and Johnny are close behind.

Me, I don't move an inch. I watch as Mom and my two sisters go into the next room where Daddy kept the very large brown boxes of paper goods. I watch as my brothers go into the back room where Daddy kept his crates of eggs. Once I know they've forgotten about me, I know what I gotta do even though I don't want to do it. Quietly I walk up the two steps that lead to the steps that lead up to the empty apartment. I run up those stairs fast as I can, cause I don't have much time. The smell in the upstairs room is even worse than the smell in the hallway and I try not to breathe as I look around. The room sort of looks like a kitchen. I stand near an old wooden table that's covered with gray ashes and dried-up spills. There's six chairs, all with dark, sweaty hand marks on the arms and faded wood on the backs. I feel like I'm taking in everything I see in this room, like I gotta take a snapshot of it in my mind. There's windows, but no curtains, a gas stove but no dishes or pots and pans. What there's lots of is glasses with dried-up wine in them, and large ash trays filled with cigarette butts and half-smoked stogies looking like witches' crooked fingers. I reach for the deck of cards sitting in the middle of the table and touch them, but I put them down cause the smell of big sweaty hands has mingled with the smell of old playing cards, and I hate that smell, too.

As I take a few steps toward the bathroom door, I notice a black Stetson hat sitting on a broken folding chair. There's a tiny white feather caught between the black hatband, and next to the chair is a black umbrella. I look at the drainboard and see the bright red, the dark blue and the dingy yellow of chips sitting in an open box.

I look again at the large empty chairs and I imagine some of the men, men with large arms and big hands, men with husky voices and Italian accents. Men with black mustaches dressed in fine clothes and men with stern faces and piercing eyes. But smells of old wine and beer fill my mouth and, as I turn toward the corner near the stove, I shake my head. There's an open gallon of Chianti and almost-empty bottles of beer standing next to it. I rub my nose again, and that's when I catch a hint of a scent of Daddy's Old Spice aftershave lotion, and I remember that it was us kids who gave it to him for Christmas.

"Rosemary! Where are you? We're getting ready to leave!" Mommy calls.

I rush out of the room and once I'm holding onto the wooden banister, I look into the middle room and there, sitting on the floor, are seven or eight black phones and there's pencils and lots of paper all over the bare floor. I just can't stand the creepy feeling that room is giving me, so I run down those steps and don't stop until I close the door behind me.

"Mommy! Some of these cans have white powder on them. What is it?" Grace asks.

Mommy's got her hands on her hips as she's saying, "Don't touch anything. It might be some of the poison that's left from your father."

I get all scared again cause I'm being reminded of how my Daddy took poison, too, and I just don't want to be reminded of it anymore.

"Mom?" Chris asks, "How are we gonna get all this stuff home?"

Mommy gives Chris her sharp eyes and says, "We're not taking anything out of the store. Do all of you hear me? I don't want any of you touching anything!"

I look to my left and all's I see are rows and rows of canned foods like crushed tomatoes, peas, corn, lima beans, soups; I look to the top of the highest shelves, I see lots of large cans of tomato puree and large pineapple juice cans; next to them there's large cans of other kinds of juices, too. I look at the cans of olive oil on the lowest shelves; they're so big I couldn't lift them, not even with both arms. And next to the large cans, there's small bottles of imported olive oil that came from Italy a few weeks before Daddy died. And on the last shelf towards the back there's boxes of laundry detergent and lots of bars of Ivory and Lifebouy soaps, and why, there's even brown floor soap, too.

Grace, now standing near the crackers and cookies, states, "Mommy, we could wash the cans once we get them home."

Mom waves her hands in the air and shouts, "I don't want to take anything home. Do you hear me! Nothing!"

I stare up at the ceiling again cause I don't want to look at cans that's got powdery stuff on them that might be some of Daddy's poison. But once my eyes catch a glimpse of Daddy's gray jacket with the European cut that's hanging on the wall, I stop staring at the ceiling. All of a sudden I'm remembering the good times at the store, like when he'd be standing outside waiting on his customers and singing or whistling "When Irish Eyes Are Smiling." And then there were times when he sang songs he made up right on the spot, or whistled made-up melodies. I get a smile on my face cause in my mind's eye, I can see him teasing his customers about this thing or that, or him telling my brothers to bring the customers' groceries to their houses. Before they'd leave with all those bags on their wagon, Daddy would say, "And don't take any money."

And I'm remembering, too, how Mommy gave me Daddy's lunch to take to him, and sat on the wooden stand. He'd ask me to get him a glass of water and I just loved watching him drink that cold water right down in two or three gulps. Then after he was finished eating his lunch he'd let me sit next to him and I'd imitate his every move. And I'm remembering how he'd tell jokes to the customers, and how the people passing by would laugh and carry on with him, too. I'm remembering how he'd make up stories that sometimes made people laugh, and sometimes made the old ladies cry a little. I'm even remembering how sometimes people got mad at him cause he pulled a practical joke on them. Even now, I don't understand why they got mad at him, but like he always said, some people just don't have no sense of humor. I'm remembering, too, how I loved walking home with him after he closed the store, and how proud I'd feel just walking down the street with my hand wrapped around his finger.

I come out of myself when I hear Mommy saying it's time to go home. I drag my feet over to the front door and find myself standing between the store and the outside steps. I turn to take one last look inside, and tears fill my eyes. Only cause I can't take it no more, I run down the steps and wait for everybody at the corner of Seventh and Mifflin cause I don't want anybody seeing me cry.

Chapter 16

I NEVER KNEW ANYBODY could feel as lonely as I do now. It's reminding me of a time when I went shopping uptown with my sister, Trudy. We were entering John Wanamaker's department store on Juniper Street side and I was holding onto her hand so I wouldn't get swallowed up by the fast-moving crowd. Imagine! Being in a crowd and still feeling lonely. But it wasn't me who was lonely then. It was somebody in that crowd. I caught a glimpse of his face as he was coming out of Wanamaker's. Now, I don't think it was a poor face, and it wasn't a rich one. It was a grown-up face with average-looking hair and average-looking skin, and it was on the young side of looking old. All of a sudden he looked at me. His eyes on my eyes. That's when I saw the only real thing I know about this soul. I saw just how horribly lonely this person was. His long, dark eyelashes blinked once, then a second time; that's when I noticed redness running through the whites of his eyes. Even though Trudy was pulling me toward her, I still kept my eyes on him. Then like a flash of lightning, he was alongside of me; that's when I saw his hunched-back. I wondered if he was crippled. Once he passed by me, I knew he wasn't, not in a physical way, that is. His hunched-back told me he had the weight of the world on his shoulders and was crippled by the loneliness of it all.

Loneliness in the heart is such a horrible thing, especially if it's loneliness that's attached to not being able to talk about what's really bothering a person. Like how awful I feel about my Dad's suicide. Loneliness is being in a whirlwind and nobody, even those who think they see me, can't see how I'm being blown every which way. Loneliness is standing in the midst of a neighborhood of people I have known all my life and nobody comes out to say "Good-bye" on moving day. But the most horrible loneliness is to live in a house full of people who I love most and watch as they do the most ordinary things and see the loneliness in their eyes, but never speak of it. Loneliness is to feel so separate from the rest of the world and not knowing how to feel a part of it again.

It's a very cold, windy morning this Saturday, December 17, 1955 and I'm standing in front of our house with Carmella and Josephine.

110

I'm wrapped in Mommy's beige cashmere coat, the one that Daddy gave her two years ago. We're watching the moving men put our things in the moving truck that's parked on our sidewalk. I laugh to myself as I watch two of the moving men wobbling up the wooden ramp as they carry Mommy's vanity table into the truck. But I stop watching when I hear Trudy saying, "Roe! Here's five dollars. Go to the five and dime store and buy two boxes of Christmas cards."

I turn towards the open front door and ask, "Why do you want me to buy Christmas cards?"

"Cause we want to give them to our neighbors."

"Huh! What I wish for them ain't gonna be in no Christmas card!"

Chris laughs her witchy laugh as she stands next to Trudy and says, "We wantta stick it right up their asses-every mother one of them!"

"It's what Daddy would do!" Trudy adds.

"Oh, come off it!" I scream. "Daddy wouldn't be giving them no Christmas cards!"

"Maybe he wouldn't be giving Christmas cards," Trudy says. "But Daddy wouldn't let them have the last word and that's for sure. If Daddy were here right now he'd say, 'Kill them with kindness!' And if we do just like Daddy would tell us to do, we'll get the last laugh."

We're all laughing then, me and Trudy, Chris, Carmella and Josephine. I laugh even louder when I think the neighbors can hear us even though their houses are closed up tighter than a drum. And there's one more thing that's making me feel alive all of a sudden, and it's how Trudy's laughter sounds just like Daddy's when he knew he got somebody's goat.

As I put the money in Mommy's coat pocket, Trudy points her finger at me and says, "You better hurry up. It's gonna take time to sign all those cards. And another thing . . ."

I don't wait for Trudy to finish. Instead, I rush down the street towards Seventh, and once I turn left at the corner I start running.

"Look at this!" Trudy exclaims as she opens one of the boxes of cards I bought. "It's a little boy throwing snowballs at a snow man! And every time he hits that snow man he jumps up and down and then he giggles!"

111

Chris laughs her evil laugh, "Look!" The snow man takes his head off and throws it so hard that it knocks the little boy right down on his ass!"

"Let me see! Let me see!" Carmella reaches for the card.

Josephine's laughing like I never heard her laugh before, and only cause I know it's going to make everyone laugh even more, I shout, "Read what it says!" Nobody hears me, so I reach into the open box. After I hold open one of the cards, I scream, "Listen!" I'm surprised at how they all quiet down. Quickly, before they start laughing again, I read, "I hope your holiday season is full of surprises!"

"And right above the word 'surprises' we gotta write 'nasty,'" Chris says.

First we all laugh. Then Trudy shakes her head and says, "I don't think that's a good idea. Remember what we're trying to do here. Kill them with kindness."

We all agree, but that don't stop us from getting hysterical again. Carmella, Josephine, me, we laugh even harder when Trudy and Chris hold onto each other and start laughing and jumping around like they're doing some kind of jig. I can't stay still, so I grab Carmella, and she grabs Josephine. Then Trudy and Chris grab us and we laugh and jump around like we ain't got a care in the world.

It's Carmella who stops jumping around first. She takes the second box of cards out of the brown bag and after she opens it, her eyes get big. "I think this one's really nice," she whispers. "It's got a picture of an angel sitting on top of a house chimney. And look how he's got his handsome wings spread open."

Carmella hands the card to Trudy, who runs her hand over it and in a soft voice says, "I like the soft blue color coming from the brick house.

"I like how the moon is so yellow and full," Josephine says.

"What's it say inside?" Chris asks.

Trudy opens the card and reads, "Every time we call out 'Merry Christmas' another angel smiles and hovers near."

I can see by my sisters' calm faces that they like this card a lot.

The mood changes fast when Pat, Georgie and Johnny come running up the cellar steps. They pass by us like we're invisible. "They got everything from the cellar. Let's go and check upstairs," Pat says.

That's when I stop thinking about giving out the Christmas cards. Something inside me wants to go upstairs with my brothers and see what's upstairs, too. Except there's nothing upstairs. I look over at where the picture of the lady angel used to hang right above the fireplace and it ain't there no more. I look into the kitchen. Grace is busy making lots of crunchy noises with old newspapers she's using to wrap the breakfast dishes.

Then Mommy runs past us. "Let's hurry up! Let's just hurry up!" She's rubbing her hands against each other like she's really nervous.

I think she can't wait to get out of here and I tell myself, "I can't wait to get out of here, too." Then I get scared when a thought I've been trying real hard not to think explodes inside of me. What if somebody in the new neighborhood finds out that Daddy killed himself? It's the most terrible thought I can have, cause if that's true then we would have moved for nothing. Except I know nobody in my family is gonna say anything in the new neighborhood about Daddy killing himself. We all know that's the reason why we're moving, even if we don't talk about it.

I'm sitting on the dining room floor watching the moving men take Grandmom's sewing machine, the refrigerator, the kitchen table, fourteen kitchen chairs and some of the brown boxes that's left out for the moving truck. That's when I hear two sets of rumbling feet running down the steps. Trudy and Chris come rushing into the dining room; in their hands, I see Christmas cards stuffed in the envelopes.

"How did you sign the cards?" I ask.

Chris pulls one of the angel cards out of its envelope and, as she opens it, she whispers, "Mike and Romania's kids."

But I barely finish reading it when Trudy demands, "Where's the boys?"

"Upstairs," I say.

Trudy, in her bossy tone of voice, yells, "Pat! George! John! Come down here right now!"

Grace comes in and says, "What's going on?"

Chris says, "We're gonna give some of the neighbors Christmas cards to wish them a Merry Christmas."

"Why?" Grace asks.

"To stick it up their asses!" Chris laughs.

113

Grace shrugs and says something about needing to finish packing up the kitchen. She walks past the three boys

Right away Trudy starts giving orders. "I want all of you, including Rosemary, to take these cards and give them out to any of the neighbors you want to."

Pat looks at her like she's nuts. "I don't wantta give nobody Christmas cards. Doing that is gonna make us look like suckers. I ain't nobody's sucker!!!"

"You gotta do it!" Trudy insists.

"Don't you understand?" Chris says and then she gives out this loud cackle. "Us doing this is sticking it right up their asses, every bitching one of them." Her expression turns serious and she adds, "We're only doing what Daddy would tell us to do if he were here right now."

Pat's forehead begins to crease and I know he's thinking hard about what Chris is saying. I bet he's starting to think in favor of what Chris said cause most of the time he does what she wants him to do. Chris is his favorite sister.

Trudy gives Georgie, Johnny and me a handful of cards and that's when Carmella and Josephine, who I didn't even know were there, scream together, "What about us?"

Trudy hands them a few, then she looks at Pat and in a silly voice says, "Well, what do yeah say, are you in with us or not?"

"Okay, I'll do it," Pat says as he takes some cards out of Trudy's hands. With Georgie and Johnny running behind him, they take off sounding like a pack of wild horses. Carmella, Josephine and I, well, the three of us almost fall over each other as we race for the front door.

Slowly walking towards Sixth Street and every time I pass a house that's familiar, I rush up the three marble steps and put a snowman card in the mail slot. After I give out all of the snowman cards, I start folding the larger angel cards and push them through the mail slots. Then I have only one left. I stand on the corner and watch Carmella and Josephine slide cards into mail slots, then jump down those steps and run to the next house. But they stop running. Mommy yells, "Hurry up! The taxicabs are here!"

I almost start running home, too, but when I see the angel card still in my hand, it's like a light bulb goes off, and I tell myself, I'm gonna give this card to Blind Man Joe. So to my sisters I say, "Go home and I'll meet you there."

I look towards Joe's house. The windows are all decorated for Christmas. And I think it's nice how he does that even though he can't see. I take small steps to his house and once I'm standing in front of it, I get a creepy feeling like spiders crawling all over me. I almost run away but then-and I don't know where it comes from-I get a burst of courage and, with lots of force, I pull open the green mail slot that's on the bottom of his door and shove the card in. I'm shocked at how the slot keeps banging so loud against the door and I take a few fast steps away from Joe's house. I ain't gone far when I hear the front door open wide. I turn and see Blind Man Joe in his long-john undershirt standing in the doorway.

"Who's at my front door?" he calls.

I don't answer cause I can't find my voice.

He keeps asking, "Who's there? Who's there? Who's there?"

I do my best to clear my throat cause I know I got to say something that's full of truth whether Joe likes hearing it or not. Once my throat's as clear as it's gonna get, I say, "One of Mike's kids!"

"Is that you, Rosemary?"

"Yeah, it's me, Joe."

He's got a shocked look on his face; his mouth drops open and he takes a deep breath. More than anything in the world I want to run up to Joe and give him a hug. I want to tell him I'm gonna miss him the most out of everybody on the whole block and that I feel just awful for the way things turned out. I don't do any of that. Instead, I say, "We're moving today, Joe."

Even though he can't see, his eyes are on me, and I got my eyes looking at him, too. I know he feels me staring cause he stumbles back a little and kicks the Christmas card. I watch him as he's slowly bending down to pick the card up.

"It's an angel card," I call out. "And it says, 'Every time we call out Merry Christmas another angel smiles and hovers near.'"

He still has his eyes on me as he's taking the card out of the envelope and even though his lips are moving, he don't say one word.

My eyes fill with tears, and in a voice that's as loud as one of the opera singers that Grandpop used to listen to on his record player, I yell, "Merry Christmas, Joe!!!"

He don't say nothing back. No Merry Christmas or Good Luck in your new house. We just stand for a few gloomy seconds.

"Rosemary, come on. I want you to sit in the second cab," Mom calls.

Without another word, I run towards the cabs, thinking how it don't really matter if Joe likes the card or not. What matters is that I like giving it to him, especially because it's what's really in my heart.

I climb in the back seat of the Yellow cab that's gonna take us to our home that's on 58th Street in southwest Philadelphia. I sit next to Carmella, who's sitting next to Josephine, and in my head I'm thinking how moving is another one of those things we don't talk about. A part of me just can't believe we're all leaving the house on Hoffman Street where we always lived. And I thought I'd always live. Just like I thought Daddy would always be here to be my father.

I look at the big window in the front of our house and I'm remembering last Christmas when Trudy decorated it with so many beautiful Christmas ornaments. As I watch Grace walk out the front door holding the cake knife, I remember so many of the Italian cream birthday cakes with lighted candles sitting on our kitchen table, and I sink into my seat. I fidget with my fingers as I remember so many of the different ways all fourteen of us were a family in this house and I sink further into my seat as I push back my tears.

Grace opens the cab door and sits next to me, but I don't look at her, not even when she says, "It's going to be so nice. Mommy took me and Trudy to see the house just the other day, and I can't get over how big it is. Across the street there's an old ladies' home with lots of green grass, and Mom said that children are allowed to go there and play."

Chris, who's sitting in the front of the cab, turns to us and says, "Most of the people in our new neighborhood look more like my old girlfriend, Joanie Murphy, with red hair and freckles. That's cause most of them are Irish Catholic."

I say with lots of hope in my voice, "As soon as we get there, we'll all be able to make new friends."

Grace puts the cake knife on the seat near the door, and whispers, "Everything is going to be just perfect."

As the cab starts, I sit up straight, rub my eyes and don't look back on Hoffman Street, not even a glimpse.

Chapter 17

BLESSED ARE THE POOR IN SPIRIT, for theirs is the kingdom of heaven. According to my catechism book, Jesus was supposed to have said this on some mountaintop near Jerusalem. Just thinking about it makes me laugh cause I definitely don't agree. For poor people there ain't any kingdom you're inheriting except maybe being more poor.

It's springtime, 1956, and one of the biggest things I learned since we moved is that I had no idea people could be so poor. There are times when my stomach hurts cause of how empty it is, and there are times when there's food on the table and I can't eat cause I stopped being hungry.

Some grown-up relatives say to me, "How come you're so skinny?"

I smile and shrug my shoulders like I don't know. But what I'd like to tell them is, "Why don't you shut up and mind your own business!!!"

But to tell you the truth, not having enough to eat ain't what bothers me the most. What does bother me the most is how awfully poor I feel when it comes to my family. It's like we ain't a family no more. We don't ever have fun like a family, and we don't take care of the house or each other like we used to, and mostly, it feels like we're not caring about each other, and that makes me feel worse than any empty stomach.

Another thing that makes me feel so awfully poor is most all my girlfriends have daddies and when I see their daddies with them, it makes me want to cry. And it ain't like I'm jealous cause I wouldn't wish on anybody that they don't have a dad, and especially not the way I lost mine. But watching them being together, well, it makes me feel powerfully empty inside, which is just another word for poor.

Another thing that makes me feel poor is how some people in our neighborhood think we ain't as good as them, and sometimes I think they're right. But most of the times I just want to get back at them for calling me "dago" and "wop" and sometimes I do. I yell that they're "harps" cause Chris says that'll get them mad, and it does, and I'm glad. But then, other times me calling them names and them calling me names, makes me feel poor inside, too, cause I don't think it's any way for God's creatures to talk to one another.

And since I'm on the subject of God, I'm being reminded of just how mad at him I am for letting my life be so empty and poor. I take great pleasure in yelling at God when Mommy sends me to Mass on Sundays. But it's not only at Mass I'm yelling at him. No sirree! I walk around the neighborhood on cold, windy Sunday mornings and I yell and yell at him in my head as I walk up and down those gloomy streets. Which makes me think about something else that makes me feel poor. That's how Mommy's always crying and talking to a blank kitchen wall, or talking to the Blessed Mother statue she's got sitting on the shelf right above the kitchen sink. I think it's silly how she talks to this statue that's made out of hard plaster, cause a piece of plaster ain't gonna be able to help us.

Oh, and before I forget, another thing about my family that makes me feel poorer than one of those black babies in Africa that the Catholic Bishop Relief Fund is always collecting for is how my oldest brother, Ralph, yells at Mommy and tells her how she's doing wrong in raising us. As far as my three oldest sisters go, I feel poor about them, too cause they're hardly ever home no more. And what all three of my other brothers do anymore is fight and then fight some more. As for me, I just sit on the couch and watch the goings-on in our house. Sometimes I have to lie down on that couch cause all's I'm feeling is a yucky emptiness in the pit of my stomach. But when I look at my four younger sisters, I push myself real hard and I try to help them best as I can. But the worst thing about being poor is having a big, fat secret in our family and never being allowed to talk about it to each other, or anybody else for that matter. Yeah, I think I am poor in spirit like Jesus said and the only kingdom I'm inheriting is the kingdom of hell right here on earth.

It's a rainy Sunday morning, April 22, four days after my Dad's birthday and I can't believe it's almost a year since he died. I'm walking on Greenway Avenue towards 56th Street and in my head I'm screaming to God. I scream things like *I can't stand you! How can you just let it keep happening over and over again? We keep getting further and further into what feels like a horrible nightmare and it's making my whole family just go away from each other. Why don't you do something about it??? Why don't you answer me??? What's wrong with you anyway??? When are you gonna do something to make it all stop??? Where the hell are you!!!*

I'm freezing cold from the wet rain hitting my face and bare calves. But I still keep walking and thinking how all my wonderful dreams about moving to a new neighborhood have fallen by the wayside, just like the way the rain is pouring off my head right now. I get a burning feeling like my stomach's on fire and I realize for the first time just how strange it is to be walking around the neighborhood on a rainy morning in April screaming my fool head off at God. I've been doing this for weeks now, but this is the first time I realize I'm doing it and I get scared. Taking off Chris's sweater, I put it over my head and, as fast as my legs can carry me, I run home. I really want to talk to Mommy about what's going on in my wacky head.

I rush in the house to look for Mom, but before I go into the kitchen, I put the fifteen cents she gave me for Sunday collection next to a picture frame with the big crack in the glass. It's the one that has a gold-and-white metal frame with Daddy's picture in it. Even though everybody says they don't know how the glass got cracked, I think somebody threw the picture on the hardwood parlor floor and it was left there until Mommy picked it up.

When I go into the kitchen, I see Mommy's hunched over the stove slowly stirring a watered-down, meatless red gravy. And even though I know she don't have money to buy meat, I think the real reason why her gravy don't smell anywhere near as delicious as it used to is cause her heart ain't into cooking since Daddy died. And the way she's breathing sounds like she's got a really bad cold, but I know she don't.

Out loud, to herself, she's saying, "Browny, why, why did you do this to me?"

I'm bursting inside like a black balloon pricked by a pin. I just can't stand listening to her calling to Daddy, and the sad, lost look on her face is reminding me that she don't have a single big person in this whole wide world to talk to. It's like everybody's blaming her for how Daddy died, not us kids, but everyone else in the family; and even though Mommy don't ever put it into words, I think she thinks they're right.

I don't want her to see I'm worried for her, so once I'm standing next to her, I laughingly say, "Whatiya doing, Mom? Talking to yourself again?"

She looks at me, smiles, but don't say one word.

My face, it's getting flushed with heat as I blurt out, "Mommy, I haven't been going to Mass and I yell at God all the time."

She looks at me, shakes her head and with lifeless words says, "You better stop doing that and go to confession."

I stare at her for what seems like forever and I want to scream, *Don't you hear how scared I am? It's not normal to be screaming my fool head off at God! Please! Mommy, please hear me, cause it's what I'm not saying is what's really scaring me.* But I don't say another word as the silence between us lengthens. She's looking at the blank wall again and tears are coming down her face. My heart feels like it's breaking, but not for her. It's breaking for me and all us kids cause what if Mommy's never gonna be all right again? What's all us kids gonna do? At the same time I'm thinking these scary thoughts, I'm wishing I could hold Mommy in my arms and wishing she would hold me in her arms, too.

I come out of myself when I watch Mom wipe moisture off her forehead with the sleeve of her faded yellow housedress sleeve as she's moaning, "If it weren't for all these kids! I'd be with you right now!"

My mouth gets wet and my tongue gets swollen in the back of my throat, and even though I want to say something, anything, I can't. I take a very deep breath, repeat her horrible words in my head and I tell myself, At least she ain't gonna kill herself. But then I think, I'm not so convinced that she won't kill herself. I want to scream, Why call out to this dead man you call my father? Why waste your tears on him? I want to punch the wall so hard and make a hole in the plaster right next to all the other holes that my brother, Pat, punched into those walls, but I come out of myself when I hear Ralph running down the stairs.

I whisper to Mommy, "Ralph's coming downstairs."

She puts a smile on her face and as she wipes her pale cheeks with the red-striped dish towel, she rushes over to the stove and reaches for the coffeepot.

Slowly, I start walking past the radiator. I don't want to be in the kitchen with Ralph. I don't want to hear him yelling how much he hates that we moved out of South Philadelphia. I don't want to hear him telling Mom that he can't stand how she's not teaching us girls how to take better care of the house. He just don't understand what's really going on around here. All's he understands is how to yell. Still, I gotta find somebody to talk to about how I yell at God all the time.

I go upstairs to my big sisters' bedroom, but soon as I walk in, I know they ain't gonna help me. Trudy and Grace are huddled together on the window seat and giggling and oohing and aahing as they lean out the window. Smoke from their Winston cigarettes is all around them. I hate their smoking, but I'm curious about what's going on outside. I squeeze in-between them on the window seat. I can't believe they're all googly-eyed over a motorcycle guy who's standing in the street next to his Harley-Davidson. He's wearing a black leather jacket, black boots and a black hat, too, and he's got his one leg slightly bent. I know he thinks he's special cause my two dumb sisters are looking down at him like maybe he's Marlon Brando. Except he ain't. The cocky look on his face just makes him look weird. "Oh brother," I moan as I roll my eyes up to the ceiling. Just then Trudy gets up and runs outta the room. Next thing I know, she's outside walking across the trolley tracks towards that weird motorcycle guy.

I scream, "Oh!!! Boy!!! There's gonna be a lotta trouble. Daddy ain't gonna like this not one bit!!!"

But it's like Grace don't hear me. She rushes over to the mirror, puts red lipstick on, then runs a comb through her short, curly brown hair and races out of the bedroom like a wild stallion.

Once I hear her throwing open the front door, I sit on the double bed, the one with the blue blanket. It's bad enough Trudy's out there acting so googly-eyed and dumb. I can't stand to see Grace chasing after some weird motorcycle guy, too. If Daddy was here, he'd be telling that motorcycle guy to get away from his daughters and don't ever come back. It wouldn't matter how much Trudy screamed and Grace cried. If Daddy was here, they'd be coming home from Mass and helping Mommy make macaroni and gravy. If Daddy was here, they'd be trying to help me not feel so scared. But if Daddy was here, I wouldn't be feeling so lost, lonely and scared. If Daddy was only here I wouldn't be yelling at God all the time, either. I just gotta find somebody to talk to.

Then, the answer comes in my head like a light bulb going on. I'm gonna go to church and talk to a priest right now. He'll be able to help me.

"Bless me, Father, for I have sinned. It has been three months since my last confession," I sheepishly whisper to Father McDermott as I kneel in the confessional. I got my hands together with my fingers pressed against my mouth and with nervous spasms in my stomach, I say, "Father, I haven't been going to Mass on Sundays for a few months, now."

In a brogue as thick as Irish stew he screams, "Doesn't your mother get you up on time to go to the children's Mass?"

I'm so shocked that he's yelling like I'm the worst sinner in the world. I ain't never been yelled at by a priest before. With my knees shaking like Jell-O, I whimper, "She does."

With lightning speed he roars, "Devil's daughter! How dare you not come to Mass on Sundays. For your penance say the rosary every day for the rest of April and all of May. I want you to get down on your knees and beg the Blessed Virgin to forgive you!! And maybe and only maybe, then God will forgive you these terrible sins."

I wish more than anything I could get off my knees and yell, My own Daddy never yelled at me like you're doing right now! If my Daddy was alive, he'd tell you to stop yelling at me and if you ever yelled at me again, he'd make you wish you didn't! But like the coward that I am, I don't say one word, and after he's finishes yelling in English, he yells in Latin, too. I know he's done yelling when he doesn't say another word and that's when I pray,

Oh my God, I am heartily sorry for having offended thee. And I detest all my sins, because I dread the loss of heaven and the pains of hell. But most of all because they offend thee, my God, who are all good and deserving of all my love. I firmly resolve with the help of thy grace confess my sins, to do penance and to amend my life. Amen.

I quietly open the confessional door, look out at the dozen or so people standing in the confessional line. I'm so embarrassed that they all heard Father yelling at me. I put my eyes to the floor and don't look up until I reach the front of the church and see the Blessed Mother statue. Putting my hands together in prayer, I ask, "I know I'm just a really bad kid since I don't go to Mass on Sundays, and especially since I yell at God when I'm supposed to be at Mass praying to him. So as you can plainly see, Blessed Mother, I definitely need all the help I can get. So if it's not too much, please, please help me be a good kid again."

Chapter 18

IT'S A CHILLY SUNNY SATURDAY AFTERNOON and I'm lying on the cement back porch of our house with my blue rosary beads wrapped around my thin fingers. I got both legs leaning against the red brick wall as I'm thinking how it's been a whole week since Father McDermott said I had to say the rosary every day for my penance. Already I'm feeling worn out from having said it six times, but I'm feeling pretty guilty, too. I know it's a very bad thing to not want to pray the rosary, especially when I need all the help I can get.

So after I stop yelling at myself, I sigh long and hard and on my fingers count, "There's five days left in April. Then there's another thirty-one days in May. That means I'm gonna say the rosary, let me see, six and five and thirty-one makes forty-two times before God will maybe, and only maybe, forgive me my terrible sin."

I push the lazy part of me out of my head and think that if I do like Father said, then I think God's going to finally let me understand why my Daddy killed himself. And I bet God's also going to help me understand why me and my whole family have to keep on suffering like this.

I clear my throat, put a very big smile on my face and with lots of happy confidence floating around in my head, I hold onto the crucifix. As I'm making the sign of the cross, I pray, "In the name of the Father, and of the Son, and of the Holy Ghost, Amen."

I take a very deep breath and I continue praying,

I believe in God, the Father Almighty, Creator of heaven and earth; and in Jesus Christ his only begotten Son; who was conceived by the Holy Ghost, born of the Virgin Mary, suffered under Pontius Pilate, was crucified, died, and was buried. He descended into hell; the third day He arose again from the dead. He ascended into heaven, sits at the right hand of the Father; he will come again in glory to judge the living and the dead. I believe in the Holy Spirit, the holy Catholic Church, the communion of saints, the forgiveness of sins, the resurrection of the body, and life everlasting to come. Amen.

But I stop praying when I see the next-door neighbor's boxer dog, Duke, running after a stray cat who accidently strolled into his yard. The grimy-looking cat with car-grease stripes going down his back jumps over the fence only after Duke misses pouncing on him by a few inches.

Once Duke quiets down, I settle down, too. I put my fingers on the first blue bead, take another deep sigh and under my breath, I pray,

Our Father, Who art in heaven, hallowed be thy name. Thy kingdom come; thy will be done on earth, as it is in heaven. Give us this day our daily bread; and forgive us our trespasses, as we forgive those who trespass against us. And lead us not into temptation, but deliver us from evil. Amen.

A chill catches hold of me, and I pull my white socks up to my knees.

Only cause I know I'm praying to the Blessed Mother do I get filled with reverence as my thumb gently holds onto the next blue bead. I pray,

Hail Mary, full of grace; the Lord is with thee; blessed art thou amongst women, and blessed is the fruit of thy womb, Jesus. Holy Mary, Mother of God, pray for us sinners, now and at the hour of our death. Amen.

I say the Hail Mary two more times. Then I look around the neighbors' back yards, then the back doors of the houses, too and only cause I can't find one thing to take my mind off praying, do I pray,

Glory be to the Father, and to the Son, and to the Holy Ghost. As it was in the beginning, is now, and ever shall be, world without end. Amen.

I look at the kitchen clock and after I make big eyes, I tell myself to forget about time and just keep praying. But before I start praying I remind myself I have to decide which one of the three mysteries I'm going to be thinking about when I start praying the decades of the rosary. This is the really hard part cause I'm supposed to be thinking of one thing, but praying another. But since Sister in school said that's how we're supposed to pray the rosary, I guess I better do it. I figure it's the only way that God's gonna explain why all these awful things keep happening in my family.

I'm just about to begin when I see our cat, Queenie, infuriate Duke by walking on his wooden fence. I sit on the porch and to Queenie I say, "You know if Duke catches you, you're a goner."

I keep watching as Queenie puts one paw in front of the other and Duke is doing his best to climb that fence. He's barking like crazy and

I start laughing. If Queenie gets caught by Duke, I'll have the perfect excuse to stop praying the rosary. Who else is gonna stop Duke from ripping Queenie to shreds?

But I ain't gonna have no such luck, no sirree! Queenie jumps off the fence into the alleyway. Soon as Duke stops barking, my mind comes back to saying the rosary and finally, I make my decision. As I lie back on the porch and rest my feet against the brick wall, I tell myself that since it's Easter time, I'm gonna pray the sorrowful mysteries which tell us about how Jesus suffered and died on the cross for all our sins. The first mystery is Christ praying and agonizing in the garden of Gesemen or someplace like that . . .

I say one Our Father and then I say ten Hail Marys, and now I got my legs relaxing against the metal railing with my head resting on the kitchen rug Mom has drying on the porch railing. I take very, very agonizing sighs in between saying the Hail Marys, and I stop once I'm done praying the Glory Be To The Father.

I remind myself again how I'm supposed to be thinking about one of the sorrowful mysteries as I'm praying the rosary. I start thinking about the second sorrowful mystery where Jesus gets beat up from the top of his head to the tip of his toes. I don't understand why Sister calls this a mystery, but it ain't too hard for me to imagine how awful Jesus must have felt knowing people don't like him.

Then it's the third decade and I pray the Our Father. As I pray the ten Hail Marys I'm trying hard to be thinking only about the third sorrowful mystery, which is Christ having his clothes ripped off his body and people making fun of him and calling him bad names. But as hard as I try to get my head to be filled with these horrible things they did to Jesus, all's I keep thinking about is how clean Mommy's wash looks as it's blowing in the cool breeze. I'm checking, too, to see if Mommy washed my school blouses and I get to feeling very happy when I see she's got my three white blouses hanging on the new clothesline that's closest to the metal fence.

More than halfway through saying the five decades, I start with the Our Father, then, the ten Hail Marys, then the one Glory Be To The Father. I smile as I look at my fingers spinning around my rosary beads like Mommy's washing machine, and it's not until I'm done saying the last decade that I look at the kitchen clock. I take another deep sigh as I see it's taken almost twenty whole minutes to say the rosary. And I got another thirty-five days of having to say the rosary.

But if I want God to tell me why my father killed himself, and if I want God to tell me why we all have to suffer like this, then I better stop doing all this complaining and just keep praying.

The back door opens and I sit up. I see it's Mom, and she's standing in the doorway with a basket of wet clothes. I run down to the bottom step and wait until she walks down those same steps, too. She passes by me barely looking at me, and it isn't until she starts hanging the white sheet on the clothesline that she finally looks at me and says, "Why aren't you outside playing in the fresh air and sunshine?"

I shrug my shoulders like I don't know why, but what's really going through my head is that there's nobody for me to play with. The girls on the block are either too young or too old for me.

Queenie scratching at the back door is what gets my attention and since I don't have any reason to stay out here, I pick her up. I don't put her down until I'm standing in the kitchen next to her water bowl. I walk into the parlor, turn the television on and I'm very surprised to see a Japanese lady dressed up like a geisha girl making tea for an American sea captain. Once she starts to sing, I know it's the opera "Madame Butterfly." Only cause the opera is reminding me of happier times when Grandpop played his opera albums on his Victrola phonograph, I turn up the volume and sit on the couch. Queenie prances over to me, purrs and jumps on my lap. I start petting her black fur, then I start tickling the white fur of her throat the way I wish somebody would pet and tickle me.

I'm walking down the middle aisle of the church to go to Communion on this cloudy Sunday morning and I get a little scared cause I see it's Father McDermott giving out Communion. But I go over in my head how I've been saying the rosary every day for the past week, and how good I've been not yelling at God in my head no more. So I tell myself to stop being afraid, and keep walking. When I'm only a few feet away from the altar, I smell whiskey. It's so strong I rub my nose trying to get the whiskey smell out of it. Then I turn and see standing behind me a very tall skinny man with lots of white hair who's barely standing straight and reeking like a sponge with whiskey.

With my heart filled with fear for this man, I start worrying, Oh my God! What's Father McDermott going to do to him for coming to

126

church drunk? Father's going to yell at him the way he yelled at me, but this is even worse cause he's gonna yell at him with a church filled with people.

I stop staring at this man once I accidently push myself into a fat lady who's standing in front of me. After she stops throwing me a dirty look for causing her pink hat with a cluster of tiny white flowers to fall into her eyes, I turn and look at this man again and I start to think that if I could, I'd hide this drunken man behind one of the pews before Father can even lay his mean eyes on him. I don't want that priest to embarrass him the way he embarrassed me.

I kneel on the red leather mat that's in front of the white marble Communion railing and wait until Father is standing almost on top of me. Then, I fold my arms over my chest, open my mouth and, once Father bends towards me, I close my eyes to show my respect as Father places Communion on my tongue and I don't open them until Father says something in Latin.

Immediately I put my arm up cause that's exactly when the drunkard man almost falls on top of me as he's wobbling trying to kneel on the red leather mat next to me. And just when the man starts slumping over the Communion railing is when Father pulls at the man's suit sleeve and, once he balances him, he places Communion into the open mouth of this man, this drunken man whose breath smells worse than a skunk. And even though the drunkard man almost pushes me to the floor as he stumbles to get up, I get an even bigger shock cause it's Father who continues to give other people Communion without saying not so much as one word to this man who came to God's House smelling like a brewery.

Once I come out of my own stupor I'm screaming in my head, Father sure has a lot of gall giving that man Communion with him being so cockeyed drunk. But to me, he yells at the top of his lungs and makes me feel like I'm the most evilest human being in the whole wide world! I give Father McDermott my meanest look, stand and I soar up the aisle like a hawk. All the while I'm thinking, I'm never coming back to church ever again!

I slam the heavy red church door, then slam the gold wooden church door and start rushing home like a wild hurricane. In my pissed-off head I'm yelling, I ain't saying the rosary no more, either. Father giving that drunkard Holy Communion is the final straw. How dare he never bother to ask me why I missed Mass. How dare he not give me the chance to tell him how scared I am that I'm yelling at God all the time, and how it scares me that even on cold and rainy Sunday mornings, I'd rather walk around the neighborhood than go to church where it's nice and warm. I think Father McDermott's a coward for how he picked on me, and I'm so sick and tired of being sick and tired of being pushed around and ignored that I think I could explode like the atomic bomb.

Seeing how there's no one else who wants to hear me, I start screaming to God in my head with more fury than I ever felt in my whole life.

WELL, WHY DON'T YOU DO SOMETHING ABOUT ALL THIS BULLSHIT? I'VE JUST ABOUT HAD IT WITH EVERYBODY INCLUDING YOU. OH! WHAT'S THE POINT IN TALKING TO YOU ANYWAY? CAUSE AS FAR AS I'M CONCERNED YOU'RE DEAD! AND I DON'T TALK TO DEAD PEOPLE, EVEN IF IT IS GOD!

It's just when I'm screaming at God in my head that I pass stupid Gene's porch. Because of all the screaming in my head, and because my bad ear is facing stupid Gene's porch, I can't hear exactly what's being said, but from the tone of the voices, I know the words are ugly. I spin around. Creepy Gene is standing on the porch with his two hoodlum friends. They're shouting with their ugly faces getting uglier, "Grease ball! Grease ball! Your kind ain't welcome here! Grease ball! Why don't you go back where your own kind live?"

Usually I'd just walk on home and ignore stupid Gene. He lives sixteen houses up from me. But today, I'm not letting even that jerk push me around. I run to the bottom of his steps, look at his snickering face and shrill, "Harp! Harp! Harp! Harp! HAAARRRPPPPP!!"

Dumb Gene and his two hoodlum friends jump down the steps. Gene hits the pavement first and screams in my face, "Skinny fucking bitch! Olive Oyl!! Yeah! That's what you are! A skinny fucking grease ball dago bitch!!!"

I tell my feet to move and with them barely touching the ground, I run faster than a runaway trolley. Gene and his scuzzball friends are behind me and even though I'm very afraid of what they might do to me if they catch me, I keep screaming, "HAAARRRPPPPP!!"

"Dago! Wop! Dago! Wop!"

"HARP! HARP!" The words keep coming out of my mouth as I run even though I'm scared cause Gene has a reputation for beating up girls. I'm feeling happy too, almost like laughing. Especially when I reach the front of my house. I know they ain't gonna come near me now. I skip up my front steps. When I'm on the porch, I turn and stare right at skinny cruddy Gene and his two scuzzball friends and in a voice as sweet as honey, I say, "Thank you so much for the compliment."

Gene punches his dumber-than-he-is friends and then he looks at me with his lunatic face and screams, "Go back to where you belong, you dumb dago!!"

I skip across the open porch and once I open the front door, I turn to Gene and shriek, "HHHHHHAAAAAAARRRRRRPPPPP!!!"

Gene's waving his clenched fist at me and screaming more curse words. I'm in absolute heaven when I see the thick vein in his throat protruding out from his neck and looking like a wiggly, blue macaroni. His face is turning the ugliest shade of red and I think I better get in the house cause he's probably crazier than a bedbug now. I push the front door open and lock it fast, just as Gene runs up my front steps. Standing at the window I shout, "Your mother must have dropped you on your head when you were a baby, Gene! Cause you're crazier than a bedbug!"

I don't know what Gene does next. Cause I'm laughing so hard, tears are coming down my cheeks; my knees go weak and I start sliding against the white door. I don't stop laughing and I don't stop my joyful tears, not even when I find myself sitting on the floor. I feel Queenie rubbing against my leg so with both hands, I pick her up, hold her like a baby in my arms, and bury my laughing head into her beautiful black shiny fur.

Chapter 19

WITH ALL THE THINGS GOING ON IN MY LIFE, school is just another one and for the first time I ain't too fond of it either. The school I'm going to is called Most Blessed Sacrament and it's nothing like the school I just came from. The kids here are Irish Catholic and there's at least 3,000 of them. There's four classes for each grade, and in my class there's around seventy-five girls, all girls because this school don't allow boys and girls in the same room. It really bothers me that there's so many of us in one class. It makes me feel the way I feel at home, which is ignored and passed over. But it's worse at school, seeing how I feel so outside of things. Sometimes I think it's cause I don't look anything like the other kids. Most of them have fair skin with light hair and lots of freckles. I got chestnut-brown hair, very dark eyes and olive skin. All and all, I got to tell you, me and my brothers and sisters stick out like sore thumbs. But even though I hate school it don't make me stop trying to make friends.

"How's it going with friends in school?" I ask as I walk to school one morning with Carmella and Josephine. It's two months since we started coming to this school and the weather is freezing cold. When neither of them answer, I say, "The worst time I'm having is at recess."

They keep walking with their heads looking down like two sad sacks and that's telling me they're being ignored just like me. So they don't feel so lonely, I say, "It feels so awful not to have nobody to play with."

They don't say one word to me, but I know they understand. "It don't really matter," I tell them. "What matters is how I'm gonna get somebody to wantta be my friend."

With questioning eyes, Josephine asks, "How are you gonna do that?"

"I don't know. But when I find out, I'll let you know."

Sister rings the bell and says, "Take out your English books." She turns towards the blackboard and writes the word, "ain't." After she's done that, she turns towards the class, fixes her eyes on me and says, "There isn't any such word in the English language called 'ain't.'"

Even though my face feels like it's beet-red cause of how embarrassed I'm feeling, I stare back at her cause she's getting me mad.

Reaching for the yardstick, she points to the blackboard and she says, "What can be used instead of 'ain't'?"

Some kids raise their hands and say words like, "am not," "are not," "is not," but she keeps staring her nose down at me. And I keep staring at her. I don't stop until she looks to somebody else to give her another answer. Then, she says, "I know some of you do this because it's a Philadelphia thing. But you can't use two negative words in a sentence because one cancels the other out."

I gotta tell you, I don't got no idea what she's talking about.

Looking right at me again, sarcastically she says, "And the sentence I hate the most is, 'I ain't got no.'"

I'm so mad for the way she's singling me out, especially since I hardly ever talk in school. I want to shake my fist at her and shout, "Whatiya looking at me for?" Instead, and I don't know how I do it, but I come up with a most brilliant idea. Once she stops talking, I raise my hand and I lie. "Sister, Sister, the school I went to before wasn't as far ahead in English as you are. Maybe somebody can help me after school."

Still looking her nose down at me, she smiles like she thinks she's being so kind when she asks, "Would somebody like to help Rosemary after school?"

I'm surprised when I see a few girls raise their hands. Sister picks Julia and I think that's cause she lives just around the corner from me. Then Sister rings the first bell, which means we got to clear our desk and put our coats on.

That's when Julia comes over to my desk and says, "Want to walk home with me so we can figure out how we're going to get together after school?"

With lots of excitement in my voice, I say, "Yeah. But I have two younger sisters that walk home with me, too. Is that okay with you?"

"That's nice. Okay."

When I stand next to Julia, I get a big surprise-my head don't even come up to her shoulder, but I shrug it off cause I can tell by the nice way she talks and by the soft smile she has that I already like her a lot. It don't even matter when I hear some girls in the back of the room laughing and saying, "They look like Mutt and Jeff."

131

I know it don't matter to Julia either. I can tell by her caring smile that we're already very good friends. All the way down the school steps, I take deep sighs of relief cause it feels so wonderful to have a friend again.

"Do you have any brothers or sisters?" I ask Julia as we walk home together with Carmella and Josephine.

"I have an older brother named Jimmy and he's one year older than I am."

"My brother Pat is one year older than I am. Maybe they're in the same room," I say excitedly.

In a slow, soft manner of speaking, Julia says, "No, they're not. I already asked my brother."

I'm full of joy just realizing that Julia must have talked to her brother about me before today. Then my heart starts to flutter cause I'm wondering what Julia would think if she came over to my house and saw how crazy everyone's acting. What if she saw Mom talking to the wall, and especially what if she heard my Mom talking to my dead father? So I say, "Since I got so many brothers and sisters, it might be a good idea if I come over your house so we can study together. That way, we won't get interrupted all the time."

"I'll ask my Mom, but I think it'll be okay."

Julia's Mom looks just like Julia; they both have medium-length, light-brown hair and a fair Irish complexion. Her Mom is even taller than Julia. She looks like she almost touches the ceiling. I don't ever remember seeing any woman this tall before.

"Mom, this is Rosemary. And Rosemary, this is my Mom."

I'm thinking about how tall she is when she gives me a big smile. "Julia says you come from South Philadelphia. I used to live there when I was your age. Where did you live?"

"On Hoffman Street near Seventh Street," I shyly say.

Mrs. McIntire then says, "That's a business district. How come you lived there?"

"My father had a produce business on Seventh Street."

"What does your Daddy do now?"

My feet shuffle back and forth and I nervously scratch my eyebrow and take my coat off, cause my body's spewing wet heat and my head's sweating, too. I don't want to tell them anything about my

Daddy, but I gotta say something. So with my eyes looking down at the throw rug, I whisper, "My Daddy died."

She takes two steps towards me and with shock in her voice she says, "I'm so sorry. How did he die?"

With lots of tears in my eyes because I'm terrified that the truth of his suicide will fall out of my mouth and we'll be thrown out of our new neighborhood just like we were thrown out of the old neighborhood, I scream to myself, "Don't say one word! Don't you daren't open your mouth and tell Julia's Mom that your father killed himself!"

The voice in my head keeps shouting these same words, and even though my Mom never said these words, I know they're her words. I know she doesn't want me to open my mouth, and I'm so afraid I might, and Mom will find out and she'll hate me and go away forever, too. I'm so scared. I can't move, and I can't stop the tears from spilling out of my eyes and down my face. I can't even see Julia and her Mom for all my tears.

The next thing I feel is a strong but gentle hand touching my shoulder. I look up and it's Mrs. McIntire who's pulling me towards her. I smother my drenched face in her blue-checkered apron as she gently pats my hair. I smell the Ajax cleanser on her apron and it's reminding me of so very long ago when Mommy's Ajax-smelling hands lovingly pinched my cheeks, too. I smell the mingled-in cooking smells on Mrs. McIntire's apron, and it's reminding me of a time that feels so far away when Mommy's housedresses smelled of delicious mingled-in cooking smells, too. After I take a very deep breath, I cry even more; Mrs. McIntire holds me tighter and I feel a caring and loving soothing strength coming from her body into mine.

"I am so sorry," she whispers. Her words sound invitingly soft and soothing to my aching heart, and I'm glad she's letting me cry; but I'm also glad that she's letting me put my arms around her.

After a few sobbing moments, slowly I drop my arms from her waist, then turn towards the stairs. Julia, who's standing on the sixth step from the bottom, has tears in her eyes, too, and she's pulling hard on her hair as she says, "We better get started. We have lots of homework." I reach for my school bag and run up the first few steps. I notice a faded picture of a man in a sailor suit that's hanging on the wall near the top of the steps. The picture has a black ribbon draping over it. Julia sees me staring at the picture. Once I reach the top step, with a red face she whispers, "That's my Dad. It's the last picture taken of him before he died."

A pain grips my chest, and once I put my school bag on the hallway floor, I look at Julia, who's running into the front bedroom. It's where she and her Mom sleep and it's where we're going to do our homework. Once I'm sitting on the double bed, the side where Mrs. McIntire sleeps, I think to myself how wonderful it was for Julia's Mom to comfort me even though her husband is dead, too. I almost start to ask Julia questions about her Dad, but I decide not to. She's wiping her eyes on her school blouse sleeve and I tell myself it's best if we get started on our English homework. That way, we stop talking about things that make us both cry like our Dads being dead.

"Mommy, can I come to the supermarket with you?" I'm saying to Mom as I stand in the dining room. I've been going shopping with her for a few months now. Mainly because I can't stand the way she talks to blank walls and plaster statues and to Daddy's ghost. The way I see it, it has to stop. For one thing her doing it makes me feel spooky. I think she needs to talk to a live human being, and I think that ought to be me. I think my going with her makes her happy. She talks nice talk as we walk to the supermarket. She even smiles, which is something she doesn't ever do when she's in the house. And every time I ask if I can go with her, she giggles just like she's doing right now. And just like now she answers, "Yeah. That'll be nice."

I grab the shopping cart out of her hand, run out the front door, and jump down the steps with the cart bouncing on each of those seven steps.

"The cart's already worn out from all the bags I carry in it. Be careful," Mommy says.

"Okay," I say and we walk towards Woodland Avenue. It feels so good walking with her that I almost want to cry for the sheer joy of it, but I stop myself. I almost start to talk, but I stop by pressing my lips together. Mommy likes the silence and so I do, too.

We're almost on Woodland Avenue when Mommy clears her throat and says, "Your older sisters are smoking. What am I gonna do with them?"

Even though Mommy's asking a question, I know she's not really asking me anything. She's just blowing off steam like her teapot does when it's left on the stove too long. I'm so glad that she keeps blowing off steam when she says, "I tell them I don't want them to smoke in the house. So they think because they smoke in their bedroom, I don't know they're smoking. Sometimes I stand right out in front of the house and I can see streams of smoke coming out of their bedroom window."

She motions her right hand as if she's pointing to cigarette smoke drifting by.

I know she's glad she's talking to me, cause I can hear it in her voice. She don't sound so heavy like the way she sounds when she talks to herself in the house. And me, well, being alone with Mommy like this makes me feel like I'm walking on air.

It's like she doesn't have anything more to say and a great big silence follows for the next few blocks. Then, like she gets a burst of talking energy, the same way an owl hoots after being quiet for so long, she says, "This time of year, your father would be selling bushels and bushels full of fresh corn. And he'd be selling lots and lots of strawberries, apples, plums and pears and fresh spinach, too. The supermarket produce can't hold a candle to your father's. His was delightfully fresh and wonderfully beautiful even to look at. You know what your father used to do almost every morning even in the dead of winter?"

Even though I know what she's gonna say cause she's told me hundreds, maybe even thousands of times already, I say, "What did Daddy do?"

"He'd get up before dawn and go to the wharf and pick out his produce for the day. That's why his produce was so fresh and so beautiful. But do you think anybody in these supermarkets does that? You know they don't. And when I look at their stuff, I get so upset, cause no matter what, it don't come close to what your father sold. You know what your father always said?"

"No, Mommy. What did Daddy say?"

With a glimmer in her eye she looks at me and says, "He always said, 'The early bird catches the worm.'"

She looks at me again and she laughs and I do, too. We both know that this is another one of her stories that she's repeated to me over and over again since we've been coming to the supermarket together.

Then, Mommy's face changes from silly to serious and she says, "Chris is starting a clerical job at a large insurance company in a few weeks. That means when I go food shopping you're going to stay home and watch after things until I get back. It's a great deal of responsibility, but I think you can do it."

My heart drops cause I know I can't go food shopping with Mom no more. But once I look up Woodland Avenue, I think how wonderful it is that she trusts me to take care of things at home when she's food shopping, which means she thinks I'm starting to grow up, which makes me feel very, very good.

Chapter 20

IT'S THE MIDDLE OF MARCH, 1957, and ever since the leaves started changing colors, my Mom's been saying almost every single day, "Life goes on." As far as I'm concerned it does. Just a few weeks ago I turned thirteen years old and officially became a teenager.

As far as my family is concerned, life is going on too. Just last September my oldest brother, Ralph, married his girlfriend, Lee. And another thing that's telling me how much life is going on is even though our father wanted all the boys to go to college and even though he wanted all us girls to finish high school, well, none of that is happening. Chris finished commercial school and has a job in an insurance company working with lots of numbers. I like watching her get all dressed up to go to work. After she puts pinkish coral lipstick on her lips, she takes bobby pins out of her chestnut-brown hair, and well, I got to tell you sometimes I think she looks older than Trudy and Grace. Mom says Chris has grown up so much since she went to work almost ten months ago that sometimes she forgets Chris is just seventeen years old.

But lately the biggest thing I'm noticing is how really different Mom is. She's got some of her old happy self back and things are starting to change. Like the way she's taking charge of everything. It's difficult finding the right words so you can understand how my Mom is different. Instead, I'll give you the perfect example of how she's got some of her old spunk back along with some things that are brand new, which I may add, I like it a whole lot.

I'm sitting at the dining room table helping my younger brother, Johnny, diagram compound sentences, and even though my eyes are on Johnny's copy book, I'm really watching Mommy. She's standing in front of Pat, Trudy's boyfriend, who's sitting on the couch waiting for Trudy to come downstairs so she can sit next to him and they can watch television together. Which is all they ever do. Once Mom turns the television off, I stop looking at Johnny's copy book.

Mom has a stern look on her face and, with her finger pointing at herself, she says in a voice that's loud, but filled with pride, "I am a widow with twelve children. My children's father is not here to protect them. But that doesn't mean I can't protect them!" She is almost shouting at Trudy's boyfriend. "I'm sick and tired of how you sit in our home night after night and never take my daughter out to a show or dinner!" Throwing her hands in the air, she shouts, "How can you be with my daughter knowing you don't even have a job? How dare you take advantage of her good nature?"

Pat's shocked eyes look down at the floor; then his lips grow tight. His arms stiffen like day-old bread as he places his black motorcycle hat on his knee. I get distracted when I hear a whisper coming out of the kitchen, asking, "Roe, what's going on?"

It's Chris and she's standing in the kitchen doorway and I forget about helping Johnny and run into the kitchen. "Mommy's reading Pat the riot act. She told him how she's a widow with twelve children. And she don't like the way he don't have a job. And she don't like the way he keeps coming here night after night. And she don't like the way he's never taking Trudy out to a nice restaurant anda-anda-I forget what else she don't like."

"Really!" Chris giggles. "Mom said she's a widow with twelve children?"

I nod, but I keep my eyes on Mom, whose hands are moving faster than her mouth.

"Oooooohhhhhhhhh!" I whisper. "Do you think Trudy's listening from upstairs?"

Chris says, "Naaaaahhh! No way. She's not hearing any of it."

"I don't wantta be around when she does hear!"

"She's gonna go off like a rocket! She's gonna cry and yell and..."

"What's a widow?" Josephine asks. She's sitting at the kitchen table eating Jell-O.

"It's a woman whose husband died," Chris says.

Carmella, who's sitting next to Josephine, swallows the biggest mouthful of Jell-O I've ever seen anybody put in their mouths except for me. With her mouth stuffed, she giggles and says, "That's for sure. Mommy is a widow that has all twelve of us kids."

Chris nudges my arm. "Will you look at Pat! Why, he can't even look at Mom."

"His whole body looks as stiff as a piece of dried codfish," I giggle.

Footsteps are coming up from the cellar and when I see it's Pat and Georgie, I wave them over and whisper, "Mom's giving it good to Pat."

My brothers hide behind the kitchen door so they don't miss a word; Johnny comes into the kitchen next and stands next to Pat and Georgie. After Pat explains to Johnny what a widow is, that's when Johnny puts a smile on his face, too.

"I know what Mommy's going to say next," Chris says as she puts her hand up to her forehead. In a voice that sounds like Mommy's, she whispers, "I keep getting headaches and can't sleep at night."

In that very moment, Mommy puts her hand up to her forehead and whispers, "I keep getting headaches and can't sleep at night."

We're all laughing so hard and trying to bury our laughter by covering our mouths with our hands or burying our heads in our laps or covering our faces with a dish towel as we keep watching and listening.

"I can't allow you to continue to take advantage of my daughter," Mommy says next. "You'll have to part company and once you have a job, then you'll be welcomed back in my home."

In no time flat Pat's up and out of his seat. I can't see his face, only his back. But for sure, I can hear his black leather boots make loud thumping noises as he hurries across the floor.

Soon as he steps down into the sun porch, Mommy's flying after him. Pointing her finger at him, she shouts, "If you come back into my home, I want you to wear regular clothes. Cause your wearing those motorcycle clothes shows just how little respect you have for all of us!"

Pat, he doesn't look back at Mommy and he doesn't speak. All's he does is open the front door and once he starts closing it, we hear Trudy racing down the steps.

She's shouting at the top of her lungs, "Mooooooooooooooooom!! You chased my boyfriend away!" She looks so angry, like I never seen her before. And she's crying and furious at the same time. I think she's going to take Mommy and shake her as she screams, "How come you never say anything to Grace! She keeps dating different guys and never stays with just one?"

Mom's sitting on the couch and after taking deep breaths, she says in a calm voice, "Grace is just having fun. But you, I can see where this is going and I don't like it. I will not allow anyone to come into my home and take advantage of any of my children and that's that!"

That's when Pat's motorcycle starts making loud noises. Trudy forgets about Mom and runs into the sun porch and screams, "Pat's leaving!!" Her long dark hair blowing every which way, she runs back into the parlor, stands in front of Mom and after she throws her red jacket onto the chair next to Mom, she kicks her black high heels into the dining room. Her face is as red as pizza what with all the fire inside her. I feel a little sorry for her, but not for long. That's cause Mom taking charge of the situation is making me feel safe and sound once again. Mommy's taking charge the way Daddy used to take charge.

"Mom! Do you want to know what Eleanor Roosevelt was quoted saying in the Life magazine Chris brought home yesterday?" Before she can answer, I blurt out, "'Women are like teabags. You never know how strong they are until they get into hot water.'"

I'm in the kitchen with Mom on this windy damp April afternoon and I'm turning the wooden handle on the new macaroni machine Mom got for the thousands of green stamps she saved from the Penn Fruit supermarket.

Mom puts her floured hands up to her face, smiles and to me, she says, "That's really funny and it's so true."

"We understand a lot about being in hot water, don't we?" But I don't say another word cause I don't want to remind her of anything that has to do with all the suffering we've been going through for almost two years now. It's so nice to be in our warm kitchen with the smell of chicken soup on the stove. And even though I know the broth has got mostly chicken bones in it, I know it's still going to be good cause Mom has some of her way of making everything taste so good back again.

With her one hand smoothing the stretched-out dough as her other hand is sprinkling flour, she rolls that dough around her macaroni stick and starts humming a tune. It's a happy melody and I sit back on my chair. My right foot's bouncing to Mom's happy humming and I almost start singing, but I don't cause with all my heart and soul I want to give Mom all of my attention. I listen to her humming and I keep staring at her flouring, then her rolling and flapping the dough. And she doesn't miss a beat as she keeps humming and rolling, then flouring and flapping. When she places five of the smooth doughy strips right next to me, I rub flour between my hands and put one of the dough strips in the macaroni machine, then turn the wooden handle. Once those thin spaghetti come out the bottom, I place them on the floured cookie sheet Mom puts beside me. They smell and look so scrumptious, I grab a few and chew, then swallow them uncooked as they are.

The front doorbell rings. It's Pat running inside from the torrential rain blowing outside. And it's Pat who leaves the front door open and lets Mrs. Donahue, scruffy Gene's Mom, in the house. We see her walk into the parlor and her nosy eyes scan the parlor walls. Mommy wipes her floured hands and rushes into the living room and before she can say one word, Mrs. Donahue announces like she's some kind of policeman, "Mr. Broderick said he'll take the two of us to the cemetery where you say your children's father is buried."

With patience in her voice, Mom says, "We can go first thing in the morning."

Mrs. Donahue's short cropped hair shows off her forehead that has a bony ridge above her eyebrows. That and the stupid gaze in her eyes makes me think Mrs. Donahue is from caveman times. Her mouth opens wide and I cringe. I know whatever is coming out is going to be stupid. Sounding like the meanest person I ever heard, Mrs. Donahue demands, "And how did you say he died?"

I sit frozen as I keep my eyes on Mom, who's now standing in the parlor only inches away from Mrs. Donahue. I bite down on my lip, praying Mom don't tell Mrs. Donahue the truth. I wait and wait and I wait some more and it's starting to feel like forever for Mom to decide what she's going to answer.

I take a deep breath when Mom opens her mouth and she says like she's an angel in front of the devil, "I never said how he died. But since you're asking I'll tell you." Right off, without skipping a beat, she tells this poor excuse for a neighbor, "He had a heart attack and died in his sleep."

I know I never heard Mommy lying before, but I don't care. I'd only care if she told her the truth. And as for Mrs. Donahue, she's so taken aback by Mom's words, she don't even ask Mom another question. She just follows Mommy to the sun porch.

"We can meet after the children leave for school and go to the cemetery," Mommy says.

Mrs. Donahue nods her head in a jerky fashion, like the weasel she is. Once they agree on the exact time, Mom opens the front door and stupid Mrs. Donahue leaves. She's got to walk by Grace and

Chris, who are coming home from working at their clerical jobs. No sooner do they come in than the phone rings.

Mom picks up the receiver and says, "Hello." She's listening real hard and once the other person's done talking, Mom says, "So you're the supervisor in charge of benefits for Social Security. Well, I am so glad you are finally returning my call. The reason why I want to speak to you is that I can't even begin to manage on what you're giving me. After all, I am a widow with twelve children."

There's a short pause, then, Mom says, "No, I'm not too proud to take charity. The nuns have given me food for the children, but they won't eat it. It doesn't matter if there isn't anything else to eat. I tell you they won't eat it!"

There's another pause, and with more annoyance in Mom's voice, she says, "All my older children work. Why, even some of my younger children have little jobs in the neighborhood. My three sons, Pat, George and John, work in a bread bakery, and my daughter, Rosemary, cleans for a woman who has multiple sclerosis. And my daughter, Carmella, why she does little jobs at a hairdresser. As for myself, I'm going to start babysitting soon for three children whose mother is going back to work. And I tell you, even with all of this, I still can't manage."

Another pause and with some embarrassment in her voice, Mom says, "Oh! I could never do that. No! No! That's out of the question. I'll never do that!" With that, she hangs up. She comes into the kitchen with Grace and Chris trailing behind, and sits on the kitchen chair that's near the stove. Much to my surprise, cause Mom never talks about anything important in front of me, she says, "The woman I just spoke to said we should go on welfare because I'd get at least four times as much money as I'm getting now. I can't believe she would even suggest such a thing. Your father paid into Social Security in case something happened and we're staying on it and that's all there is to that."

I look at Grace, Grace looks at Chris, and Chris looks at Grace, and in between me looking at them, I look at Mom's determined face, but not a one of us says one word.

When Mom talks again it's not about Social Security or welfare. She's telling Grace and Chris what happened with Mrs. Donahue and how she told her Daddy died in his sleep. "Mrs. Donahue thinks you all have different fathers. And since she's the self-appointed mayor of our neighborhood, it's best if I show her where your father's buried. That way she'll tell the whole neighborhood and that will put that rumor to rest."

Even though Mom doesn't say it, I know she's glad that she told Mrs. Donahue that my Dad died in his sleep from a heart attack. Now that bucket-mouth Mrs. Donahue can tell the whole neighborhood how Daddy died, too.

I know if Mom thought it, she'd say, "Mission accomplished," but since she didn't, out loud, I say, "Mission accomplished!"

Grace and Chris smile cause we all understand even though we don't talk about it. They go over to the stove and pour hot water into two cups for tea. Mom starts rolling and flapping the dough, and I start turning the wooden handle on the macaroni machine. Chris and Grace tell us their day.

My friend, Julia, and I are the best of friends cause we really like each other. But another reason why we're the best of friends is because we have one very big thing in common which is, of course, that both of our daddies are dead. It's not like we talk about it or anything like that. We don't have to cause we both know how awful it feels.

The kids at school call us Bobbsey twins cause like they say, "Where you see one, you see the other." We still do our homework together, but now, Julia comes over to my house. I don't worry anymore about her seeing Mommy talking to walls and ghosts. Stuff like that is over. And we're a family almost like we used to be.

This afternoon Julia and I are upstairs in the front bedroom. We have our arithmetic homework books open cause we still have five more word problems to do. I put my head down on Trudy's pillow and watch Julia jabbing her pencil through one of her ponytails while she's lying across Grace and Chris's bed. With her long thin legs up in the air, her long fingers under her chin and with her big blue eyes on Trudy's poodle skirt that's hanging on the closet door, she says, "That's the skirt I saw Trudy wearing last Saturday when she was going on a date with that cute guy. Who is he?"

I sit up and say, "His name is Pat. Mommy lets him be Trudy's boyfriend again cause he got a job and cause he's wearing regular clothes like my Mom told him he had to do if he wanted to come back into our house. Last Saturday was their first date since Mom let him back in the house. I like that Pat's back cause I missed him play-fighting with my brothers and me, which is something we've done four times since he's been back."

"Do you think they're going to get married?"

"My Mom thinks so. Do you want to try Trudy's poodle skirt on?"

With scariness in her voice, she says, "We'll get into trouble."

"No, we won't. I'll lock the door."

"Okay."

Once the bedroom door is locked, I put the skeleton key on the bureau and reach for Trudy's absolutely beautiful poodle skirt. After I take it off the hanger, both of us got our hands all over the felt part of the skirt and then we rub our hands over the very large black poodle and between the both of us, we're saying lots of "oooooh's" and "aaaaah's!"

I hand it to her and say, "I bet this skirt fits you even though you don't have hips like Trudy, yet."

Julia takes off her maroon uniform and after she puts the skirt on, I hand her Grace's cinch belt and help her tuck the skirt under the belt. I give her the once-over and say, "You look all grown up. I can't wait until I grow up cause when I do I'm gonna get married and have a family with a Daddy, Mommy, and with kids, too. I just can't wait until I can have a regular family just like everybody else."

She doesn't look at me but I know she hears me even though she's twisting and turning as she's looking at herself in the mirror that's hanging above the gray double dresser.

I keep my eyes on her and what's going on in my head is all this wondering about how Julia's father died. I wonder how old Julia was when he died. I wonder what her Daddy was like. I wonder if she misses him. I wonder if I ask her about her Daddy, if it's gonna make her cry. I wonder. I wonder. Only cause I want to know all there is to know about Julia cause she's my very best friend, do I softly ask, "How did your Daddy die?"

For a minute, I don't think she's going to say anything, then with her eyes still looking at herself in the mirror, she whispers, "He died somewhere in the Pacific during the Second World War."

I get shocked. I don't know what I expected her to say, but I didn't expect it was the war that killed him. But as long as I got the conversation going, I ask, "What was he like?"

She turns and stands in front of me. I feel sad for Julia cause I see her brown eyelashes glistening as they catch the last of the day's sun rays. "He died before I was born. But my Mom says he was handsome and nice and gentle and he took very good care of her."

I can't move off the bottom of the bed and I can't take my eyes off her either, cause I know my questions upset her and the nice part of my heart is crying for Julia. I can't believe that not even as a newborn baby did she feel his love for her. Never did she know his gentleness and never did she feel his wanting to protect her. My eyes get all wet, too, and I look away from Julia. I know the tears I'm feeling are for Julia's sadness. I just can't believe her Daddy never saw her. At least I had a chance to know my Dad and spend time with him. At least I have memories of my Dad.

She takes the poodle skirt off and hands it to me. Once I have the skirt on, I hide the extra material behind my back and pretend the skirt fits. That's when Julia asks, "How did your Dad die?"

I look up at the faded ceiling wallpaper and just like a trained parrot I say, "He died in his sleep from a heart attack."

My heart is beating fast and my hands are as wet as a wash cloth cause I'm scared she'll see through my lie. I swallow hard and only because I can't stand anymore, I sit at the edge of the bed.

"What a nice way to die." Julia smiles sadly.

What I'm thinking is how repulsed and horrified she'd be if I told her the truth. I catch a glimpse of Julia as she's putting her arms through her school uniform and a great sadness falls over me. I know what the sadness is about: today I pushed myself away from my best friend, and I did it with an awful lie.

Chapter 21

ALLELUIA! ALLELUIA! That's what's screaming in my head since I turned fifteen a few days ago, on February 23, 1959. I'm starting to feel like I'm finally growing up, not only cause of how old I am, but cause Mom's allowing me to do things that I couldn't do a year ago. I'm allowed to go to parties and dances, stay up late and watch "The Late Late Show" on television-provided I keep the volume down. Mom says, "I don't wantta hear that television when everybody else including me is either trying to get to sleep or already sleeping."

There's something in our family that's really different. Remember Pat, the guy who used to ride around on a motorcycle? He and Trudy got married last year, then ten months later, they had a baby girl and named her Ramona after Mom. It was only the day after baby Mona was born that Pat had to go away to the National Guard for two whole weeks. I couldn't believe it when Trudy asked if I'd stay with her and help take care of baby Mona. I was so excited whenever baby Mona was in my arms. It made me smile inside of myself, especially when she made cooing sounds like a beautiful white dove. Helping Trudy take care of my niece, well, it's one more thing that's making me feel almost all grown up, too.

But even better is spending lots of time talking with my two best girlfriends, Julia and Emily. We spend hours talking about clothes, make-up, hairstyles, school, and sometimes we even talk about, well, I mean we whisper about our once-a-month period. So it makes me really mad that Mom won't let me talk to them on the phone. "It's foolishness to talk to your friends on the phone when you just saw them at school, or just came back from walking up the avenue with them," she says.

I don't think Mom understands what it's like being a teenager in modern times. I think it's because she grew up in the olden days when women wore long dresses that went all the way down to their ankles and hardly anybody had phones in their houses.

There is something else that makes me feel almost grown up and that's starting West Catholic Girls' High School last September. The thing I like most about going to high school is the pure enjoyment of after school. That's when I walk almost three blocks to Market Street where the "American Bandstand" television studio is. *Bandstand!* It's the same Bandstand where Dick Clark is host and it's where I dance and dance and dance until I can't dance anymore. Sometimes when I'm walking in my own neighborhood, kids point their fingers at me and yell, "I saw you dancing on Bandstand!"

So all that's happening being fifteen, staying up late and watching TV, my friends Julia and Emily, being in high school and going to Bandstand, well, it's making me think this is the most wonderful time in my whole life. It feels like I'm being set free.

We don't care that it's a bitter cold day in March. Emily, Julia and I are sitting on my front steps and waiting for two of our other friends so we can all walk up Woodland Avenue and flirt with the boys as they drive by in their fathers' cars. Emily, with her long brown hair pulled back in a ponytail and with a laughing smile on her face teasingly says, "Roe, how come you've never been out on a date yet? I know boys like you, but you don't encourage them. How come?"

I'm getting angry cause this is at least the sixth time this month Emily's teasing me about boys. I don't understand why she doesn't tease Julia cause Julia can't even say "Hello" to a boy without her face turning a hundred shades of red. I give Emily one of my pissed-off looks and state, "When I find a boy I like, I'll go out with him!"

She rolls her green eyes, slaps her hand on her brown wool pants leg, laughs and says, "Oh yeah, right away! When we were up the avenue last Saturday afternoon, I saw you looking at that boy. So how come you didn't talk to him when he got out of the car and stood next to you? Huh! How come? How come?"

"Who do you think you are, criticizing me?" I shout at her.

Acting like she didn't hear one word I said, she shouts back, "Why? Why? Just tell me why you didn't talk to him!"

I get off the step, stand inches away from Emily, then put my hand on my hip. "You think you're my Mom, don't you? Well, you're not! And just for your information my mother said that when I'm ready to start dating boys, I'll know. You think you know better, but you don't! And one more thing! I don't want you talking about boys and me in the same sentence ever again!"

"Will the two of you just cut it out!" Julia says. "Here comes Irene and Roseanne. Let's go!"

Even though I always make it a point to sit next to Emily when we take the bus to school and when all us girls go to Savitz drugstore for cherry Cokes, once Irene and Roseanne catch up to us, I walk near the curb with Roseanne alongside of me. I just hate Emily teasing me about boys. I hate it more than anything.

The dismissal bell rings, but I stay seated at my desk because Sister Marie Joseph, who was a debutante before she became a nun and who we call "Big Joe," told me she wants to see me. Once the classroom is almost empty, I get out of my seat and start walking up the aisle towards Big Joe. We call Sister that cause she's very tall and very, very skinny.

Once I'm standing in front of Sister's desk, she whispers in her usual prissy way of talking, "How come you stopped getting A's and why are you failing history?"

I try not to roll my eyes as I look at her. I can't believe she's asking me about my grades today of all days. Today is the day I finally convinced Emily and Julia to come to Bandstand. I try to stop biting my top lip, too. I'm trying to hide what I'm screaming in my head, which is how much I'll die if Emily and Julia go home cause I'm not waiting for them by the lockers.

Again, she says in her prudish way, "Why are you failing?"

I'm afraid to tell her it's because I hate studying about King Henry VIII and his family. What I hate most about him is how he had his first wife's head cut off so he could marry another woman. And then, when his second wife couldn't give him a son just like his first wife, he had her locked up in the castle tower never to be seen or heard from again. And then, he married another woman and I'm not sure, but I think she couldn't give him a son either. So even though he was king, I think he was one of the most evil persons that's ever existed. I don't want to hear about him, much less being forced to study about him.

I squint my eyes almost shut as I watch Sister's mouth moving faster than a locomotive. But I don't hear one word she's saying. All I can think about is getting out of here so I can go to Bandstand. I have to stand in line for almost two-and-a-half hours, but I don't care. I'll do anything to dance on Bandstand. And I think that from now on, while I'm waiting in line, I better do my history homework so Sister won't be bothering me anymore. *Bandstand!* I just love Bandstand!

"You're spending your free time going on that television show when you should be home doing your homework! What does your mother think about you going on Bandstand and making a spectacle of yourself?" I look up and see Big Joe looking at me with pitchfork eyes and I can't believe what she just said. Not for one moment do I like that Sister and a bunch of other nuns in some convent are watching me dance on television. But I cover my aggravation by making sad eyes. Though I know I'm hoping against hope that she'll take mercy on me.

She starts thumbing through her plan book, and I think she's ignoring me. Which only makes me madder. Cause who is she to say anything about my being on Bandstand when my own mother says it's okay. In fact, when some of the neighbors asked Mom why she lets me go to Bandstand, she always said, 'I don't understand what the problem is. I can see where my daughter is and I can see what she's doing and who she's doing it with. None of you can say that about your children when they go out.'

I search my brain to find a way to get out of here, but I get mad at myself; I can't come up with one thing. The only thing I know is if my best friends don't wait for me because Sister is taking forever torturing me with all her words, I won't care if I flunk out of this class. Then I won't have to look at Sister's prissy face anymore.

Pulling out a yellow piece of paper the size of note pad from her plan book, Big Joe states, "Since you insist on going on that television show where you all look ridiculous jumping up and down and call it dancing, I want you to cover your school emblem so no one can see you're from West Catholic." Then she goes on to repeat herself again and again, which is her way of punishing those of us who don't do exactly what she thinks we should being doing. I look at her nose twitching in unison with her mouth and wonder if she ever had fun when she was a teenager like going to dances and parties and walking up the avenue with her best girlfriends flirting with boys. I tell myself, I don't think so.

She does get me to stand at full attention once she hisses, "If you don't keep your grades up, I'll see to it that you won't be allowed to join the glee club next year!"

My eyes look hard into her cold blue ones. I hate that she's got me under her total control. I hate it so much I want to aggravate her more than anything, even if I don't get to be in the glee club next year. So I shrug my shoulders and look away. Big Joe's mouth is going a mile a minute and my head is spinning. I just can't wait til she shuts up.

I get scared for being so cocky in my head, so I put a smile on my face, put my sickening sweet eyes back on her and, after I let out a very deep breath, I'm fantasizing that even when I'm walking through the hallways from one class to another, I'm daydreaming about dancing. Even when I'm sleeping in my own bed without me being able to control what's going on in my silly head, I'm dreaming about dancing, too. So, whether it's daytime or nighttime there's no end to me fantasizing about going to Bandstand so I can dance and dance and dance some more! Bandstand! It's the only place where being a silly, giddy, dancing fool of a teenager is the most important thing in the whole wide world.

Sister, she pulls her thin lips together, then hands me the piece of yellow paper and says, "Bring this home and have your mother sign it. I want to make sure she knows you're failing history."

I take the paper from her hand, read my failing marks, and as I'm placing it between the pages of my history notebook, I look up at Big Joe and say, "Okay."

"When are the two of you going to come to Bandstand with me?" I ask for the hundredth time to Emily and Julia as we walk home from school on Kingsessing Avenue. Once we cross at the corner on Cecil Street, Emily says, "I've been wanting to go to Bandstand ever since you started to go a few months ago, Roe. But I know if I go with you then Julia will never go. She thinks you won't ask her anymore." I stop dead in my tracks and stare at Julia. I don't even have to say one word. Julia takes a few steps away from us, stands next to Mrs. Robinson's cement steps and after a few quiet seconds, she turns to look at me and says the words I've been dying to hear. "Okay, I'll go." I scream like the howling wind for the sheer joy of it. Emily giggles, then says, "It would be so groovy if we wore our black wool skirts with our sweater vests." With pure excitement in my voice, I say, "Yeah. Anda-and we should pull our hair back into ponytails, too. And another thing, we have to wear our t-strap shoes with bobby socks. Sometimes the cameras go to the floor and show our feet dancing to the beats of the music." Julia, now walking alongside of me, mumbles, "I'm going to wear my mother's cinch belt to show off my tiny waist." I look at Julia and Emily and only cause I don't want them to be saying yes just to get me off their backs, I run a few steps ahead and face them. With my hand on my hip, I state, "Let's go next Wednesday after school." Emily giggles and says, "That sounds great to me." I look at Julia and with her face as red as sunburn, she whispers, "All right, next Wednesday." I blink back the shocked look in my eyes and only cause the reality of my best friends going to Bandstand with me is making me feel wonderfully jittery inside, I drop my books and stretch my arms to reach for them. Emily, she drops her books, too, and once Julia lets go of hers, we hug each other and crazily dance as our laughter screams into each other's ears.

I'm so excited I can hardly compose myself as Emily, Julia and I are standing at the entrance of Bandstand with about thirty kids in front of us. Emily's nervously giggling as she has her wide eyes looking past the entrance way into the studio. She's watching a man on top of a ladder change a really big light bulb. I look at Julia, who's in front of Emily, and she won't look at anything, not even the floor. That's cause she's nervous. But I know she'll be all right once she gets inside and starts dancing. The three of us come out of ourselves when the line starts moving and once inside, what captures our attention is very loud screeching noises coming out of the ten or so overhead speakers that are attached to the ceiling in the studio.

Once the loud noises stop, I start pointing to the bleachers that's about ten feet away from us and whisper, "We better hurry cause the show's gonna start soon."

We run up the bleachers and, after we settle ourselves in the middle row, Julia, who's sitting next to me and Emily's sitting on her other side, pulls at my gray school sweater and with quiet excitement cries, "I can't believe I'm really here at Bandstand!" Her crystal-blue eyes have a glow in them that's as shiny as a going-steady ring. She looks away from me as her eyes wander to the bulky lights hanging overhead and I watch as she looks at the hundreds of wires, some thick, some thin, some hanging from the ceiling, others taped to the floor.

I stand so I can get a better look at Emily, and smile to myself cause she's got her eyes opened wide as she stares at Connie Francis, who's rushing towards the stage door where Dick Clark comes out of before the show begins. Once the stage door closes behind Connie Francis, Emily turns her head towards the front of the studio and Dick

151

Clark's podium where he stands when the television cameras are on. Come to think of it, he stands there when the cameras aren't on. He never comes down from that podium, not even when kids want to talk to him. Oh! That's right, there is one time when he comes down-that's when he's doing a commercial about something us kids might want to buy like chocolate candies, hair spray, things like that.

"I thought the studio was much bigger than this!! I can't get over how small it is!!" Emily says.

"I know just what you're talking about. I couldn't get over how small it was the first time I came, too!"

Just then Dick Clark comes walking out from behind the gray curtains, the ones that glitter like stars. The three of us can't take our eyes off him as he steps up to the podium. That's where the ten best songs in the country are posted. I nudge Julia with my knee and say, "'Personality' by Lloyd Price is number one in the country!! I can't tell you how much I love that song!" With my arms outstretched, I sing, "Well, she's got *Boom* personality!! Charm personality!! Looks personality!! Plus she's got a great big caaaarrrrr!!!"

Julia pinches me hard on my leg to keep quiet. I give her an unfriendly smirk as I sit down, but quickly forgive her for being such a goody-goody cause I'm so happy she's finally here. Dick Clark smiles his big I'm-on-TV smile and I think how he looks more like a banker than a host for a teenage dancing show. That's cause he's wearing his usual dark suit with a white shirt and a tie. His dark hair is combed straight back with every strand in place. "Looks like he's got tight-fitting rubber bands for hair, don't it?" I whisper to Julia. She doesn't think I'm so funny.

With lots of distant friendliness, Dick Clark says, "Hi, everybody. Thanks for coming today. Just a few reminders. When you're dancing, don't dance past the yellow strip of tape going across the floor. That area is for the three cameras and you'll never be on television if you do that. One more thing, even though it's cold in here right now, it's going to get hot under these lights. It might be a good idea if you take off your jackets and sweaters and hang them on the rack. But whatever you do, don't leave any of your things on the bleachers."

Music starts coming over the speakers and I jump up and yell, "'At The Hop' by Danny and the Juniors!" I point to the ten top tunes. "It's number seven!"

Julia gets giddy, jumps up and with her feet already dancing says, "Roe, come on! This is my absolute favorite song! Let's dance!" She turns to ask Emily if she wants to dance with us, too, but stops herself. Emily's already got some guy talking to her.

I look at Emily and think, Emily finds it so easy to talk to guys. They find it easy to talk to her, too. I wish I knew how to do that.

"Come on," Julia says. Together, we run down the bleachers and once we're on the hard cement floor, we start dancing like whirlwinds. One of the cameras that's only a few feet away has its red light on. That's the one that's taking everybody's pictures and sending them across the country. With a tilt of my head, I motion to Julia and we dance over to the big bulky black camera. I smile right into the camera's eye and elbow Julia, and she does the same.

Soon we're forgetting about the camera cause the music is starting its wilder, louder beats. We tilt our heads back and start singing, "You can rock it. You can roll it. You can really start to grove it at the hop. Let's go do the hop! Oh Baby! Let's go do the hop . . ."

I come to an immediate halt when I feel a very, very, very hard push against my right hip. I turn and my eyes get small cause it's Terry, one of Bandstand's regulars, who's doing all the pushing. The same Terry who has lots of pimples and bleached-blonde hair that always has dark roots.

I start dancing again and to Julia I scream, "Terry's always pushing people so she can be on television."

Terry pushes harder and I push, too. It's like it's a Mexican stand-off, cause neither of us is budging not one solitary inch. I don't know how it happens; I couldn't have made such a perfect move if I'd thought about it, but all of a sudden my elbow is pushing into breast-excuse me, I mean her falsie, which flattens like a pancake. She pulls away and even with the music playing, I can hear her falsie popping back into shape.

Terry's madder than a hungry lion and she pokes me on my shoulder, but before she can touch me again, I look into her tiny eyes and yell, "Camera hog!! Camera hog!!"

Someone else nudges me. This time it's Julia and rolling her eyes, she motions me to the guy Terry's dancing with. He's a jerk from South Philly named Al, who also happens to be a regular at Bandstand. From the grin on Julia's face, I know what she's thinking. Al looks like a wannabe gangster with his black shirt and a tie that has an ugly kaleidoscope design running through it. His dark hair's slicked-back with a pumped-up pompadour and once he sees the camera is on him, he rolls his one eyebrow up like maybe he thinks he's some kind of model or movie star but he looks more stupid than he is.

Only cause I want to aggravate him, I shout to Julia, "If conceit were consumption, he'd be consumed!"

Julia and I are laughing hysterically as we stroll-like walk our way over to just inches away from the bleachers and start dancing again. The camera with the red light shining is in front of us, and Julia and I, we dance our wildest and our craziest ever. Almost halfway through the song Emily starts dancing with us to the terrific rocking sounds of this most wonderful song. The only time we stop dancing is when the music stops. Julia, barely catching her breath, huffs, "Iah Iah neeeed to sit doowwn." She rushes up the bleachers with Emily racing behind her and me, I'm trailing behind Emily trying to catch my breath, too.

I'm between Julia and Emily as we sit on the top bleachers listening to the soft dreamy sounds of "All I Have To Do Is Dream" by the Everly Brothers. My eye catches Carole, who's been a regular on Bandstand for almost two years now, and she's slow-dancing with some guy who I never saw before. Once she sees me she gives me a warm smile, waves and I wave back. I point her out to Emily and Julia and whisper, "It was just last week that Carole asks if I wanted to become a regular. I told her . . ."

Before I can say what I told her, I hear an almost-grown-up man's voice say, "Hi! How are you?"

I look up to see an almost-grown-up man who looks like a handsome football player with sandy-blonde hair and the bluest round eyes looking at me. "Would you like to dance?" he asks.

Him being so grown-up makes me scared and embarrassed at the same time. And not knowing what else to say, I nod, "Okay."

He offers his hand to me and, once I'm standing straight, I feel Emily tickling my leg. I smile politely at him while bending and pushing Emily's hand away like shooing away a fly. Then I start walking down the bleachers as I hold onto this guy's hand. Once on the dance floor, my stomach gets all queasy when he puts his left arm around my waist. For a brief second my knees go weak. I feel as nervous as a cornered cat and wish I could run and hide when he takes my right hand and holds it tightly against his big chest. His one foot moves to the smooth rhythms and I move with him. As we begin to slow-dance he rests his head against my hair and I get a very big surprise cause I'm feeling a tingly feeling going throughout my spine. And it's only cause being scared is all that I'm thinking about, I keep stepping on his ox-blood shoes.

He pauses in his dancing and says in his dreamy deep voice. "I'm from Harrisburg, Pennsylvania. I came here today because I wanted to meet you."

I look at his clear blue eyes and I can see he's the serious type, so I know he's not making a joke. I keep watching this good-looking guy and I barely breathe cause my stomach's puckering inside of me. He pulls me closer and we keep slow-dancing; slowly my insides relax and, only cause I've seen this in some movie with Katherine Hepburn, I chance putting my left hand gently against the back of his neck and my fingers brush against his short hairs. That tingling feeling shoots from where I'm touching him all the way down to my toes.

I know it's time for me to say something cause I don't want him to think I'm stupid. I take a very deep breath and in a sweet tone, I ask, "How long did it take you to get to Philadelphia from Harrisburg?"

"Over two-and-a-half hours."

I put my chin on his shoulder to hide the doubting wrinkles on my face, and in my head, I'm thinking, Don't they have any girls in Harrisburg that he can dance with? Then I wonder if I should invite him home since he came all the way from Harrisburg. But I remind myself that I'm not interested in having a boyfriend. Besides, the thoughts of taking him home reminds me of my big sisters and what they have to go through when they bring a boyfriend home. Soon as that boyfriend comes in the door, Mom sits on the couch next to him asking him a million questions about him and his family. Then, when my older sister, whose boyfriend it is, sits on the couch next to him, my four younger sisters don't take their eyes off them until it's their bedtime. I'm not ready for anything like that.

The music's playing softer now and my heart goes into a dreamy world; it feels like we're standing on a soft white cloud rocking from side to side. He pulls away from me and I'm filled with surprise as he whirls me around and my feet lift off the ground. My heart soars and I think more than anything else in the world I'd love to have him for my boyfriend.

Once the music stops, he lets go of my hand and asks, "What do you do for fun when you're not coming to Bandstand?"

The words fall out of my mouth so easily, they surprise even me. "I'm going steady."

I see the stunned look on his face, and I hear the disappointment in his voice, when he says more like a moan, "Ohhh . . .!"

Without giving him a second look, I make a beeline up to the bleachers and sit next to Julia. Emily isn't here, so I guess she's on the dance floor.

"Do you believe that guy?" I say like I'm really disgusted. "He says he came all the way from Harrisburg to meet me. There must be something wrong with him that he has to come here just to meet a girl. He even wanted to know what I do for fun when I'm not at Bandstand!"

Julia looks at me and, with wrinkles going across her forehead, asks, "What did you tell him?"

"I told him I have a steady boyfriend."

Julia shakes her head and with disgust on her face, looks towards the dance floor where Dick Clark is setting up a table to do a commercial for pimple medicine.

With seething anger, I say, "Look! The only reason why I come to Bandstand is because I want to dance. I don't want to be bothered with some guy. I mean what's the point cause once you like them, that's when they leave you high and dry. It's nothing more than a set-up for getting really hurt." She doesn't answer.

"And another thing," I cry. "He lives so far away. Do you really think this guy's going to stick around? Let's get serious, he won't. So why waste my time?"

Even as I'm talking, my eyes search the studio looking for him. Finally I see him standing next to the camera that's got its lens focused on Julia. I hold onto my stomach that feels like it's being gnawed at by a savage beast while I watch this guy from Harrisburg looking at me with longing in his eyes. I don't know why but I get to feeling very sad.

We don't take our eyes off each other until the studio mike is turned on, and in his usually calm voice, Dick Clark says, "The next song is the last song of the day and it's going to be a spotlight dance with Kenny and Arlene. They're going to dance to 'Put Your Head On My Shoulder' by Paul Anka."

Julia grabs my hand, "Hurry up! I want to get a close-up view of Kenny and Arlene dancing." She locks her arm under mine and only lets go once we're flying down the bleachers. In no time flat we're on the floor and standing as close to Arlene and Kenny as we can get. They're on the dance floor waiting for the music to start. I accidently push against the person standing next to me and when I turn to apologize, I get embarrassed all over again when I see it's that guy from Harrisburg. Even though I don't want to, I feel that same tingling that I felt when we were dancing and I wish we were dancing with his arms around me and my hand on the back of his neck.

Julia grabs my arm and pulls me closer and whispers, "Look! Look how Arlene's eyes light up when she looks at Kenny. Anybody can see she really loves him. And just look at Kenny. He's looking at Arlene with so much passion, it just takes my breath away. Look at his dark, romantic eyes and his devilish smile. And his curly dark hair. Ohhh, he's such a hunk!"

Her swooning almost makes me forget how things really are between Kenny and Arlene, and I begin to chuckle. "They're acting all mushy with each other for the cameras. Watch what happens when the cameras are turned off."

"What's wrong with you?" Julia demands.

Emily, who's now standing next to me, pulls at my skirt and whispers, "You know what your problem is? You can't accept a tender feeling between a guy and a girl."

Emily's words catch me dead in my tracks and even though I know she's right in what she's saying, I glare at her with sarcastic eyes. I don't stop glaring at her until the music stops, the camera light goes dim, the spotlight goes out, and the kids start running towards the two open doors.

Then I nudge Emily and Julia and with glee in my voice, I say, "Watch how lovey-dovey Arlene and Kenny are." I point first to Arlene, who's leaving by the double doors with not so much as a good-bye to Kenny. Then to Kenny who's leaving by the side door without so much as a good-bye to Arlene. "They hate each other," _I say as I start across the dance floor. I start giggling, but Emily and Julia, they don't giggle until we're in front of the podium, and that's when Dick Clark says, "Good-bye, Roe. Hope to see you soon."

I proudly say "Good-bye" too, and a big smile covers my face cause I feel really special that Dick Clark called me by my name and right in front of my two best friends.

"Wantta come back to Bandstand again?"

Julia looks away, but Emily, she says, "Let me know when you wantta come back, Roe. We'll come together and we'll drag Julia with us."

Chapter 22

I ALMOST FORGET TO GET OFF THE BUS cause the sounds of rock and roll music and the visions of me dancing on Bandstand is what's going on in my head. Only the jolt of the bus makes me look up and realize it's my stop. I jump up, run to the side door, pull on the string to sound the buzzer and, once I'm off the bus, I run up 58th Street towards my house. I open the front door, run into the dining room and balance my books on the typewriter that's sitting on a metal table. Chris, she's teaching me how to type cause of this saying Mom's been expressing a lot lately: "A young girl can always get a job so long as she can type."

But right now I'm thinking about finding out if Mommy's been crying like Chris says she does whenever she sees me on Bandstand. I know if there's ever a day that she's been crying those happy tears it's today, when I danced the spotlight dance with some guy I don't know. Smiling, I race into the kitchen where Mom's sitting at the table drinking coffee with Chris.

"Well, Mom! Did you see me dancing the spotlight dance on Bandstand today? Did you? Did you?"

I get taken aback cause Mom's not looking at me with happiness in her eyes like she does when I come home from Bandstand. She's looking at me in a way that makes me feel like something horrible is about to happen. I look at Chris and get even more anxious, cause I know the only reason why she's staring at her coffee cup is because she doesn't want to look at me.

With a deep furrow between my eyes, I ask, "What's going on?"

Mom doesn't say anything. She walks over to the stove, takes the lid off the big pot that's on the big burner. She puts the lid back on the pot, turns towards me and in a voice that's as anxious as a mother cat giving birth, she says, "In September you're going to go to St. Monica's Commercial School."

My mouth drops open and I fix my eyes on Mom. "What are you talking about? Why do I have to go to commercial school?"

Mom walks over to the sink, reaches into the sudsy water and as she squeezes the washcloth, she says, "But you'll have to take a test first to see if they'll accept you."

"Take a test! What do you think I am? Stupid? I have Latin for Christ sake! And wait a second! Why do I have to leave high school?"

Mom points to Chris. "Your sister quit school to help out around here, and that's what you're going to do! And you want to know why? It's obvious, isn't it? We need the money!"

"But Chris hated school and wanted to go out to work. I don't want to quit school!"

Mom goes on like I haven't said a single word. "It's a two-year program, but you're only going to go until you turn sixteen."

I punch the wall where the calendar is hiding a big hole and I scream, "Huh! I'm not even going to get to graduate. At least Chris got to graduate!"

Mom sits on the kitchen chair again and in a stiff voice, says, "You'll do what I tell you to do!"

"I can get another part-time job besides my babysitting job. That way I can stay in high school."

"That's ridiculous. I need you to have a steady job and that's what you're going to do!"

"What about Pat?"

Mom places her hands on the table and, once she stands, reaches for the unfolded dish towels resting on the table and starts folding the white one with the red lines going through it. Then she folds the one with the blue line going through its center and murmurs, "He's a boy. He needs a high school diploma."

Chris says, "Just think of all the clothes and the money you can have if you work full time."

Through my clenched teeth, I yell, "I don't want clothes and I don't want money! What I want is somebody to listen to me! I'm sick and tired of being told what to do all the time and nobody even bothers to ask me how I feel about it. The only time I get noticed around here is when somebody wants something from me!"

"Stop being so dramatic! You'll get over it in time," Chris snickers.

At this very moment I realize the awful truth and I yell, "You knew all along Mom wanted me to go to commercial school and quit when I turn sixteen. That's why you've been teaching me how to type on that stupid typewriter! Don't deny it!"

"All right! I won't deny it!" She turns her back to me, pretending she's looking out the kitchen window.

I turn towards Mom and catch her placing the folded dish towels in the dish towel drawer. Once she closes the drawer, she looks at me and says firmly, "You'll do what I tell you to do and that's final!"

My heart starts to drop cause Mom's rushing down the cellar steps. I know it's cause she doesn't want to hear what I have to say. Filled with the rage of a caged animal, I rush and open the dish towel drawer and throw them one at a time onto the kitchen floor. Once the drawer is emptied, I slam it shut and start stomping on those dish towels like I was killing bugs and screaming, "Aaaaaaaaahhhhhhh!!!" Then I kick those towels all over the kitchen. Once there's no more to kick, I look at Chris and scream, "It's the same old shit all over again! I'm supposed to be seen doing and not ever heard! Just like the day Daddy died, we had to go back to school! Just like the day of Daddy's funeral, we were sent to Aunt Mary's house!"

Chris doesn't answer me. She runs out the kitchen door. I take a few deep breaths and all of what Mom's telling me I must do sinks in. But I can't do it. I won't do it. And I know I'll have to do it. It makes me so furious, I kick the dish towels as I run out of the kitchen, and go screaming through the house. I don't stop until I slam the front door behind me.

Everybody in my house keeps missing the point. I'm fifteen and I'm being told by my Mom that I have to go to business school next year, and once I turn sixteen, I have to get a job so I can help out around the house. Even though there's lots about this whole situation that I'm upset about, the thing that's got me the most upset is that my own Mom won't listen to how sad and angry I am about how my life keeps changing like the moon. But there is one very big difference in how the moon and me keeps changing. The moon changes the way it's supposed to change, month after month, year after year. My life keeps changing in ways that have nothing to do with what a young girl my age is supposed to do, like going to high school with my friends and going Bandstand, and just having lots and lots of fun. I really don't think my mother wants to understand how awful this is for me. Because if she did, then I think it'd make her feel very sad, too. Yeah, but it's okay for me to feel sad. It just makes me so crazy mad not being able to share what's going on in my heart with the one person in the world who I love the absolute most. It just makes me go off in my head, and then I get very, very nuts.

If I had my way all I'd be doing is lying in my bed with the covers over my head on this soft, breezy, bright, sunny Monday afternoon in the middle of May. But my mother won't let me rest in peace.

In a voice that's telling me I better do what she wants, she yells, "Rosemary! Your girlfriends are outside sitting on the front steps! I want you to go out and sit in the sun. You look as pale as a ghost!"

I can't stand listening to her anymore so I get out of bed and, once she sees me coming down the steps, she leaves me alone and goes back into the kitchen. I'm tempted to run back upstairs, but I don't, and once I'm in the sun porch I open the front door and see Julia and Emily sitting on the bottom step. I put a phony smile on my face, walk down the six steps, and, after I sit, I wait for a few awkward seconds to pass between us before I say just above a whisper, "Hi. How yeah doin?"

"Roe, where have you been?" Emily asks.

They both look at me with so much concern in their eyes that it makes me want to cry, but since I don't want to cry, I look away and say, "I've been very busy."

"Doing what?" Julia asks. "I haven't seen you playing box baseball with your brothers and you haven't been hanging around with us either. So what have you been doing?"

I murmur, "What's it to you what I've been doing?"

Julia says, "I called you Friday afternoon and you never got on the phone."

"You know my Mom won't let me talk on the phone. Besides . . ." I put my hand up to my forehead the way Mom does and, in a voice that sounds almost like Mom's, I say, "It's foolishness to talk on the phone with friends you see almost every day."

"Yeah, then how come I heard your Mom telling you I was on the phone!" Julia demands.

"Well, I didn't hear her!" I say, even though I did.

"And another thing," Julia goes on. "Emily and I wait for you almost every day at your school locker so we can go to Bandstand together. But you're never there. You're avoiding us!"

"Yeah," Emily says. "You're avoiding us the same way you avoid boys!"

"What the hell are you talking about?" I shout.

Before Emily can answer, Julia nudges her, then shakes her head like she agrees with her and, after she fixes her convinced eyes on me, she shouts, "Yeeeaaah!!! I never thought of it that way before. But you're right! You're avoiding us the same way you avoid guys who like you."

"Is that why the two of you came here? So you could gang up on me?"

"Answer the question," Emily goes on in that know-it-all attitude of hers. "I know boys like you, but you don't encourage them. How come?"

I feel my face first turning red, then turning a very deep shade of purple as I scream in my head, This has to be the hundredth time this year that Emily's saying this to me! Instead I point to Julia, but I'm shouting at Emily, "Well, what about Julia? The only boy she can talk to is her brother!"

That does it. Julia's on her feet and, looking angrier than I've ever seen her, she says with a snarl, "What about the time at Bandstand when that boy from Harrisburg asked you to dance? And when he told you he came to Bandstand just to meet you, you lied and told him you were going steady. I would never do anything like that no matter how shy I felt."

Julia doesn't take her fuming eyes off me until Emily pushes her away; with her green eyes blazing at me, she yells, "You did *what*? I can't believe you did that!"

My shoulders almost sink into my lap as shame and sadness fill me. I look at my friends and, hating that I feel as naked as a newborn, I stand and demand, "If the two of you came here to torture me, then I'm going back into my house! And besides it's a waste of time bothering with guys even if we're attracted to each other. What's the point?'

They look at each other with hopeless eyes and I yell, "Why did you two really come here anyway? And . . . And if you want to know how I'm doing. I'll tell you. I'm doing just awful!" I look down the street and that's when my eyes catch the sun's rays and all of a sudden I can't hold back my horrible feelings anymore. Like a dam that burst wide open, I cry and cry and cry.

Julia sits next to me and once she puts her arm around me, I sob, "I have to quit school."

Emily slaps her beige capri pants leg. "Oh my God, you're pregnant!"

"How could I be pregnant? You know I don't go out with boys!"

Julia elbows Emily as she looks at me and says tenderly, "Why do you have to leave school?"

"I have to go to commercial school in September and once I turn sixteen, I have to go out and get a job." It's so horrible saying these words out loud. My voice is only a whisper and it's like someone's knotted up my insides. But now that I began, I must keep on going. "What I want more than anything in the world is to stay in high school. And what else I want more than anything is to go to dances and parties and walk on the avenue just like everybody else. But once I go to commercial school I'm never going to see any of you. I'm going to have to leave early in the morning and I won't get back until late afternoon. So when am I going to see any of you? Never! I tell you. Never!"

"It's not going to be that bad. We'll still see each other," Emily begins.

"Stop it!!" I shout. "Don't you remember how we used to say how stupid and lazy all those kids are who go to commercial school? So don't even try and make this seem like it's all right cause you know as well as I do that it is not. I'm going to be one of those dumb kids now."

Emily opens her mouth and it's only cause she can't think of anything to say to make things any better for me, she shuts up.

It's Julia who breaks the thickening silence. "Isn't Grace and Chris already working?"

I wipe the tears from my face again. "My Mom says Grace is getting married in September and as for Chris, she's already giving Mom her whole paycheck."

Emily, in her no-nonsense approach, asks, "How come your brother Pat isn't quitting school and going out to work?"

"He's already working part time at that bread bakery. And my Mom said that Pat's got to get his high school diploma because one day he's going to get married and he's going to have to support a family. But me, I don't need a high school diploma cause I'm going to stay home and raise a family. But you know what?" I ask, giggling as to what I'm remembering. "Last week I wrote a letter to Frank Sinatra asking him for three thousand dollars cause I think that's how much money my Mom needs until I finish high school. I also wrote that when I grow up, I'd pay him back with any amount of interest he wants. And if he wanted, I'd swear on a stack of Bibles or anything else that's holy to him promising him I'll pay him back."

Emily and I laugh, but Julia asks, "Have you heard from him?"

"Nah, I didn't mail it. I tore the letter up and flushed it down the toilet."

All the laughing changes the mood for Julia and Emily. They start talking away, but I'm not paying attention to what they're saying. I'm staring at Emily's flaming-red fingernails, and I look at the friendship ring that was given to her by her steady boyfriend, Joe. I look at the without-a-care-in-the-world expression on her face and I wonder why that can't be me, and it takes everything inside to hold myself back from running up and down the street screaming like a raging lunatic. Instead my eye catches sight of the pretty silver earrings that Julia's Mom gave her for her sixteenth birthday, and I think, But when I turn sixteen what I'm going to get is a job.

Looking at both of them being so young and carefree, I feel like I don't belong with them anymore. I just feel so old.

I come out of my strange head when Emily says, "Let's go to Savitz drugstore and get a soda and play some records on the juke box."

I say, "I can't cause I don't have any money left from my babysitting money."

In a comforting tone, Julia says, "We'll treat you."

"It's not that. I really don't want to go."

Emily says, "We're not leaving until you come out with us."

"I can't go anywhere until my half of the bedroom's cleaned. It's got dust balls the size of half-balls and I've got dirty clothes thrown all over the floor."

"We'll help you clean your half of the room. Right, Julia?"

Julia smiles like she thinks they finally got me cornered and I give her one of my cocky looks as I shout, "I can't let either of you up there. It's really filthy."

"Oh, stop it! We've seen your room a mess before."

"Not like this. It's really disgusting."

"Okay," Julia says. "How about if the three of us plan on going out tomorrow after school? We can walk up the avenue and stop off at Savitz drugstore on our way back. How's that sound?"

Just so I can get them to leave me alone, I say, "Okay." Without another word, I stand, open the front door, and say, "I'll see you tomorrow."

I watch as my two best friends start walking towards Greenway Avenue and I know that means they're going to Savitz drugstore. For a split second, I have a change of heart and almost run after them. But I stop as I tell myself I don't have enough energy and I close the door behind me.

Once inside, I run up the stairs to my bedroom and stare in the mirror. "Look at this face! I angrily whisper. "It looks so old!" I pinch my cheeks again and again and again, and frantically mutter, "Look! Just look! No color! What good is having high cheekbones when they protrude with a sickening shade of pasty skin."

Reaching for Chris's pink make-up bag, I keep my sinister eyes on the reflection of that long face in the mirror. I open the bag and pull out a compact and frantically smear lots and lots of biegy powder over my ugly face as I laughingly scream, "Now you look just like one of those powdered-up old ladies that live in the old ladies' home across the street."

I get sick to my stomach cause some of the powder has caked onto my hairline and I frighteningly whimper, "I don't want to look like an old lady. I'm only fifteen. I want to be young cause that's what I am. *Young!*" I pull at my bottom lip until it hurts and after I let go, it stays wrinkled and I get mad cause the parched skin reminds me of just how dried-up the rest of me is, too. I pull at the corners of my eyes, look in them and tell myself, Your empty eyes have the same blank look that senile old ladies have. See! You really are old! Look! Look at these eyelashes! They look just as brittle and lifeless as whiskers on an old alley cat. Everything about you is old!

I grab my stomach cause of the gnawing pain in it and only let go when I look at my profile. With seething self-loathing, I scrunch up my nose and whisper, "Just look at your nose. It's so long and skinny. It's the ugliest thing on your face. That's why it's in the middle. That way everybody can see the ugliest part of you first."

I straighten my nose, and change my thinking as I encouragingly whisper, "Your nose is fine just the way it is. And your eyes, you have such nice eyes. But you really do need to smile more."

I do smile and I smile again and I'm thrilled to be seeing my sparkling white teeth. Then, I remind myself there's really no reason to be smiling cause I don't have any reason in this world to be smiling about. I open my vanity top drawer, reach for my black eyebrow pencil and, with all my might, push the point of it hard into the tip of my nose. It hurts like a cutting knife and I pull it away. After seeing the huge black blob on my nose, I put another black mark on my forehead, and another on my chin. "Now you look just like an ugly old lady with moles and warts and all!" I cackle.

With my bony cold fingers, I push my brittle dark hair to one side and what's reflecting back at me are the twenty or so white hairs I've had since I was a baby. In an agonizing wail, I scream, "Look! Look at yourself! You were born old!"

I scrunch my forehead and with my black eyebrow pencil, I pencil in the creases. Then, I pencil in the deep furrows between my eyebrows and I pencil tears coming down my long face and I scream at the top of my lungs, "Just look at yourself! You're so ugly! No boy could ever be attracted to you! Cause they can see just how old and ugly you really are!"

I reach for my pink lipstick and on the mirror in big bold letters, I write, I'M TOO YOUNG TO BE SO OLD!

I stare at the words written in pink and scream, "Aaaauuuggghhh!"

I get jolted out of myself when the bedroom door opens and Chris walks in. "What the hell's going on in here? I heard you before I even came in the house!" Once she gets a good look at the vanity table, she frantically says, "I'll kill you if you used my make-up!"

I run out of the bedroom, and as I'm running down the steps, I hear Chris yelling, "My powder puff has pink lipstick on it. You ruined it! Oh my God, look what you wrote on the mirror."

I almost run into Mom on the bottom step. "What did you do to your face?" she demands.

"Just trying to make myself look like what I am!"

From the top of the stairs, Chris yells, "You should see what she wrote on the mirror with her pink lipstick. In big bold letters, she wrote, 'I'M TOO YOUNG TO BE SO OLD!'"

Mom's one eyebrow raises as she states, "I want you to go up and after you wash that face, clean that mirror and clean that room, too! Go do it right now!" She turns her back to me and rushes into the kitchen.

I run in behind her and scream, "Don't you want to know why I did this to my face? Don't you want to know why I wrote that on the mirror?"

Chris walks in and angrily says, "Mom, she ruined my powder puff! I need a new compact and she's going to have to pay for it! Right, Mom?"

With lots of cockiness, I say, "Oh *Mooooom!* I know you don't hear what I'm saying. But don't you hear what Chris is saying? *Mooom!*"

Mom doesn't answer either of us, but she turns towards me and begins to wipe the kitchen table. A hard chill runs up and down my spine cause of the cold, rigid look in her eyes. After I take a few calming breaths I say, "Mom, all's I want from you is for you to listen."

Mom stares at me as she's biting down on her teeth and says, "See all the trouble you're starting. What's wrong with you anyway?"

"You think this is starting trouble? Watch this!!" With the strength of a madwoman, I lift the brown table and send it flying across the kitchen. The crashing sounds of the table's porcelain top slams against the pink tile floor and sends shocking vibrations throughout the house. A huge smile forms on my face as I happily look at Chris clenching her powder puff. I'm pleased, too as I watch Mom drop her washcloth onto the kitchen floor; her eyes twitch and her chin quivers as she stares at the turned-over table.

Finally she says through her clenched teeth, "I can't believe you did this!"

I put my open hands to my cheeks and yell, "I've got to get out of here!"

As I run out of the kitchen, Mom yells, "I'm going to see about having you put away!"

"That'll suit me fine!" I run out of the house, down the front steps, and once I'm on the pavement, I hear Chris yelling, "Roe! You're coming back, aren't you?"

I turn to see Chris standing in the sun porch with the front door open. Laughingly I say, "Of course I'll be back. Where else am I going to go?"

"I'll calm Mom down. But you got to stop expecting Mom to do something she just can't do. She feels bad enough."

"Well, what about how I feel? How come nobody ever wants to know about how awful I feel?" I don't want to hear any more of Chris's awful words of how I'm supposed to be dealing with our mother, so I run across the trolley tracks and climb over the stone fence to the old ladies' home. I walk up their tree-lined walkway, the same walkway where I've come hundreds of times before to sit and talk to some of the old ladies. Once I'm near the porch of the smallest house that's hidden behind some old maple trees, I quietly walk up the five wooden steps. I sigh in relief that none of the old ladies are outside, rocking on the old wooden rocking chairs. I sit on one, the chair with the broken arm, and once I got myself fitting comfortably into its white wicker seat, I start rocking and rocking. I reach for the light-blue shawl draped over the rocker's arm, then lift my legs and wrap my whole body in the old lady's shawl, then rock some more.

I look out at the manicured lawns that go almost as far as my eyes can see. I look at the knitting needles lying on a pile of pale-green wool and I listen to the wailing of one of the sickly old ladies coming from inside the house. I turn and look through the open window of the gray stone house and a cooking smell is coming out the open window. And even though the cooking smells are unfamiliar to me, everything seems so inviting, and I tell myself that this is exactly where I belong. I bury my head in my knees and rewrap my old body in the woolen shawl and slowly rock back and forth.

Chapter 23

"NO MORE HOMEWORK! No more books! No more teachers' dirty looks!" I hear West Catholic High School girls screaming as they run across Chestnut Street on this hot, sticky last day of school in June, 1959. Me, I'm the last one left in the room. Even the teacher's gone and I think I should go, too. But it's hard knowing that this is the last time in my whole life I'm ever going to be in a regular high school. And seeing what a terrible report card I just got, it's probably just as well. And maybe if I sit here long enough, Julia and Emily will walk home without me.

The giggling of girls just below the classroom windows keeps drawing my attention. Finally, I shove my report card back into its beige envelope and hurry over to one of the four open windows. Leaning out, I can't help giggling as I watch some juniors ripping off their red-and-white uniform emblems and throwing them into the air as they race across Chestnut Street. Thankfully, Julia and Emily are nowhere in sight.

The noon heat is getting to me, and I start fanning myself with my report card, which reminds me again of what's on my report card, and I think, I didn't do as well as I could have. Eh, what's the big deal anyway?"

Wouldn't you know, just as I think that, my eye catches a girl in her green uniform waving her report card as she's running and yelling, "There's my Dad! I gotta go!"

An old black car parks next to the curb, close enough for me to see her Dad's bald head as he leans out the car window. She places her report card into his inviting hand; he gives it a glance, then in a voice that sounds as deep as the ocean, he says, "First honors! I'm so proud."

My eyes fill with dry tears as I remember the many times I showed my Dad my report card, and how proud he'd make me feel for all my nineties and hundreds. He sure wouldn't be proud if he saw this report card. It's so terrible. I can't believe I got a seventy-five in Latin. If my father were alive, I never would have gotten such a horrible report card. I would have wanted him to be proud of me, too.

I don't take my eyes away from the girl and her father, even though my eyes are starting to burn. I don't blink either. Then it's like the girl and her father vanish.

I'm watching another girl with long chestnut-brown hair pulled back into two ponytails blowing in the soft spring breeze of another last day of school. I know it's me I'm seeing when I was nine years old. Just a few minutes earlier, Miss Basil dismissed my third grade class, and I'm running down Peirce Street. I'm so happy, I think I can fly all the way to my Daddy's produce store. In my head I'm shouting, When he sees the hundred I got in history, he's gonna be lost for words, which is something I can't wait to see cause even though I always get honors, he don't think it's any big deal. Like he says, 'If you do what you're supposed to do then you'll get honors. Why don't you get some hundreds?'

"Daddy," I try to explain as I put my hand up to my forehead. "Sister don't give hundreds cause when I asked her she said nobody's perfect!"

Even though I know I'm not perfect, it still don't stop me from trying to get hundreds. And now that I got one, I can't wait to see the expression on his face. I keep running until I turn the corner at Moore Street and race past the tall old maple tree with roots pushing up the cement sidewalk. I run past the soda water factory, and the screaming baby in the playpen. Once I'm at the corner of Seventh Street, I turn to see who's calling my name. I'm not at all surprised it's my very best girlfriend, Carole, who yells, "Wait for me!"

"I can't cause I gotta go to my Daddy's store!"

I run past the store that has a stuffed peacock in the window, past the five and dime that still has two Halloween masks hanging on its door, past the grocery store that sells dried fishes and Italian cheeses. I run past the suitcase store and, after I breathe in the smell of the leather goods, I run faster and don't stop until I'm standing on Siegel Street in front of the fish store, the one with the two large fish tanks in it. That's when I see my Dad. He's standing in front of his produce stand smiling as he hands a lady customer a bulging brown bag that has a head of iceberg lettuce sitting on top. As she starts walking towards the shoemaker store, Daddy stands near the green pears and starts talking to his friend, Angelo, who's smoking a fat cigar that I can smell all the way over here.

I comb my bangs to make myself presentable. I comb my two ponytails, too. I button my blue sweater, pull my navy-blue socks up to my knees, put a big smile on my face and, after I look down Seventh Street, I cross. Slowly, I walk past the butcher shop, and as I pass Angelo, I give him a smile and once I'm standing in front of my Daddy, I stop.

He doesn't see me cause he's busy straightening out the pear boxes that's sitting on the stand. "Hi, Daddy. Wantta see my report card?"

He lifts his shoulders like he's surprised I'm here, but after he turns and sees for sure that it's really me, he says, "Yeah, let me see."

After he wipes his hands on his pants legs, I hand it to him. He puts a serious expression on his face and, before he looks at it, gives me a side glance which is telling me he's giving me the once-over. When he opens my report card, I start to feel anxious in every part of my body, especially my breathing. But the smile forming on his face, the same smile that always warms my anxious heart, fills my eyes with happy tears. "Daddy," I whisper, "look at the other side. The side that has my history grade."

He states, "Let me look at your report card the way I want to." In a very, very slow manner of moving, he puts his hand up to his chin, slowly shakes his head up and down and says, "Uuuummmmmmmm!"

I jump up and say, "Let me see!"

He waves his hand up towards the sky and says, "I want to look at your marks on obedience and especially self-control. Those marks tell me everything I want to know about the other side."

I roll my eyes, then stand on my tippee toes and as I touch my report card, I say, "Daaaaddddy! What's taking you so long!!"

He laughs, then says, "Oohhh! I see you finally got a hundred. Do you think next time you could get two hundreds?"

My eyes get big as I shriek, "Daaaaddddy! Getting one hundred was hard enough!"

He leans against the produce stand, then hands my report card to Angelo and with his nose in the air says, "Smart kid! She takes after me."

Angelo shakes his head and says, "I've never seen a better report card."

Daddy takes time to look at it again, then pretends he's handing it back to me, but when I reach for it, he lifts me high into the air. He looks into my eyes and my heart flutters like a contended butterfly as he brings me to his chest and whispers, "Nice job."

I bury my head into the cavity of his neck and I breathe in the scent of my father and, only after precious time passes, he lowers me onto the sidewalk and says, "You better get yourself home. The church bells are ringing, which means it's noon. That means your mother has lunch on the table."

He hands me my report card and as I start skipping towards Mifflin Street, I wave "Good-bye" to my father, then wave "Good-bye" to Angelo, too. Once at the corner of Mifflin and Seventh, I wait on the sidewalk for two cars to drive past and only cause I feel eyes on me, I turn, giggling when I see my Dad looking so happy and proud.

"There you are!" Julia's voice snaps me out of my memory. Quickly, I wipe my tears from my face with the sleeve of my uniform blouse.

"What are you doing all alone in here?" Emily asks.

Then they're both hurrying toward me and Julia says, "I wantta see your report card!"

"No! It's a horrible report card!"

"Oh, just stop it! You always do well!" Julia lunges towards me.

I run to the back of the room screaming, "Never in a million years will I let you see my report card!"

Once they have me catty-cornered near the closet door, Julia grabs my report card. Waving it in the air she shrieks, "I got it! I got it!" and runs towards the front of the room.

"Give it back to me right now!"

It's too late. They've opened my report card and stare at it like they don't believe what they're seeing. Only cause the quiet in the room is making me feel nuts in my head, do I finally say, "I hate that I got a seventy-five in Latin. I told you it was bad. I'm just stupid. I just don't do well anymore."

My whole body feels like it's exploding, so I sit down at a desk and bury my head in my hands. In my mind I cry out, I feel so lost inside of me and nobody knows that I need someone to come and find me!

When I lift my hurting head, I see Julia placing my report card on Sister's desk and Emily sitting in Sister's chair. "What are the two of you up to?"

With a very serious look on her face, Emily lifts her hand, the one that's holding her black fountain pen, and says, "We have decided, Rosemarie, you are not a seventy-five person. In fact, we believe you are a ninety-five person. So by the power vested in me by Julia, one of your best friends, and I, who is also one of your best friends, I now will perform a feat worthy of your status in high school."

"What are you doing?" I gasp as I stand and start walking towards them.

"Remember when you first moved around here?" Julia says. "You asked our sixth grade nun if someone could help you with your English homework."

"I remember, and it was you who volunteered."

"Yeah, but you didn't really need my help. Even though you used lots of double negatives and the word 'ain't' back then. Remember how much you helped me write a short story about a nurse who took care of wounded soldiers during the Second World War?"

"Come here," Emily says. Her voice is as serious as her expression.

I run to Sister's desk and watch as Emily slowly places her pen down on the far tip of the number seven and, with a gentle stroke, she draws a line that closes that number tight.

"It looks great! No one will ever know!" Julia exclaims.

Emily hands my report card to me and, with pride in her eyes, murmurs, "I can't get over what a great job I did."

Once I rub my finger over my new grade, I place my report card back into its beige envelope and say, "Let's go to Savitz drugstore and get cherry Cokes. My treat."

Slowly, we walk into the hallway. As I close the creaking door, I give the Latin classroom a once-over as I breathe in the smell of mimeographed test papers and powdery chalk. This is the last time I'm going to be in high school, I tell myself. I close the door and I catch up with Julia and Emily, who are racing each other down the stairs that lead out to the main doorway.

With quick "good-byes" to Julia and Emily as they leave me in front of my house, and with the taste of cherry Coke still on my lips, I run up the steps and open the front door. Once in the parlor, I see near the kitchen doorway a tiny wooden rocking chair with tiny feet dangling from it and my heart fills with warmth cause I know my niece, Mona, is here. I run into the dining room, toss my report card onto the white table cover and that's when I hear Trudy and Grace laughing.

"Remember the last day of school how everybody from Hallahan High School always jumped into the city water fountain and got totally drenched?" Trudy gasps.

Grace laughs harder. "The first time I jumped into the water fountain it was the end of my freshmen year. I jumped in with my Latin and French books, too. I didn't even care that they were totally ruined. My wool uniform shrunk so much that Mom had to cut it off me. Remember, Mom? Remember? Remember?"

I walk over to the kitchen doorway and that's when all my good feelings that came from spending the afternoon with Julia and Emily vanish. I hate seeing my two sisters sitting at the kitchen table with Mom.

"I still can't believe what Daddy did when I went to my senior prom." Trudy goes on. "I was at the Latin Casino and he called me at midnight and told me to get on home. I wanted to crawl into the woodwork."

Baby Mona comes running over and throws her arms around my leg. I bend down, pick her up and that's when Trudy, with a faraway look in her eyes, whispers, "Those were the days."

As I hug Mona, a disgusting smell fills my nostrils, and fury I didn't know I was feeling makes me put baby Mona down on the floor. "Didn't they teach you anything in high school?" I shout. "Like how to take care of your daughter when she has a shitty diaper!"

Mom's the first one who looks at me, and the shocked expression on her face tells me she didn't know I was here. Grace takes one look at me, stands and runs towards the cellar steps.

Trudy jumps out of her chair and yells, "I'm a good mother! I just changed her ten minutes ago."

I put my hand on my hip, roll my eyes and moan, "No shit, Sherlock! Everybody knows that. It's your nose that has to be checked out!"

As Trudy pushes the chair out from under her, Mom reaches across the table and gently touches her arm, but Trudy furiously shrugs Mom's hand away. Turning to me, she yells, "Whatdiya gotta talk that way for?"

She picks baby Mona up and when she takes a few steps away I laugh. "Pew! That's disgusting."

Rushing over to the couch, Trudy yells, "Whatdiya have your period again?"

"Oh! That's real cool, blaming me for your daughter's shitty diaper!"

Mom rushes past me and gives me big eyes and I know she's telling me to "shut up." I do, but not because of Mom. I'm trying to figure out what else I can say to aggravate everybody. I just love seeing crying Trudy putting baby Mona on the couch at the same time that she's reaching for the wet washcloth Mom's holding out to her. Mom, with a calm look on her face, sits next to Trudy and whispers to her, but I can tell by Trudy's red face that she's not buying any of what Mom's saying.

After Trudy pins Mona's diaper, she lifts her to her chest and yells, "She fights with everybody. Enough is enough with this shit." Trudy turns towards me, "I'll smack you silly you keep talking like that!"

I put my hand on my hip and shout, "Queen Trudy has spoken?"

"See, Mom, that's what I'm talking about."

Trudy gives baby Mona to Mom, then she runs towards me as she's yelling, "You talk so stupid anymore. You're aggravating everybody."

My eyes, they start blinking like crazy cause Trudy's got her face in mine, and even though I'm afraid of what she might do, still at the top of my lungs, I yell, "Well, that's what I am-stupid! Don't you know? I'm gonna go to a stupid school."

Mom, carrying baby Mona, rushes towards us and places herself between Trudy and me. With a puckered mouth, she looks at me and yells, "I want you to go up to your room right now!"

I open my mouth, but before I can say another word, Mom whispers, "Don't let me tell you again!"

I walk out of the dining room and it's not until I'm near the steps that I start yelling, "Poopy diaper! Poopy diaper!" I start running up the steps two at a time cause Trudy's coming towards me with an open hand. I know if I don't get out of here really fast, she's going to rip my face off. Once I'm near the top step, again I yell, "Poopy diaper! Poopy diaper!"

Once inside my bedroom, I slam and lock the door. As I plop on my bed, tears come into my eyes as I'm thinking, "Trudy had it all and she doesn't even know when to change her daughter's shitty diaper." I roll over to Chris's side of the bed, the tears stream down and what keeps rolling around in my head is the gray of my father's wavy hair and the warmth of his smile and the thought that if my father were alive, he'd never let me go to a commercial school. He'd do anything in the world to make sure I finished high school.

I pull the covers over my head and as my exhaustion catches up to me, I close my eyes and I sigh as sleep claims me.

Chapter 24

I'VE BEEN GOING TO COMMERCIAL SCHOOL since September and there isn't much I like about it. One of the things I especially hate is having to get up at the crack of dawn and travel on two buses and one trolley car to get to this stupid school. And coming home is no picnic either. Another thing I hate is how the only reason why any of the other students seem to be here is cause they hate the idea of even setting foot in a high school. So most of them come fresh out of eighth grade, and I think if it wasn't against the law to leave school before the age of 16, they wouldn't be here. Another thing I hate about this place is how everybody ought to win an Oscar for acting like they're stupid. Soon as Sister William Marie starts talking about anything interesting, that's when everybody in the class starts nodding off. Which is fine by me. Sister and I have had some very interesting discussions-sometimes even heated, which is about the only thing I like about being in this school.

The very first day, when I was sitting in front of my gray typewriter, Sister stood alongside me and asked, "Do you know what your last name, Pasquarello, means?"

I shook my head as I said, "No."

She wrote my name on the blackboard, PASQUARELLO, and under that she wrote, PASQUA and she said, "Pasqua in Latin means Easter or life." Next to it she wrote, "RELLO" and as she placed the white chalk on the ledge she looked at me and said, "Rello in Latin means religion and together your name means religion of life."

She smiled, then walked to the front of the room and asked us to open our typing books, but I kept my eyes on Sister William Marie. She's a tall Irish nun who must be in her late seventies or early eighties. I've never seen so many wrinkles on a face; it's like she's got wrinkles on top of her wrinkles and when she smiles at me, her teeth look worn down like an old horse. But I just love looking at her, not just because she told me that my last name is about God and life, but because she talks to me like I'm a person who's got interesting thoughts. Like the conversation we're having right now. Even though it began with a question she asked the entire class, she looked right at me as she said, "There's no such thing as a teenager."

Right away, I raise my hand, "Everybody in class is a teenager."

"What is a teenager anyway?"

"It's a time in our lives that's between being a child and a grown-up."

She looks at the class through her bifocal glasses and says, "What do teenagers do?"

Nobody else raises their hands even though this is a lot more interesting than the other day when Sister tried to convince me that God can do all things.

"Rosemary," she calls on me.

"Teenagers go to school," I say. "Go to parties and dances. They have fun."

"What about responsibilities? Don't teenagers have any?"

"Yeah. Babysitting. Doing chores around the house. Maybe even having a part-time job."

She folds her long arms across the large cross resting on her chest and says, "There's no such thing as a teenager. What you describe sounds like a spoiled brat to me."

I don't know how to answer that. I know for sure I'm not spoiled, but as I look around the room at the other kids, I think that no matter that we all look identical in our navy-blue uniforms, we're different as night and day.

I look at Maria, who always makes it a point to talk to me, and I talk to her, too, cause I got to talk to somebody. I look at the friendship rings she has on a chain that's attached to her uniform belt and I tell myself, she's boy-crazy. I look at the seat in front of me, at Joan with her skinny body and the always-tired eyes. Her head's leaning on the typewriter and, once I nudge her, she sits up. After she's done rubbing the sleep out of her eyes, she takes a handful of tiny white pills out of her uniform pocket and says, "Want a few? It'll keep you up."

"No, thanks. If I'm tired I'll go to sleep."

She whispers, "I've been up all night. I have to take them."

"Your Mom and Dad wouldn't let you stay up all night!" I say in disbelief.

She laughs. "They don't know I was out all night."

I roll my eyes and think that I never in my whole life heard of anybody doing anything like that. I stare at her straggly blonde hair, her unwashed white blouse and wonder what the hell I'm doing in this school.

Just then the classroom door opens and Sister says, "Everyone please stand and welcome Father McMillan."

I know our discussion about teenagers is over for now, which is okay, cause I don't have any real good answer for Sister.

Once the class sits and quiet fills the room, Sister looks at me and says, "Class, do you remember the other day when we discussed the dogma of the church that teaches us that God can do all things? Father is here to continue that particular discussion. Would anyone like to say anything about this particular teaching of the church?"

I take a very deep breath, raise my hand and before I realize what's coming out of my mouth, I say, "If God can do all things, then how come He doesn't stop a father from dying so he can raise the twelve children he brought into this world?" I sit on the edge of my seat and, as my eyes start filling with hot tears, I yell, "I can't believe I said what I just said!"

I don't think Father can either. He keeps staring at me. I get fidgety and I sigh a great relief when he turns his gawking eyes to Sister. She looks away and he takes a piece of chalk. As he's drawing a square on the black board, he says, "God can do all things. But he can't make a square into a circle." I nod, pretending I understand what Father's talking about, but what I'm really thinking is, Just what I thought. God can't do all things.

Father keeps talking about all the wonderful things that God can do, like making the sky blue, the oceans deep, some animals fierce. I'm not even listening. None of that has anything to do with my question. Which doesn't surprise me. No one, it seems, ever has an answer for that.

It was just last month that I had my sixteenth birthday and me and everybody in my house ignored it like the plague. Everybody knows how crazy I can get in my head. Whenever I think about me turning sixteen, my heart sinks into my stomach cause it's reminding me that I have to go out and find a job. But I don't want to think about having to do that. I want to think about how it was yesterday morning after prayers, Sister said that St. Patrick was Irish. I said, "There's no way he could have been Irish. Everybody knows that all of Ireland was pagan until he converted them to Christianity."

She kept insisting that he was Irish, so when I went home I looked up St. Patrick in the Encyclopaedia Britannica that my Dad bought during the Second World War. Right now, with the "S" Encyclopaedia Britannica in one hand and a white piece of chalk in the other, Sister has me standing in front of the blackboard copying right out of that book, "St. Patrick's mother was French and his father was Roman."

As I wipe the chalk off my hand, Sister smiles and with her lively blue eyes fixed on me, she says, "Rosemary, can you stay a few minutes after class? I'd like to talk to you."

Seeing how it's the last class of the day and I don't have anything better to do, I say, "Sure."

I don't know what she wants to talk about, but I sure am surprised when, after everyone else leaves, she motions me over to her desk. For a moment she looks at me and I feel such love coming from her to me. Not the kind of love when you know somebody, because we hardly know each other at all. But I think she understands me even though I've never told her anything about me.

Then she begins to talk. Her voice is different somehow, softer, more friendly and she says, "Since you turned sixteen, I know it's just a matter of time before you'll be telling me you found a job. There's two things I want to tell you. The first is that I wish I would have recognized when you first came how fast you catch on because I would have given you shorthand. You would have been able to get a better job. There's something else, too. I know how much you enjoy helping Mrs. Bianca mark her third grade test papers. I think you ought to think about becoming a teacher someday."

That's all she said but I know I'll remember those words and the way she touched me with her eyes for the rest of my life.

I feel so proud that Sister thinks so highly of me, and for a brief second I try to imagine how it might feel to be a teacher in front of a classroom filled with lots of students. But then, anger fills my being. An anger so big it comes between Sister and me as loud and clear as if a door slammed shut between us. But all I do is collect my books and say, "Thank you, Sister."

I know I got to get away from Sister and her touching me without touching me, her understanding me in a way no one in my whole family does. I got to get away because in a few days or weeks I'll be leaving her class and getting some stupid job. And I'll never be a teacher. And I'll never see Sister again. As I close the classroom door, I feel the rage of his suicide pulling at me like the ocean's undertow.

I run down the street to the bus stop and when I see a soda bottle on the sidewalk, all I can think of is that my father used to sell that exact brand. I pick up the green bottle and throw it in the middle of the street and smile as it smashes into a zillion pieces. And when the first car drives over the broken glass, I hold my breath and giggle. I hope that glass makes a tire go flat. I'm so disappointed that it doesn't. I stand against the black pole waiting for something to happen, but after ten or so cars drive by, I give up on anybody getting a flat. Suddenly, I got to get moving. I'm walking in the same direction as the cars and once I'm almost at Broad Street I forget about taking two buses and one trolley car home. All I can think about is Sister and how I could have been a teacher one day if he hadn't killed himself.

I open the front door and see Carmella sitting on the gold couch; tears are streaming down her face. She looks up soon as I walk in and she jumps up. "I was so scared something awful happened to you, Roe!"

Her eyes turn fiery and she screams at the top of her extremely very powerful lungs, "Mooooom!!!! Roe's home!!"

It's Chris who comes in first. She looks like something terrible has happened and she says, "Thank God you're all right! I was so afraid."

"What the hell are you talking about? Of course I'm all right. Why wouldn't I be?" I toss my blue sweater over the green Queen Anne chair near the parlor door.

Chris makes a mad dash for the stairs and, in a high-pitched voice, she says, "I'm getting the hell out of here. I wouldn't want to be in your shoes."

But it's Carmella's laughter that's bouncing off the parlor walls that chills me to my bones as she squeals, "You think you're hot shit since you turned sixteen!"

Only cause I can't stand how she's always minding my business, I give her my meanest look ever and scream, "So who asked for your opinion?"

With me still giving Carmella my evil eyes, I throw my two books onto the dining room table, and even though I see my typing book sliding off my notebook, I don't make any attempt to stop it from slamming onto the floor. That's cause I'm too busy listening to Mom stampeding up the cellar steps.

I'm very surprised at how it's taken her only a few seconds to be standing in front of me and yelling, "Where the hell have you been! I've been worried sick about you!"

"I was just walking around."

She puts her open hand up to my face and yells, "If you don't tell me right now where you've been, I'm gonna rip your face off!"

I think she really means what she's saying, so I answer, "It was taking forever for that dumb bus to come. So I started walking and I didn't realize how far I walked until I was standing in front of the Delaware River. I didn't have enough money so I had to walk back to the bus stop near school."

With wildness coming out of her eyes, she pounds the table and yells, "What the hell's wrong with you? Remember how Elmo Smith raped and killed that young girl last year! The things he did to her. Why, they couldn't even put it in the newspaper."

"What are you worrying about? Nobody would want me." I'm half-laughing, but mostly out of nervousness. I don't ever remember Mom being upset like this.

With her fingers clutched together, she shakes her hands and screams, "There's some sick people out there! What in God's name is wrong with you?" She turns and looks at the black phone on the credenza. "I even called Sister William Marie to see if you were still at school. I better call her. That way she won't worry."

That does it. All my worrying about Mom being so upset vanishes. I kick the chair, the one with the arms, and I don't stop kicking until it starts making crashing sounds on the floor. With my hands shaking furiously, I scream, "This is exactly what I'm talking about! You care more about that nun than you do about me! Uuuooohhhh! And not only that! You listen to everybody else, but you never listen to me! You don't even want to know how much I hate how everything is different since I left high school! You don't want to know how I hate that I now have to get a job!"

She squints her eyes and as quivering wrinkles form on her chin, she murmurs, "Everybody in the house is telling me how you're arguing with them all the time. You better cut it out."

Even though I'm crying hysterically, and even though I can hardly catch my breath, and only cause I want her to know exactly what I was thinking when I was standing in front of that river, I cry, "I'd rather be dead than living this rotten life. What's the difference if I'm dead or alive? Nobody cares about me anyway!"

A chill runs over me as the silence of a cemetery fills the room. Mom turns her back to me, then stumbles over to the chair near the closet. She's wringing her hands as she cries, "I try to do what's best for everybody. But it always seems to turn out wrong." Once she stops her hands from shaking, with bewilderment in her eyes, she asks, "Why are you saying those horrible things?"

I don't get a chance to reply. The front door opens and Pat runs into the house yelling, "Roe, where the hell were you? We looked all over for you." He stops only inches from me. I know he's raging mad and wants to yell at me again, but he won't cause of Mom. I watch him bite his bottom lip and, in a strained voice, he says, "We even went to Julia and Emily's houses to see if you were there."

A lump forms in my throat as I remember my last day of high school when I was with my two best friends. All those lonely, miserable feelings rush over me, the feelings that make me wish I'd jumped into the Delaware River and was already dead. Waterless tears burn my eyes as I start making soundless noises in my dry throat. Just when I think I can't stand it anymore, I feel a tender touch on my lifeless hand. It seems like I haven't felt Mom's gentle, tender touch for so long. And it's so sweet. She clasps my hand and I think I don't ever want her to stop touching me. Waving everyone else into the kitchen she says, "There's pastafagioli on the stove." Then she looks at me and intertwines her fingers into mine as she leads me into the parlor. Once we're sitting on the couch, she looks at me and, with the biggest tears in her eyes I ever did see, she says, "I want you to tell me right now what's making you say you'd rather be dead."

I can't say anything and she gestures for me to place my head on her soft lap. As I rest my legs on the couch, she starts massaging my temple, smoothing my hair, then patting my forehead as she whispers, "What's bothering you?"

I let go of my pent-up tears and I don't stop crying until I choke on my words as I whisper, "I miss not being in high school. I miss not going to dances. I miss not having friends. I just feel so lonely and scared all the time. And now, I got to go out and get a job. And Sister reminded me of that today and then she said I should think about

184

becoming a teacher. Well, how am I supposed to do that when I can't even finish high school?"

I don't have anything more to say, and we stay like that awhile, all the time she keeps smoothing my hair, patting my forehead and massaging my temple. I listen to the only sounds between us which are my very quiet sobs. Her gentle touches stop, and she says, "You think I don't understand what a horrible thing I'm telling you to do. Well, you're wrong, because I do. It breaks my heart to see you so upset. But I can't let on. You must understand that everybody in the family looks to me to be strong. But I want you to know I cry in my heart every time I think about what I'm telling you to do. I don't want to take you out of your world, but I don't see any other way for the family to stay together."

I sit up and stare long and hard at her as I'm thinking, My God, she's never told me what was going on inside of her until now.

I get another very big surprise as she buries her eyes in her hands; tears fall between her fingers as she cries, "Maybe it would have been best if I had given some of you to different family members who wanted to help me by raising some of you. You could still be in high school doing all the things girls your age do. I don't know! Maybe it's really selfish of me to want to keep all of you with me."

My insides start jumping around as I cry out, "Whhhhaaaaatttt! Did anybody want to take me?"

She sits straight as an arrow and with weariness claiming her voice, she says, "Your godmother, Aunt Mary, offered to take you. But I wouldn't hear of it." She looks away from me and with new tears forming in her eyes, I can see for the first time how sad and how scared she is. I want to touch her face, her graying hair, her trembling arms, and I want to tell her not to cry, but I can't. I wait until she dries her tears, then I put my arm around her and say, "I love you, Mom."

Even though she doesn't say anything, I can tell by the way she starts crying again, and I can tell by the way she keeps the family together that she really loves me, too. I lean towards her and kiss her red cheek. I watch as she gazes at my father's picture, the one she has sitting on the television. I listen, too, as she mumbles something under her breath, but I don't ask her what she's saying cause I know it's not for me to hear. I look at my father's picture, then back at her. For the life of me I don't understand how it is she never gets furious with him.

Chapter 25

TODAY IS APRIL 20, 1960, and I'm sixteen, one month and twenty days old to be exact. Today is also the day I start working as a file clerk in the Central Index department of the Philadelphia National Bank. It wasn't hard to get the job. In fact, it was the very first interview and the only interview I went on. Today is also the first time I've come into center city by myself. It's also the first time I'm walking through the back door of the bank, past a dumbwaiter that has lots of large flour-sack-looking bags piled on top of each other, and through the gold-colored door. Even though I hold it open with both hands, it still slaps against my shoulder, causing me to stumble.

Once I steady myself, I look out at the first floor of the bank, a room that's almost as large as a football field, and my stomach stirs like witch's brew. I see thirty or so teller cages with mostly men behind them. I look into the farthest corner behind the tellers' windows, the ones that have metal bars across them. There I see three men dressed in black tailor-made suits with stiff white shirts and gold chains hanging from tight-fitting vests that cover their big bellies. With my eyes stuck on these men like glue, I rub my nose cause the smell of old money is in the air. Unnoticed, I slip behind the tellers' windows and once the metal gate closes, I hear a man say, "I'm going to need at least fifty one-hundred dollar bills." Off in the distance, I see three elevator doors and only cause I feel like a fish out of water, I leap towards them. But what slows me down is the slapping sounds of paper money being counted. I stop for a brief moment and watch tellers count money faster than the speed of light. Another few steps and I hear coins sounding like breaking glass as they crash into each other. I turn towards a corner almost hidden by an imposing white wall. That's where large men are lifting barrels filled with loose change, dumping it into metal drums that wiggle as half-dollars, quarters, dimes and nickels fall into their proper slots. I tell myself, It's the first time I've ever seen so much money.

I stride over towards the brass elevator doors and I feel my black heels sink into the thickest rug I've ever felt. Beyond is a black marble floor dotted with specks of white. My stomach turns again and I look down at the marble floor, not wanting to make eye contact as I feel lots of curious eyes on me. Lifting my head, I look past those eyes. Green money, silver coins, brown wood carvings, gold pocket watches, wingtip shoes, the empty chatter of successful people is what I see, hear and smell. With wet eyes, I tell myself this is a cold, hard place. A place where money is everything and being a scared teenager means nothing. A place where they don't even know I exist or care to know how my heart is aching.

I pass a very large window that's facing Chestnut Street and my heart sinks further when I see a girl running with her friend, both in their high school uniforms. The one with her red hair scrunched up into a ponytail is wearing a green-feathered parrot on the side of her head. I tell myself that from the way she's laughing, she must be wearing it on a bet. I think about my hair being cut short just last week cause Mom said, "You have to look the part when you start your job at the bank. So your ponytail and bobby socks have to go." And I know I'd give all the money in the bank to be back in my teenage world. I walk closer to the elevators and as I touch the black marble wall, coldness fills my being.

I hear a ringing sound coming from one of the elevators as a tall, thin man with gray at his temples and soft eyes stands next to me. Following him is a woman in her forties wearing a mink coat and gold bangle bracelets, and she's taking down his every word on a steno pad. "Young lady, the elevator door is open." He gestures, then continues, "After you."

I smile at him as I walk into the elevator and wonder why God couldn't give me a Dad like him. A Dad who's successful and caring and tender. A Dad who didn't want to leave all of us by killing himself. I look at this tall man's broad shoulders and I tell myself that sometimes I hate my father more than I ever loved him.

I was only a few days on my job when I realized that in this particular world of commercial banking the clientele are either very, very wealthy people or very, very wealthy corporations. And now, just a few months after I started working at the bank, I'm very proud to say I've gotten a promotion. I've become a statistical typist, which means I work with numbers all the time. I'm on the other side of the credit department, too, the side where there's lots of accountants and certified public accountants, some of whom come from very wealthy families. So every day I'm surrounded by lots of high finance talk coming from these wealthy men, and I just can't believe it, but I just love the way things have turned out. Just think. At first I just hated that I had to get a full-time job. But now, I just love this world that's so very different and far more exciting than the world I come from.

But if I'm going to be completely honest, there are still those friendless times when I'm missing Julia and Emily and loneliness fills my being. But then I remind myself that no matter how demanding and exhausting life is for my mother, she doesn't give up; she can't, she won't because that's who she is. And I know I'll never give up on life again.

I'm sitting at my desk typing and I'm very absorbed in what I'm doing. Not because typing numbers is so interesting, but because I'm working with lots and lots of numbers and I don't want to make any mistake. But I stop as soon as I hear a man's voice say, "Hi, my name is Ray."

I know it's not the voice of someone who wants to give me work because it's too friendly. It's deep and smooth and it makes my fingers stop their furious typing, my breath stops in my throat and my heart beats a little faster. I know that voice because I listen for it when I walk through the accountants' office. I can pick it out above the other men's voices cause it sounds like music, a kind of music I don't think I've ever heard before. It's a music that sings to my body and I hope my face isn't as red as it feels when I look up and see Ray.

He's a tall, thin man in his early thirties with hair the color of sand in the sun and soft blue eyes that always seem to brighten when we pass or say, "Good morning." I've noticed how long his fingers are too, and how they look so handsome with the white cuff of his starched shirts against the dark blue of his suit. I imagine he'll be president of the bank one day because he looks so good. Today he's standing only a few feet away from me with his beautiful hand extending out to mine. As I place my hand in his, my body shudders. It takes everything in me to stop myself from doubling over cause of the knot in my stomach as I tell myself that I don't ever remember feeling like this before. My hand relaxes out of his, and that's when I know my face is turning all shades of red as I say, "My name's Rosemarie."

He leans his long arm on my adding machine and smiles. I've never seen such a beautiful smile, such smooth lips and white, straight teeth. "Nice name. Mind if I call you Rosebud?"

I feel like jumping up and down and laughing and screaming but I say with a confidence I definitely do not feel, "That's cool." Quickly I look back at the keys on my typewriter.

He sits on the chair next to my gray desk, and in a soft but teasing voice says, "I want you to look at me."

What amazes me is that I do look at him and after he stops staring into my dark eyes, he whispers, "I don't want to embarrass you, but I think somebody should tell you. In the banking world we don't say 'cool.'"

I tell myself I should feel embarrassed, but I don't. Instead, I watch Ray as he puts his slide rule on my desk and after he opens one of his brown files, I forget how surprised I am that he doesn't ask my supervisor, Mrs. Keswick, if he can give me his file to work on. And even though I know he's saying what needs to be done, all's I'm listening to is the song in his smooth voice. And even though I know I should be looking at the file, all's I'm doing is staring at his sandy-colored hair, his incredibly large blue eyes, and in my head I'm thinking how drawn to him I am and how much I love that he's talking to me even though it's just banking talk.

Ray leans back in the chair and becomes very silent when Mrs. Keswick, who's sitting at her desk, three desks in front of me, in a stern voice states, "Rosemarie, I need you to type this balance sheet immediately!"

Mrs. Keswick keeps going on about what she wants me to do with the balance sheet, and I give her most of my attention except I don't stop watching Ray even though it's out of the corner of my eye. I pretend that I don't feel him staring at me as he's placing the file on my desk. But I stop pretending when Ray's soft hand touches my thin arm, and I don't know why, but I can't hardly move, not even an inch. That's all he does. Touch my arm. It's only a second but I feel as if his touch will be burned there forever. He lets go of the file, turns and walks away. I don't take my eyes off him until I see his office door closing behind him.

Immediately, I face Mrs. Keswick, and hoping I'm not smiling too much, ask, "Who is he?"

Mrs. Keswick opens her bottom drawer and, after she puts her polio-stricken leg over it, she starts massaging it as she looks at me and says, "Ray's the nephew of the President of the bank."

I put my hand up to my chest and as I try my best to catch my breath I'm thinking, Imagine that! The nephew of the President of the bank was talking to me! I remember how sweetly he talked to me. I remember how he called me "Rosebud" and I say, "He's such a gentlemen."

With cigarette smoke circling around her auburn hair, she says in a scratchy voice, "Ray's family name is in the blue book, which means Ray comes from very wealthy old money, which is better than very wealthy new money any day."

I don't understand what Mrs. Keswick is talking about but what I do understand is that there's something magical between Ray and me. I lean my elbows on my desk and keep my eyes on Ray's office door, which is about twenty feet away from my desk. After a few quiet seconds, I jump out of myself when Mrs. Keswick clears her raspy throat and, in a voice that sounds as gutsy as the March winds, she says, "Hand that file over to me!! It's my job to give out the work in this department and not Ray's."

There is one thing that bothers me since I started working at the bank. It's how stupid and uneducated I feel. I don't have the vocabulary that most everybody else has and I especially don't have the vocabulary that the men with all those college degrees have. So I bought a book called Word Power Made Easy, and every night after dinner I review the spelling of ten words and their meanings. When I'm at work, I use these words so I can impress people. Sometimes, I don't use them correctly and that's when Ray explains their proper use. He's so nice to me. Another thing I'm working on is my diction. I pay close attention whenever Ray speaks and I do my best not to drop the "ing's" at the end of my words. He told me I must open my mouth wider and pronounce the sounds of my words more clearly. I also do my best not to use slang words like "yo" and "man" and definitely not "cool."

Ray said if I really want to increase my vocabulary what I need to do is read more, so I joined the Doubleday Book Club. I'm very proud to say I have a favorite author, Taylor Caldwell, who wrote *The Last Love*, which I just adore. It's a story about Napoleon being exiled on that island after he lost the battle at Waterloo. He fell in love with this young girl who lived on that island with her family, and she fell in love with him, too. I read it twice already and as soon as I'm done reading the book that came yesterday called *To Hell In a Handbasket*, I'm going to start reading *The Last Love* again. Another book called *Wuthering Heights* is one of my all-time favorites. I just love Heathcliffe.

I can't tell you how helpful Ray's been when it comes to helping me develop a really good reading list. Why, he's even lending me some of his college books like Plato's *Republic* and *The Greek Way*. I go to the public library, too, and I found a book that's really a play and it's called "My Fair Lady." I just love the story of how this very educated man helps this very uneducated women to become very refined. He teaches her how to fit into a world of people who are not of her kind. In some ways it reminds me of Ray and myself. After all, he's teaching me how to get along in this banking world where there is none of my own clan, my own kind of people. Sometimes I feel like a fish out of water, and if it weren't for Ray being so helpful, well, I don't think I'd be fitting in at all. He's so kind and such a gentlemen. I'm glad that Ray and I are such good friends.

I'm closing the bedroom door as I'm singing along with the tune of "Wouldn't It Be Loverly" from Chris's album, "My Fair Lady." Chris is sitting in the middle of our bed looking through her Mademoiselle magazine and only cause I really want her to look at me, I screech more than sing, "All's I want is a room somewhere, far away from the cold night air. With one enormous chair, oh, wouldn't it be loverly. Lots of chocolates for me to eat. Lots of wood making lots of 'eat."

When I finally get her attention, which is filled with dirty looks, I put my chest out and state, "Ray's up and done it this time!"

Suspicious like a fox, she leans towards me and, once her magazine drops half-open onto the bed, she sneers, "What are you talking about?"

I stand, lift my beige skirt, and after I start unsnapping my garter belt, I say, "Ray's taking me to dinner Saturday night. We're going to the Union League."

She slaps the magazine hard onto the floor and as she squints her eyes she asks, "Have you told him you're only sixteen?"

I fold my arms across my chest and state, "No! And I'm not going to." I know she's going to start sounding like Mom about Ray being too old for me, so I scream, "If I'm old enough to go out and work full time, then I'm old enough to go out with whomever I want!"

"Do you know what the Union League is?"

Even though I don't have the foggiest idea, I put my nose in the air and in a piercing voice, I say, "It's like a restaurant!"

She holds her thin open hands in front of her and with her know-it-all attitude yells, "You gotta be delirious! It's a place where wealthy people hang out. The Union League is not a place where our kind of people get invited. WE'RE NOT WELCOMED THERE!"

I get surprised at how red her face is getting, too, especially when she puts her hands together and screams, "Don't you understand? It's a place for people whose grandmothers were daughters of the Revolution or whose families came over on the Mayflower. The only way our kind get invited is if something needs to be fixed or cooked or cleaned. We don't fit in with snobs like that!"

I want to ask her how she knows so much about the Union League, but I don't. A knot is forming inside me that goes from my throat to my stomach as I think, I don't have a clue as to what to wear.

Chris leans against the beige headboard and, after she screams for me to look at her, she stares me down and states, "There is only one reason why a rich single man in his early thirties would be interested in taking you to a fancy place like that. Do I have to spell it out?"

It's easy to block out what she's saying when I hear coming over the hi-fi the most beautiful song, "I Could Have Danced All Night." Already in my head I'm floating around dancing with Ray as I think how wonderful he treats me. I have to make Chris see this. Sitting at her end of the bed, and with my hands shaking every which way, I say, "You have Ray all wrong. Why, he explains things to me that I don't understand. He teaches me how to speak correctly and he tells me what books to read. He's showing me how to fit into this world that doesn't have our kind of people in it. He's a really nice guy."

I can tell by the stern look on her lips that she doesn't buy what I'm saying. I just have to convince her to my way of thinking, so with teary eyes I whisper, "Ray's just like Mr. Higgins in 'My Fair Lady.' Mr. Higgins taught Miss Doolittle how to speak properly and he taught her how to act around people that were not from her class, and he didn't take advantage of her even though she was living in his house. Ray's my Mr. Higgins. It doesn't only have to happen in a play or on a record album. It can happen in real life, too."

Her piercing eyes follow me as I reach for the hairbrush on my vanity table, but before I can even brush my hair one stroke, she screams, "Don't you understand the important thing here is that you could really get hurt. Once he's had his way with you, he'll toss you aside like a piece of loose change. What if you get pregnant? Did you ever think of that?"

My shoulders drop as I shake my head and say, "You just don't understand."

"You mark my words! If you go out with this creep the only tune you'll be singing is, 'I Should Have Danced All Night.'"

Even though I know my fantasies about Ray don't agree with what I'm about to say, and only because I tell myself I'll never act on those fantasies, I look in Chris's furious eyes and state, "You have to do something in order to get pregnant. I decided a long time ago that I'm saving myself for my wedding night! Why can't you accept that we're just friends?"

She throws me one of her know-it-all looks and wails, "For somebody so smart, you sure act stupid when it comes to this guy!"

It's that mean look on her face that make me furious as a hissing cat. I'm so sick of her thinking I'm stupid. Throwing my hairbrush across the room, I jump up, open the bedroom door, run down the steps and once I run out of the house, I take a fast walk up to Kingsessing Avenue.

As Ray closes his brown Mercedes car door, he slips into his leather car seat, then glides his arm effortlessly over my jittery shoulder and in a voice as sensual as a haunting melody, he whispers, "I'm so grateful that you stayed and typed all that paperwork on that South American country. That enabled me to present it to the Board of Directors Friday morning."

With my back to Ray, I remain stiff like a wax figure as he massages my neck and murmurs, "You had a great deal to do with the Board of Directors granting the eight-million-dollar line of credit to that South American country. Thank God you picked up how their accountants were trying to make accounts owed look like accounts received. I would have been in a mess of trouble with the Board. But now, they're ecstatic. I'm on my way to becoming an officer."

My body relaxes just a little as I tell myself, It's so wonderful knowing Ray appreciates me for how smart I really am.

His hand tenderly touches my chin as he whispers, "Turn and look at me."

My body relaxes as I feel almost Ray's equal and, as I look into his caring eyes, I sigh as I'm thinking, Just imagine, I saved Ray from a horrible fate. The Board never would have trusted anything he presented to them again.

With his warm breath playing in my ear, he whispers, "I want you to go to college in the evening. Once I become an officer, I'll make you be my assistant."

My quivering hand slips from Ray's arms and, with butterflies filling my being, I tell myself, I'll never tell Ray I can't go to college. I'd rather die before I'd tell him I'm a high school dropout. I look through the car window up to the heavens and say, "Look! Look at that lonely star up there. It's so beautiful the way it's shining so brightly."

Silence falls between us, but only for a short while and my legs grow weak as I watch Ray stretch his long legs over mine. Then, as he presses his brown-vested chest, white shirt and beige silk tie against my shoulder, he gives me a quick kiss on my lips. "We make a good team, you and I."

I sigh, look into his big blue eyes and think, It's the first time Ray's kissed me. It's just a little peck, but still it's so exciting. He's so wonderful.

"Rosebud," he whispers. "My little Rosebud."

As his moist lips press against mine, I fling my arms around his neck and, with this burning belief that I am so much his equal it sends shocks of electricity running through my body, I kiss him, too. The passion of a thousand volts flows between us. As our lips part, I feel every movement spin ecstatically. Body heat, his and mine, tells me to remove my black velvet coat, and as I do, I look at Ray. Caution feeling like darkness grips my being as I remember Chris's warnings about how Ray could destroy me. But as Ray wraps his strong arm around my tiny waist, I blot out these black waves of gloom. My breath is taken away again as he presses his chest against my firm breasts, and a lustful chill runs down my arms as our bodies intertwine.

He runs his fingers through my dark fluffy hair and, as he whispers, "My intelligent, unspoiled one," he effortlessly slips me down onto the seat. Chris's dark warnings float across my mind again and I freeze like a mannequin as Ray bites on my ear while his one hand clutches my breast and his other plunges between my thighs.

I push at his suddenly brutish hands and scream, "No! No!"

He pulls me into his arms again and, as he relaxes his cheek against my shoulder, he whimpers, "I neeeeddd yoouuu! Don't you understand? I need you!!"

I feel his hands under my dress as they paw for the fullness between my thighs and I scream at the top of my lungs, "Sttoooopppppp!!"

He doesn't and the savageness of his assault collides with the horrible truth of all Chris's warnings. Disappointment, humiliation and rage well up in me. Pressing up against the car door, I raise my leg and slam my bare foot twice into his face. In a deep guttural whisper that sounds more like the voice of a wild animal than a young girl, I tell him, "If you touch me again, I swear on my father's grave I'll scream rape!!!"

He pulls back and as I sit, I watch the venom in his eyes as he sneers, "I never needed your help. It was always you who needed mine. I made you who you are today. You're nothing but a little bitch from the wrong side of the tracks, South Philadelphia no less. So go back! Go back to where you belong!"

Fumbling for my shoes and purse, I grab my coat and yank open the car door. Once outside I scream, "Remember one thing. It's a girl from South Philly who just stopped you dead in your tracks!" As I stumble to put on my black heels, I look at his pathetic shadow, and add, "I was stupid enough to think you were the perfect gentlemen, so refined and all. Ha!! With all your money, your smooth talk and your Ivy League education, it doesn't add up to you being much of a man!"

Turning, I run across the lawn of the old ladies home and as I pass the old cottage where the three rockers are sitting on the porch, I stop to put on my coat and straighten my hair. Then I hurry home. I open the front door and, as I check the huge run in my black stocking, I see Trudy standing in the parlor doorway.

With open arms and a worried look, she asks, "What happened?"

I fall into her arms and sob like the sixteen-year-old girl that I am. Once I stop crying, I tell her all of what Ray did to me, but mostly of what he tried to do to me.

Chapter 26

I'M SITTING AT MY GRAY METAL DESK and as I look out my window, the one that goes from ceiling to floor, my body shivers as I start sneezing into a handful of white tissues. Without so much as looking into my box of menthol cough drops, I place my fingers into the half-filled box; as soon as a honey-colored cough drop rolls out onto my desk, I pop it into my mouth, sit back and thoroughly enjoy this moment of clear breathing. As I swallow, the dryness in my throat forces me out of my gray swivel chair and sends me flying in the direction of the water cooler, the one that's five desks away from me. I fill the tiny cup with cold water and as I begin to sip, I notice Ray standing alongside of Ernie's desk.

Ernie, she's the new girl who's been working at the bank since she graduated from high school six months ago. She's about 5'10", thin and very attractive with medium-length brown hair and a very warm smile. Sometimes we go to lunch together and other times we go on coffee breaks, too. At 5'4' I'm lots shorter than she is, but I still think we're like two shoes from the same pair. It's just so easy and natural between us and that's cause she's from my own kind of people, my own clan.

But anyway, let me come back to what's going on right in front of my suspicious eyes. Wanting to get a good look at the big brown open file sitting on Ernie's desk, I step closer. Just as I suspected, it's Ray's file and he has much of it spread out all over her desk. So, he's been here for quite awhile. I don't know how I missed it.

I step back, stand near the cooler again and watch Ray as he slides himself behind Ernie like a snake getting ready for the kill. It's been over a month since Ray tried to molest me in his car and now the only time I speak to him is when it comes to banking matters. As I watch Ray softly rest his hand on Ernie's shoulder, she flinches. I know she's uncomfortable and as much to aggravate Ray as to protect her, I say, "When Mrs. Keswick comes back from her meeting and realizes Ray gave you a file, she's going to be madder than a wild dog. She can't stand the way some people disregard the simple fact that she's our supervisor."

Ray sighs like I don't know what I'm talking about.

Leaning on the water cooler, I snicker, "I know you know better than that, Ray!"

He sighs again, louder, but his face is puckered like a raisin. Soon as our eyes meet, he looks out the mezzanine as he tries to hide his fury behind a facade of pretended stoicism.

I know he's trying to get one up on me by sitting on the black chair that's next to Ernie's desk. I know he wants me to go back to my desk, too, but I don't move. It makes me cringe as he speaks in his well-bred manner and explains to Ernie the criteria the bank uses in lending large sums of money.

I'm impressed how Ernie's able to remain composed even after Ray gently brushes his black wool suit sleeve against her bare arm and says loud enough for me to hear, "You're such an intelligent person. We can do great things together."

I feel like I'm going to vomit all the sweet things he ever said to me as I wonder what I ever saw in him. I know just as soon as he's gone, I'm going to tell Ernie what he did to me that horrible night.

I crush my paper cup and after I toss it into the nearest trash can, I stand near the closet door and watch as he pats her upper arm and only cause I can't stand any memory of his touch, I furiously rub my upper arm.

Slowly, he stands and with his phony-caring eyes still on Ernie, he passes by me. I don't breathe, not one breath as I plaster myself against the closet door. He strolls into his office and as he closes his door, my shoulders relax and my heart finally stops pounding. I take a deep breath, clear my raspy throat and sit on the chair near Ernie's desk. Looking hard into her dreamy eyes, I point to Ray's office door and state, "I want to tell you what that creep did to me." Nervously, I push my hair behind one ear and untangle my bangle bracelets from my shaking hand. "He said he wanted to take me to the Union League for dinner. Dinner at the Union League!!! That's a laugh! He never even bothered to turn the car engine on before he started putting his hands where they didn't belong. I screamed for him to stop, but he didn't. I screamed, again but he kept pawing me like I was a toy thing."

She looks at me with doubting eyes and in no uncertain terms states, "What are you talking about? Ray's such a gentleman."

I don't blink, not once, as I say, "I thought he was a gentleman too, but boy, was I wrong."

She rolls her swivel chair closer and I can tell by the way her mouth is open, she wants to say something, but before she does, I add, "Look, the only reason why I'm telling you is because the way I just saw him sweet-talk you, well, he used to do that to me, too. I know it for what it really is. I'm telling you, I couldn't get him to stop until I kicked him really hard in his face."

She pulls away, sits straight and with angry eyes exclaims, "What were your feet doing near his face?"

Wondering if I made a mistake telling her, but convinced that I need to let her know what a horrible human being he is, I exclaim, "It all happened so fast . . . He started kissing me and before I knew it, I was leaning against his car door and his hands were moving faster than a jet engine. His hands were between my legs and no matter how much I screamed, he just wouldn't stop. So, I kicked him really hard in his face. Not once! But twice!"

"You really kicked him in his face???" she gasps.

I nod and we both begin laughing. "It felt soooo good!!!!"

My laughter stops as Mrs. Keswick's phone rings, and it's me who rushes to her desk and hurriedly writes down a message.

Ernie's laughing so hard, tears begin to run down her cheeks. Not even waiting for me to hang up, she shrieks, "You really kicked him in his face?" Again she's dissolved into peals of laughter.

Soon I'm half-wheezing/half-giggling because of my cold. I'm laughing so hard, I grab my sides the way I did as a child. More howling seconds go on between us and even when she puts a serious look on her face, I can't stop myself from having another fit of laughter-for the first time I see just how totally ridiculous and absolutely absurd Ray really is.

"He didn't hurt you, did he?" Ernie asks, very serious now.

I snicker, then squeal, but when I look into her sincere eyes, I remember the seriousness of it all, too, and say, "Just my pride. That's all that got hurt."

She leans back on her swivel chair and questions, "What did he do when you kicked him?"

I crease my forehead and I'm glad it helps me not to laugh again. Then I moisten my parched lips and I don't know why, but I look away from Ernie as I say, "I think he wanted to tear my heart out. He did the next best thing, though. He insulted me by calling me a little bitch from South Philly. But I got him back when I told him I'm the South Philly babe who stopped him dead in his tracks."

She takes her eyes off me and I watch as she sits frozen, staring at Ray's closed door; after a few quiet seconds, I interrupt her thinking by saying, "I got myself out of the car faster than a rabbit and ran home. Pat wanted to take George and John and go break his legs. But my Mom, she stopped them before they ran out the door."

I start feeling silly again cause I'm remembering what else Pat said that night, so I snicker and add, "It was after my sister Trudy calmed me down that Pat said one good thing came out of all this. I won't be using those big words anymore and that's fine with him cause now he'll be able to understand what I'm saying."

I look away from Ernie and as brief seconds pass, the only thing I hear is my soft wheezing. I'm glad when Ernie breaks her silence as she starts rustling a bunch of papers into Ray's file. She slams the file closed and with both hands sends the file flying through the air; it crash-lands on Mrs. Keswick's metal-top desk. We both sit still as mannequins as we wait for someone to tell us to not make so much racket cause we are now in the banking world.

When no one comes, I say, "I've got to get out of this place!"

"Yeah. I agree. I just hate the way they look down their noses at us."

I place my thin fingers on eight of the red keys of Ernie's gray adding machine. I push all eight of those keys, then pull the black lever and exclaim, "The only thing I like about working here is how some of the other employees from different branches treat us with some respect. I know it's only cause they know we work where the big money is brought into the bank. But if we go anywhere else, we lose this look of dignified respectability."

Ernie tears off the curly piece of white paper hanging from her adding machine; after she fastens it to the utility company file that she's been working on all morning, she looks at me and whispers, "That's not respect. Not really. And we definitely don't get any respect from the people we work for every day."

"Yeah," I say, leaning closer to her. "Last Friday morning I was wheeling one of the green carts filled to the brim with files and ditto papers into the board room. You'll never believe what I overheard. Mr. Randolph, the officer who wears stiff white shirts and a pocket watch in his black vest, was placing new one-hundred-dollar bills on the table for the men who were coming to sit in the board meeting. Well, every time he'd place one of those crisp bills down on the table, he'd clear his throat and in his conceited voice, he was bragging to Mr. Dunbar, the trust officer who has the fat belly. He was saying what a wonderful deed the bank is doing offering banking services to the middle class cause there's no money to be made from it. I wanted to scream how come the bank is opening thousands of accounts to the middle class if not to make money. But I didn't." I sit back in the chair, then with sly eyes, I state, "This isn't the first time I've heard these snobs talk like this! Uhh! The sheer gall of it all!"

Ernie clenches her teeth, then says, "I can't believe how stingy they are, too. They should be ashamed to call what they give us a salary. I think they actually believe they're doing us a favor by having us work here. It just makes me so crazy in the head."

She holds her breath for what seems like an eternity. Once she starts breathing again, I tell myself that I can trust Ernie. I know she'll never repeat what I'm going to tell her. So with my nose wrinkling, I whisper, "I haven't told anybody in the bank about this, but I'm going to tell you. I went on a job interview last week at a company that needed someone with my statistical typing background. The woman in their personnel department told me the job was paying a lot more than what I'm making now, and she also said I was the most qualified out of everyone she's interviewed. But she couldn't offer the job to me. I was very confused and sat frozen on the chair. I think she thought I wasn't going to leave so she called the personnel director. He told me that the federal government wouldn't give their company any more contracts until they hired a minority. It took me a few moments to get over being unbelievably shocked. But once I did, I reached for my handbag, excused myself, and went right back to the employment agency who set up the interview. I told the lady there that I wasn't going on any more interviews cause it's a waste of my time."

Ernie puts the brown file in her "OUT" box, then as she mindlessly takes her yellow pencil between her hands, she looks past me as if in a daze. Twirling the yellow pencil, she says, "We should apply for some of those teller positions that's posted in the lunch room. Some of the openings are in branches in neighborhoods where our kind of people live and work."

I perk up and say, "That's a really good idea! Hell, the starting salary is more than what we're making here. And not only that, the hours are much better cause once the branch locks its doors and everybody balances their drawers, they get to go home. And you know what else? The people we come from regard being a bank teller as something that's very respectable. So no matter which way you look at our situation, working as a bank teller is much better than working here!"

Suddenly I'm feeling furious and stupid for working here, and I blurt out, "There's another very good reason why we should get out of here as fast as we can. Our busy season is going to start in another month and we'll be very lucky to be leaving any earlier than ten-thirty on Wednesday nights. Hell, last year one Wednesday night, we were here until after midnight."

With a frown in her eyes, she asks, "Why did you have to work so late?"

"Because Mr. Lenox, who became our new boss last year, well, he doesn't have enough backbone to tell the officers to give us the paperwork before noon on Wednesday like they're supposed to. Huh! The officers will be bringing their work up to us at four-forty-five with their hats, coats and gloves on and you know where they're going? They're going home! But we have to stay until all the work is typed and collated. And guess what else, we don't get paid one extra cent for all the overtime we work."

My throat feels like it's on fire. Coughing, I add, "I really have to get out of this place! One particular night last year I didn't get home until one o'clock in the morning. My mother was furious with me. She didn't believe I was working late. All's she kept saying was those aren't banking hours."

"Why didn't she believe you?"

"I don't know. Maybe she thought if she believed me then she would have to tell me to quit. She needs my help. Who knows?"

I'm surprised how quickly Ernie picks up her black phone and, as I push my hair out of my face, I listen to her talking to personnel. "Uhhhuh. Okay. Sure thing. Okay! Good-bye." She barely hangs up the phone when she kicks her long legs in the air. "I have an interview next week! Eeeeeehhhhhhhhhh!" Once she stops kicking and shrieking, she reaches into the bottom of her file drawer and as she lifts her handbag, she says, "My Dad would really be proud of me if he knew I was going to become a bank teller."

"It was my Mom who told me to look for a job at a bank. She said my Dad wanted his daughters to work at insurance companies and banks cause those are respectable places. Huh! I never realized until right now, that must be why Chris works in an insurance company." I stare at the black geometric designs running through the tiles as I add, "I wish my Dad were here, too. He'd be so proud." I look at Ernie and say just above a whisper, "But he can't because he's dead."

Ernie removes her gray-framed glasses and, after she rubs her deep-set eyes, she meticulously examines her glasses and whispers, "My Dad's dead, too."

I don't let a heartbeat skip between us as I effortlessly whisper, "Sorry to hear that. How did he die?"

She clutches her black leather bag under her right arm, looks out at the mezzanine and declares, "I'm freezing! I'm going to the coffee shop and get a cup of coffee. Want anything?"

I shake my head. "No!"

She rushes to the elevator and once in front of the closed door, she keeps hitting her knuckles against the elevator button.

I don't take my eyes off her until the elevator door closes and as I put a new tissue to my nose, I clear my hurting throat, then sit straight, call personnel. I don't hang up until Miss Lynch, the personnel director, tells me I have an interview for a bank teller job in two weeks.

Even though we're tellers at different branches, Ernie and I have become the best of friends. We do lots of things together, like going away for weekends to the Poconos when it's freezing cold or down the shore when it's very hot. And when we're not going away on weekends, we go ice skating, dancing or horseback riding. On payday, sometimes we go out to a fancy center city restaurant and then off window-shopping at the best of stores on Chestnut Street. Something else we also have in common is that we both enjoy reading novels. Ernie's borrowing one of my books called The Prologue of Love by Taylor Caldwell and she's lending me a book called Mrs. Mike but I don't remember the author. It's wonderful having so many things in common with Ernie. Even the deaths of our fathers binds us together; except whenever I ask her how her Dad died, she never gives me a straight answer. I decided, though, the next time the opportunity presents itself, I'm going to coax it out of her one way or another.

It's Ernie who heard about a bunch of girls going in together to rent a very large room down at the shore over Memorial Day weekend. When she asked if I was interested, I jumped at the chance. The shore house only allows females to stay in these rooms and since there's twelve of us, Mrs. Kramer, the owner of the establishment, has rented us her largest room.

The very first thing that struck me when Mrs. Kramer opened the large brown door is the two rows of six single beds made up with only white sheets and lined up one after the other. Mrs. Kramer gave me one of the four keys to the room and after she left, Ernie and I opened our suitcases on two of the last six unclaimed beds.

Within a few hours all twelve girls arrive and ever since, there's been so much yelling, laughing and carrying on, Ernie says she wonders if this is what it's like living at a college dorm. I told her I hadn't the foggiest idea, but it sure sounds like my house when all twelve of us are home. I don't know half of the people who keep coming in and out of our room; Ernie said she doesn't either. But it doesn't matter cause everybody's having such a great time.

Out of all the new girls I'm meeting this weekend, it's redheaded Karen whose sense of humor I'm enjoying the most. With her laughing green eyes scanning all us girls, she tells us that whenever there's a lull in a conversation, anything that the person says next becomes dirty in her mind. So when Ernie says, "Stick it in there!" it's Karen who starts laughing. One by one we join in and, once Ernie realizes what she said, she laughs, too.

Ernie and I left the beach early this afternoon so we can take our showers before the mad rush. It's peaceful in the room with no one else here and I sit on the wicker rocking chair, the one with the faded pillow, and rest my feet on the bottom of my bed. Ernie collapses onto her bed and, after I light up one of my two-week-old stale "Kool" cigarettes, she takes the crunched cigarette pack out of my hand, lights one, and takes a drag. Immediately, she starts choking on the filtered smoke, and once her chest stops having spasms, she takes another drag, but this time, she blows the smoke out of her mouth in a most relaxing way. She positions the cigarette in the clam shell sitting on her end table, the one that's a makeshift ash tray, rests her head against her pillow and tries to make smoke rings, but without any success.

I exhale the flat-tasting smoke, place the cigarette into the makeshift ash tray, too, and sit in my chair and rest my legs over one of its side arms. I sigh a little as I look at the beautiful alabaster horse figurine sitting on Karen's bed. I remember Karen telling me how her father helped her when she was buying her brand-new blue Volkswagen and I remember, too, how she told me she bought that beautiful figurine so she can give it to him on Father's Day. I tell myself this is the opportunity I've been waiting for. I stare at Ernie and once I catch her eye, I motion for her to look at Karen's bed and say, "What a beautiful figurine. Karen said she bought it in one of the stores on the boardwalk. It's for her father for Father's Day. He loves horses."

The jerky movement of Ernie's long body pulls the corner of the top sheet from under the mattress and, after she kicks the sheet off her foot, she turns away from the figurine and looks at me with sad eyes.

I put my bare feet onto the floor and as I dig my heels into the white throw rug I force myself to ask in a soft voice, "How did your father die?"

She rolls over on her side and as I watch her fidgeting feet, I twirl my fingers as I tell myself that with us doing so many things together it just seems to me she should be able to tell me how her Dad died. But listen to me! I've never told anyone how my father died. But if I tell her, I know it would be wonderful. Finally, there'd be someone to tell. I stop twirling my fingers and with a new conviction, to myself, I think that if she tells me how her father died, I'm going to tell her how mine died, too.

I catch a full view of her lost eyes and her painfully long face as she says, "It was a long time ago. I was just a kid."

In a voice as warm as a summer breeze, I state, "If you tell me how your father died, I'll tell you how mine died, too. It's ridiculous that we don't tell each other, being that we're such good friends."

She looks at me with hesitation in her eyes, then, as if transformed in body and mind, she stares at me with a child-like expression and says, "I was in church making my First Holy Communion and he was home having a fatal heart attack."

Watching her moist eyes, her flinching cheek, her pulled mouth is making my nervous stomach tremble even more, so I look at the clam shell that's serving as an ash tray and slowly I put out my cigarette. Once the heat coming off my face cools down, I look at Ernie and catch a glimpse of her perspiring hairline as she turns her sunburned face towards the window, the one with the distant ocean view.

With my eyes resting on her, my mind is thinking, On my Communion day I ran into my parents' bedroom to show my Dad my dotted Swiss white dress that Mommy's friend made. I showed off my white veil and white prayer book and he made such a fuss over me with his oohh's and ahhh's and that was after he kissed me on my cheek . . .

I come out of myself when Ernie starts sitting up and, after she takes an emery board out of her make-up case, ferociously starts filing her broken thumbnail. She doesn't speak, not one syllable, and I know she's still in her sadness. I push down on my cigarette again and as the stale tobacco pops out, in my head I'm thinking how her Communion day was supposed to be one of the happiest childhood memories and it turned out being her most painful one.

Only cause bitterness is filling me do I push even harder on my smashed cigarette and the only thing that makes me stop is when Ernie moans, "You told me you were going to tell me how your father died. So tell me!"

I tell my chest to relax, I take my cigarette out of the half clam shell and break what's left of it in half. After a few awkward seconds, I drop the remains of the cigarette, then open my mouth to speak. I look at Ernie and try to find the right words, but instead my mouth closes like a vise. I tell myself I really want to tell her, so after I swallow, I allow the chair to support my aching back, and the words start flowing out of me like a babbling brook. But the thing that surprises me is how I'm in shock as I find myself saying, "He died of a heart attack, too, but in his sleep."

I feel a deep furrow between my eyes and a huge knot in the pit of my stomach as I yell in my head, *I can't believe you lied to her like that. Especially after you promised her you'd tell her if she told you!*

I don't look at Ernie and I can't stand being in the same room with her either, so I whisper, "I'm going to take my shower before everyone comes back."

I reach for my white towel that's folded on the bottom of my bed and, after I bury my wet eyes, I tell myself that I can't stand how after all these years I still can't bring myself to speak of his suicide.

Chapter 27

IT'S THE LAST DAY OF THIS GLORIOUS Memorial Day weekend and I'm standing underneath the Ninth Street boardwalk with about fifty college kids watching some guy with honey-colored hair sitting on a metal milk crate and strumming Peter, Paul and Mary songs on his guitar. But once he starts playing "If I Had A Hammer" some guy with long hair and cut-off dungarees sits on the sand near the guitar player and starts playing his bongos. That's when all hell breaks loose. My insides do eager flips when almost everybody, including me, do our best to sing louder than the person next to us by screaming, "If I had a haaaammer, I'd hammer in the moooornin' all over this land. I'd hammer out justice! I'd hammer out freeeeedom! I'd hammer out love between my brothers and my sisters aaaalllll over this laaaaannnddd. WWWWOOOOHHHH! WWWWOOOOOHHH!"

But I stop singing and start laughing when somebody, anybody, almost everybody starts hitting lots of sour notes. I mosey away from the growing crowd and move closer to the rock jetty, the one that separates Ninth Street beach from Tenth Street beach. I step onto the only rock without jagged edges and, once I have my footing, I put my arm above my eyes and look in the direction of the blue sky.

I don't get a chance to look at that sky cause without any warning, I feel an awakening within me like the sun bursting a lazy dawn. I don't understand why I'm feeling this way, but I know with everything in me it has to do with my first glimpse of this nice-looking guy who's standing on the black boulder only twenty or so feet away from me. My body starts shivering as his piercing dark eyes look directly at me. I watch, too as he takes a drag from his cigarette and, as smoke pours out of his nostrils, he flips his cigarette between his fingers and it lands fifteen or so feet into the rip tide. He tilts his head to one side and with him still making eyes at me, he folds his muscular arms across his chest. Jitteriness is filling my insides and I start to lose my footing and slide not once, but twice off the slippery rocks of the black jetty. Once standing on the hot sand, I stop blushing and come back to watching him. That's when I put a really big smile on my face cause I'm very glad to see he's still watching me. He leans his broad back against the larger boulder and turns his eyes away from me, but I tell myself not to worry cause soon enough he'll be looking at me again. I seize the moment and quickly remove six hairpins from my wind-blown hair. I pull my shaking fingers through my thick hair, but I stop once I feel penetrating eyes on me once again. I fasten the ends of my hair into a french twist, then smooth the front of my one-piece white bathing suit and stand as tall as a beached seagull balancing herself on one leg.

I can hardly catch my breath as I feel his masculinity oozing from all that he is and the promise of what he is yet to be, and once I get up enough nerve, I look at him again and stare at his round, sun-tanned face. I notice his short brownish hairs standing at attention on his broad chest and even though I know I shouldn't let him see me staring at him, I tell myself to stop worrying cause for the life of me I can't think of one good reason why I shouldn't let him see.

I watch as he starts talking to Ernie and as they're talking and laughing together, I realize they know each other and I'm going to get Ernie to introduce me to him.

I take those twenty or so steps towards him and once I'm standing on the edge of my green Army blanket, the one my brother, John, received from the Army recruiting office when he spoke to them about training to become an airplane pilot after he graduates high school, I look at this guy, this guy who now is staring at me as he continues talking to Ernie.

Suddenly she looks from this guy to me and back to him and says, "Sorry, John. I should have introduced you."

I tell myself his name's John. I like that name.

Ernie, she leans her body towards me, then pulls at my hand, points and says, "These are my twin cousins, Jim and John. I told them we'd be here this weekend."

I say, "Oh, that's nice."

Sitting next to Ernie, but near the jetty is Ernie's cousin Jim, who I didn't see until now and, after I give him a smile, I immediately look at John and whisper, "Hi. Nice to meet the two of you. You're not identical twins, are you?"

With lots of cockiness in his standoffish posture, and in a voice as deep as a well, John states, "Of course we're not! We don't look identical, do we?"

With my one eyebrow arched I sigh as I look out towards the dark-green ocean thinking I'd love to ride a few waves in, but it's

John who seems to undergo a major change when in the smoothest voice I ever heard he whispers, "We're born three minutes apart."

I gawk without any shame at his dancing eyes, the folding and unfolding of his arms across his broad chest and I listen, too, to hissing sounds made between his teeth before he says, "On the day we were born, I kicked my brother out so he could be born first. I wanted to make sure the coast was clear."

I laugh. Jim gives John a dirty look and Ernie smiles, too.

I look at the pack of cigarettes John's handing his brother. I look at the cut of his hair, the black leather band of his silver-faced wristwatch and think he doesn't look like he's in college.

John's dark eyes rest on me; he takes a step towards me, and with a little-boy smile on his mouth, he whispers, "How about if we go for a walk, you and I?"

With me standing as still as marble as my feet sink into the moist sand, I tell myself to say "Yes" but I can't, so I look at the sand and nod. As if in a silent movie, I place my hand into his and he closes his hand over mine. He stands with his back against the ocean and places my hand against his chest, then we start walking along the shore.

After we've taken a few quiet steps, he looks out towards the large waves, and only cause I want him to look at me, I ask, "Do you live near Ernie?"

He looks straight ahead and says, "Yeah. The Little Italy section in North Philadelphia." He looks at me with sexy glances and I hide the excitement I know is in my eyes with my hand as I say, "The sun's in my eyes."

Speaking faster than a speeding bullet, John asks, "Wheredeyeli?"

"What did you say?"

"Wheredeyali?"

I half-wonder if it's my loss of hearing that's causing the problem, and nervously ask, "I'm sorry, but I didn't hear what you just said."

He lets go of my hand, faces the ocean again, and after an uneasy silence, turns and in no uncertain terms, states, "I said where do you live?"

"In southwest Philadelphia on Fifty-Eighth Street," I say as I stare into John's marvelous face. I see his dark thick hair that encircles his round face, his dark eyes that look so inviting, yet very dangerous, and I know I desire him in ways I never thought I could desire any man. And I am well aware just how frightened I am and not because

I'm afraid of what he might do, but rather what I may allow myself to do with him. Almost as if he feels me willing his touch, he slips his hands, with great gentleness, on the bare back of my waist, and we start to walk again. It's in his sensitive eyes I feel his dark intensity. I wonder what he does with himself and, only cause I don't know what else to ask, I ask, "Are you in college?"

He kicks the wet sand and after he nervously wraps my arm around his, he whispers, "It's not in the cards for me to go to college now. But someday I will."

I sense his awkwardness, his sadness around this subject, so I don't question any further.

He looks out at the ocean again, and then back at me, "Are you serious about anyone?"

"No. Are you?"

"No. I don't believe in going with anyone unless it's the person I want to spend the rest of my life with."

I kick the wet sand from under my toes and only because I'm really glad he isn't going with anyone either, I nod and say, "I agree."

We hardly realize the tide is coming in until it rushes up over my legs. I scream and run backward. He chases after me and when we're up on dry sand, I ask, "What's your last name?"

He looks at me with a silly grin on his face, then with command in his voice, he states, "Manes!! It means Roman god of Death!

I laugh. "Oh really. My last name is 'Pasquarello' and it means 'religion of life.'"

"Our last names together make a life and death situation."

We both laugh like this is the funniest thing we've ever heard. We fall silent only a moment before, with twinkling eyes, he asks, "How about if I call you?"

I don't hesitate, not one second. "That'll be great!"

He commits my phone number to memory before we start climbing back on the jetty. Once we're on the other side, I run to my empty blanket and I'm glad when John catches up and sits next to me. I breathe in the sulphur smell of his match as he lights a Pall Mall. I watch as he blows cigarette smoke out of his mouth, and I think, What I feel for John is good. What I felt for Ray was sick and I thank God I never acted on that perverted desire. Ray was never really warm or kind. He pretended to be the perfect gentleman when it was nothing more than a clever cover-up for how cold and calculating he is . . .

My heart starts to sink when John buries his half-smoked cigarette into the wet sand and says, "Come on, Jim, we better get going."

The sadness I feel over his leaving ceases when he touches my bare shoulder and whispers, "I'll call you before the week's out."

I say, "Looking forward to it." I hand him the red pack of cigarettes with his book of matches and heat rushes through me as he touches my fingers with the softness of his own. I watch as he walks to the edge of the ocean and says good-bye to Ernie. I watch, too, as he walks alongside of his brother, Jim, and the only time I take my eyes off him is when I see him climbing the steps to the crowded boardwalk.

I'm holding the black receiver of my telephone and sitting on the edge of my bed with my door closed cause I don't want anybody listening in on my conversation with John, my boyfriend of five months, as I tell him, "I have a newspaper article sitting on my lap and it's saying how the Art Museum has just constructed a Buddhist temple. I'd love to go see it this Sunday?"

He mumbles, "Oh brother!"

"Jooooohhnn! I really wantta go!"

"What do you want to do something like that for? It's a waste of time!"

Once the quiet that falls between us stops buzzing in my ear, I demand, "If you really don't want to go, just tell me. Chris will come with me cause we've been to the museum before and she likes things like this, too."

Twitching sounds come over the phone, then after a short pause, he states, "Huhu! How do you get me to do these things?"

I don't answer cause I don't understand what he's talking about. But all's I do know is that I'm tickled pink he's going with me.

I don't say another word as I listen to his muttering, but I do perk up once he clears his voice and states, "Find out if the museum is open Sunday morning. In the afternoon my aunt's throwing a surprise birthday party for my uncle and I want you to come with me."

"That sounds really nice. I'd love to go." I roll my eyes for the sheer joy of his invitation. I know he must be thinking serious thoughts about me if he's inviting me into his family.

211

John closes the car door of his blue-and-white 1956 convertible Chevy and once we start walking up the Art Museum steps, he reaches for my hand; as our fingers interlace, my body shudders with pure delight and I remind myself this happens every time he touches me. We climb those huge number of steps and as we approach the last one, we wait until we catch our breath before we walk through the massive double doors.

Once in the museum, it's John who approaches the guard standing at the bottom of another massive set of stairs and asks, "Yoooo, buddy! Where's the Buddhist temple in this place?"

Pointing to the fifty or so steps, the guard says in a heavy Italian accent, "Itza on the topa floor."

"Thanks." John takes my hand again and as we start climbing the stairs the guard calls after us, "Youa tuuu, brroootther and seeiister? Eh?"

We look at each other and laugh. John calls back, "We get that all the time. But we're not related at all."

He starts walking ahead of me up the stairs. As I hold onto the white marble banister, I say, "How come people ask us that? Don't they see we're holding hands?"

John laughs again, then shrugs his shoulders like he doesn't understand it either.

Once we're in the darkened room that's the size of a large catering hall, John wraps his arms around me. I shake from the cold feel of his black leather jacket, but as he kisses my lips, my body starts pressing against his chest and I feel the heat of his heart pouring into mine and I soften into his embrace. Remembering where we are, I pull away and take a few steps back as embarrassment washes over me from the sheer thought that there may be others watching. He comes towards me and I hold his arms at bay as I look throughout the temple, even behind the four pillars that are holding larger-than-life-size charcoal-colored Buddhas. Once I see it's only the two of us, I relax my shoulders as I let go of his arms.

John clumsily reaches for the back of my neck and I allow the kiss. But this time, I don't close my eyes and I find myself staring at the black Buddha five feet away. I'm overwhelmed with the reverence of the Buddhist temple, so I turn my face away. In a hurt voice, John whispers, "What's wrong?"

I let go of his arms and say, "It feels creepy making out in a Buddhist temple. It's like making out in church."

I find a black bench near one of the walls where paintings of bamboo trees are hanging, some with birds perched upon their branches, and a serenity comes over me. My eyes adjust to the darkness in the room and I read how these paintings come from an art form that has been going on in China for over 5,000 years. I sit marveling at the paintings' great simplicity. When John sits next to me, I ask, "Remember when you and I went for a walk on the beach and I asked you if you were in college? You said that someday you will go, but not now. Why not now?"

He rests his elbows on his legs, looks at the painting, the one with the sparrow flying off the bamboo branch, and says, "My father had two strokes and lost his very successful factory where making bleach and other household cleaners were the order of the day. Now, I have to help out financially at home." Silence falls around us as John focuses his gaze on a white feather standing in a bowl of sand. Finally he looks at me and with intensity in his eyes, says, "I'll tell you something I've never told anyone. It's been my dream since I was a little kid that someday I'll be a lawyer. Someday I will."

I feel in his words, his voice and in the way his shoulders hunch, the pain of denying who he is for the sake of his family. My eyes fill with tears and I'm overwhelmed by a strong desire to tell him that someday I know he'll become a lawyer cause I know someday I'll become a teacher. Instead I ask, "Did you finish high school?"

He won't look at me, so again I speak, "I couldn't finish high school. I had to go out to work when I turned sixteen because my Mom needed me to help out at home, too."

Swiftly, he turns towards me and says, "I'm sorry to hear that. But I did finish high school."

Feeling great relief cause I see he understands what it means to have to walk away from something you want for the sake of the family, I am overcome by the knowing that one day I will have his children.

John stands, takes my hand and says, "We better get going. I want you to meet my family."

Feeling somewhat nervous knowing that I'm going to be meeting his parents, I ask, "Is Ernie going to be there?"

"Yeah, she is."

I look into this row house that's packed wall to wall with boisterous people and I feel my throat closing like a clam. With his hand extended, John gestures for me to go in first, and after I roll my eyes, I take one small step inside and plaster myself against the parlor wall. John follows me in and nudges my waist to make room for him, and the room falls silent. My face feels like one of Mom's hot flashes and as I see that everyone's staring at me, I wipe my moist top lip; after my shoulders drop, I start staring, too, but at the gray living room rug that's splashed with ugly, large pink flowers. My eyes follow the rug's fringes into the dining room. The smell of a burning cigarette leads me to an older man straddling a dining room chair; his arms are resting on its wooden back and smoke is encircling his round face. As I look at his white socks, his dark trousers, his white shirt with rolled-up sleeves, I feel something pulling at me in some long-forgotten way, but I can't imagine what it possibly could be. I hear a young boy about the age of ten asking me for my jacket and I manage to hand it to him without taking my eyes off this older man with the powerfully dark eyes.

He takes his cigarette from his mouth and, as he holds it between his fingers, the corners of his mouth turn up. In a commanding voice that fills the room, he bellows, "Everybody knows the Pope pulls the President's strings and every time he does, Kennedy dances to his tunes!"

Before he has time to put his cigarette back in his mouth some of the men, but mostly the women, start yelling while others point at him and still others roll their eyes.

But it's this pretty dark-haired woman with fiery eyes who puts one hand on her hip as she yells, "Nick, you can't be serious! You're Catholic too!"

He takes the cigarette out of his mouth and laughs as he blows smoke towards the ceiling. The woman swings her hands every which way and in an operatic voice, shouts, "Hell! Everybody here's Catholic and I don't think anybody would allow the Pope to interfere!" She breathes out of her nose like a wild bull, then she waves her hand as if she's slapping the air. "The Pope would never do any such thing and the President wouldn't listen either!"

I move a few feet further into the parlor and once I get a better view of him, this man in his late forties or early fifties, I can't understand for the life of me how he's not ruffled not even a little by how almost everybody's throwing him some kind of dirty look. I watch as he flicks the ashes off his cigarette and with laughter coming from his throat, he rests his cigarette in the ash tray. "Renee!" he calls in an authoritative voice. "That's why the Pope won't let women become priests. You're all so God damn emotional!"

I look at John hoping he can read my mind cause all's I really want to do is go home where I belong. I know it's not cause I'm not used to everybody yelling at each other, cause I am. It's not cause I'm not used to everybody having very strong opinions on everything that can possibly happen in the world, cause I am. And it's not cause my family doesn't have lots of arguments around world events, cause we do. It's just that I can't take for the life of me how this man with a commanding presence has me shriveled up inside like a scared little kid.

It's clear John isn't reading my mind; he's standing next to his brother, who's sitting on the green velvet chair that's closest to the front door. It's Ernie's Mom who takes notice. She comes over, gives me a kiss on my cheek and after she pushes her dark curls away from her eyes, says, "Don't pay John's Uncle Nick any mind. He likes getting everybody's blood moving." She then turns her back to me and yells, "Nick, cut the shit out! You're scaring people away."

Her words don't budge Nick one bit; he's laughing and laughing. Suddenly he puts on a very serious face. With his right hand making the sign of the cross and in a voice that sounds like a drill sergeant, he roars, "All you young ones, you better get your foot lockers ready cause there's a war brewing in Asia someplace called Viet Nam and you're all going to be called up soon!"

As if I'm not scared enough by this man, now he's got me thinking about Georgie and Johnny being called into the army once they graduate high school.

"Nick, just because you've been in the Second World War and the Korean War, too, and just because you're a colonel in the National Guard doesn't give you the right to be scaring the young ones with your bullshit! Stop it right now!" insists an older woman with light hair and blue eyes as she gives him a clean ash tray.

He starts with a silly grin, then laughs as he throws his hands in the air. "I'm telling you right now, you better all start packing real soon! It won't be long!"

I pull at John's shirt and ask, "Why does your uncle keep saying all these weird things?"

"It's his way of having fun. Just ignore him."

It's as if a light bulb goes on in my head and I laugh as I remember times when I was a little kid and my Dad sat in a chair the same way John's uncle is sitting. I remember, too, how my Dad, with sinister looks in his eyes and laughter in his voice, enjoyed taunting people the same way John's uncle is doing. My eyes are fixed on John's uncle as if for the first time in a very long time, I'm remembering the olive color of my father's skin, his short wavy hair, his mocking eyes, his white shirt, his unbuttoned collar, his commanding presence, his jeering laughter.

I watch in amazement as I catch a glimmer of John's uncle's soft side: a young girl about the age of nine, a pretty young girl with big blue eyes and long dark hair, comes to sit on his lap. She calls him "Dad." I watch as his leg dances with her sitting upon it and I see, too, how his open arms are inviting her into his protective world. My eyes close as I remember my father's inviting arms and secure lap and only cause I find myself swallowing my hot tears, I turn my back to everyone and look out a nearby window. But the outside world won't leave me alone. I feel a tug on my sweater sleeve and as I turn I see Ernie reaching for me. I wrap my arms around her and bury my face in her shoulder and don't stop until the pit in my stomach is gone and my face has a relaxed smile upon it again.

"Mom, I'm telling you right now John's family is a lot of fun and one thing's for sure, they really like to eat. The only thing they don't do like we do is sing and dance. But other than that, the women like to cook and everybody likes to laugh and joke and especially tease each other." It's later that night and I'm sitting at the kitchen table with my mother.

She takes a mouthful of her coffee, and I burst out, "I'm going to marry John someday. It's like I have x-ray eyes cause as clear as anything, I know underneath all his cockiness there's a heart that's as good as gold."

She smiles, then says, "Tell me everything you know about his family."

I take a sip of my milk and say, "John has the same round face as his Mom. But he has his Dad's long legs and piano fingers . . ."

Mom and I, we talk for hours, and before I go to bed, she smiles and says, "They sound like family people. That's good."

It's ten of nine in the morning on this cold day in late March and even though I'm wearing a smile on my face as I say "Good morning" to my boss, Mr. Smith, there isn't anything pleasant going on inside my head.

The simple truth of the matter is I'm sitting on my very high stool at my teller window feeling like a time bomb just went off cause of all the crazy things I'm starting to think about again. But it's Mr. Smith who interrupts my tortuous thoughts by rolling my money drawer into place. He hands me brand new fifty-dollar bills that are wrapped with a white-and-yellow $2,000 band. After I stop quietly sighing, I sit straight, reach for those spanking new bills, and start flipping through them, making sure they're all facing the same way. I remove the band, and start counting, "Half, one. Half, two. Half, three." I place six of those new fifty-dollar bills near my coin machine and as I thumb the rest of the fifties, I go back into my disturbed head.

I'm remembering last night. John was really upset with me. We were sitting in his car and he was saying how he can't stand how I had that faraway look in my eyes, and he swore I didn't hear one word he was saying. I was lying when I acted indignantly by folding my arms as I told him I heard everything he said. But the reason I lied was cause I didn't want to tell him I was thinking about my father's suicide. I'm terrified he'll turn away from me like the people in South Philly did.

I give Mr. Smith another smile as I glance at him; dipping my fingers into the wet sponge, I start pulling at each fifty-dollar bill and counting, "Half, four. Half, five. Half, six. Half, seven. Half . . ."

Mr. Smith gets my attention again, when, with gentleness coming out of his blue eyes, he says, "Roe, you're not yourself today. What gives?"

In a shaking voice, I say, "I'm just tired." I slide off my stool cause I don't want Mr. Smith standing so close to me and again I start thinking about how at first John would try to be nice just like Blind Man Joe tried to be nice. But after he had time to think about it, he'd pick an argument with me like Blind Man Joe did when my brothers and I wanted to pet his German Shepherd dog. But what John really will be screaming about is how he can't stand being around me anymore cause my Dad killed himself.

I go to wet my dry fingers again, but once I take a good look at that dirty old sponge, I say, "Ick" and tap my fingers against my moist tongue, instead. With my fingers moving faster than a card dealer in Las Vegas I start counting fifty-dollar bills again. "Eight. Half, nine. Half, ten."

Inside, I'm screaming in my demented head, *The way it is now John always wants to spend his free time with me. So why ruin a good thing? Once I tell him, he'll start laughing and looking his nose down at me. He'll start saying some mean things like my whole family and I are all off our rockets, all loony, all living in the same nuthouse! Why, he might even start giving me an attitude of his being better than I am and I know for sure that will only make me feel lower than a rat in a sewer!*

With my teeth grinding and my hands sweating, I continue pulling at each one of those new bills and in my head scream, "Half, eleven. Half, twelve. Half, thirteen. Half, fourteen. Half, fifteen. Half, sixteen. Half, seventeen. Half, eighteen. Half, nineteen. Half, twenty."

It's Mr. Smith who taps my shoulder and laughingly says, "It's a good thing they mix in old rags with paper money. That way they don't tear so easily. The way you're handling those new bills, if they weren't, we'd have to send them all back."

Once my face stops feeling like it's on fire, I giggle and give Mr. Smith a big smile.

He says, "That's what I like to see. A big smile. You need to smile more often."

I'm glad when Mr. Smith dashes towards the security guard who's calling him as he stands near the open bank vault. Only cause I don't want the new bills to cling to each other, I mix them in with some of the old bills, then place all of the fifty dollar bills neatly into the money drawer. I sit on my stool again, look out at the people passing by the two very large bank windows and start ruminating . . .

Even if he can see just how awful it is for me to have had my own father kill himself, once he tells his Mom and Dad, they're going to tell him to get as far away from me as possible. And I know it won't really be because they don't like me or anything like that. It'll be because they won't want any nutty grandchildren in their family. And not only that, I might even lose my girlfriend, Ernie. It'll spread like wildfire in his family and she won't want to be friends with me anymore just like my girlfriend Carole didn't. It was Carole's mother who told her to stay away from me and once Ernie's Mom finds out, she'll tell her to get as far away from me as possible, too.

In this raging moment, I take a dollar bill out of the money drawer and after I start snapping it between my fingers, I look at George Washington's picture and in my throbbing head, I cry, "I can't stand how my father's suicide keeps haunting me like a bad dream."

I stop snapping that dirty old bill when my chair gets shaken just a little as Mr. Smith rolls the night deposit table towards my window and, even though he's placing the table alongside of me, I still don't look at him. That's cause I'm listening to what's tossing in my brain, which is how John and I have been dating almost ten months now and the thing we do so much of, which is something I absolutely love, is talk.

Mr. Smith places a bank voucher in front of me and I sign it cause it states I just received $2,000 worth of new fifty-dollar bills. Once he's done distributing the night deposit bags between all six of us tellers, that's when a smile starts to form on my face. I can't help but smile when I think of how John and I can talk for hours on end about this thing or that. And my most absolute, favorite subject I talk to John about is marriage. Now I don't want you getting the wrong idea about me being the one who always brings this subject up, because I only bring it up about half of the time. But if I'm going to be completely honest, if John even hints at this topic, I'm on top of it like icing on a cake.

When it does come up, which is more often than not, we always end the discussion with John saying first, "I'm ready for marriage. I just need the right person to come along."

Then, with my eyes still on him and only cause I don't want him thinking I'm being pushy, I repeat those very same words. But what's always floating around in my head is that the right person is already in my life. And I really believe John feels the same way about me.

I get off the stool as the handles on the clock approach 9:00 AM and once the bank alarm goes off announcing that the bank is open for business, I watch as the guard unlocks the revolving doors. Three customers, a businessman in a suit, a construction worker with a hammer in his tool belt and a housewife with a black wool scarf around her head, hurry in. Since none of them come to my window, I go back into my head and start thinking how it is that John and I love going out on the town. And this Saturday night promises to be one of our hottest dates ever. John's taking me to see the play "Golden Boy" with Sammy Davis, Jr. at the Schubert Theater. But before we're going to the show, he's taking me to the Bellevue Stratford Hotel restaurant for dinner. I love all the attention he's lavishing upon me, and I'm living in pure ecstasy and sheer joy cause of the great love I have for John. It makes me feel as light as a falling rose petal caught in a sweet-smelling summer breeze.

I sit on my stool again and only cause I want to make sure all the bills in my cash drawer are facing the same way, do I start thumbing through the twenty-dollar bills. As I start putting pennies in the change machine, I remind myself of the times when I look at John's lovely face and think that if there was ever anyone I wanted to tell about my Dad's suicide, it's John. And I'm driving myself crazy trying to decide if I should tell him or not. Even in the mornings before I open my eyes, in my scrambled head I'm screaming at myself for how wrong it is not to tell him. He has every right to decide if he wants to have his genes mixed in with mine.

I come out of my head when I hear a baby crying and when I look, I see a young mother holding a fidgety toddler and after she hands me a check, she utters, "Cash please."

I count out fifty dollars, three tens, three fives and five ones, and hand it to the woman. I'm glad to see the offer of a lollipop quiets the little boy and as I watch his mother remove the cellophane from the red lollipop, I resolve to stop torturing myself. I'm going to tell him Saturday night. It's the only decent thing to do.

It's almost midnight and John and I are parked in front of my home. I remind myself that now's the time I promised I was going to tell him about my Dad. My heart starts palpitating as I see the car headlights dim, but a calmness comes over me when I hear coming out of the car radio a song, a simple song called "I Wanna Hold Your Hand." It's sung by some group from England. They call themselves The Beatles, which strikes me as being a very funny name for a band that has four guys in it. I listen to the words of the song and smile, as John, winking, reaches for my hand.

I gently squeeze his hand, too, and a comforting silence passes between us. After I stop sighing, I say, "The play was really good and dinner was excellent."

He smiles and I know it's cause my compliment pleases him and I don't take my eyes off him as he says, "Thanks. I had a good time, too." He stretches his long legs, then leans forward and kisses me. I fight my worries and kiss him, too, so that I may enjoy this delicious moment.

He holds me closer and our kiss becomes more passionate, but once I pull away, with confusion in his eyes, he asks, "What's wrong?"

I look out the car window thinking how I hate that I'm going to take a perfect evening and turn it into a nightmare. I just hate it! I jiggle the door handle and tell myself that maybe I'll jump out of the car, run into my house and barricade myself in my bedroom and never ever come out again.

But I let go of the door handle when John says, "Hey, there you go again! You're a million miles away. What gives?"

I look at John and whisper, "I need a minute."

"I don't understand-what's going on?"

"John, please, I need a minute!"

John wistfully places his soft fingers gently across my cheek and tenderly says, "Roe, I can't stand when you get that faraway look in your eyes. I can't reach you when you're like this. What are you holding back from me? Is there somebody else? Tell me. Is it something I've done?"

I smile. "There's nobody else. And it's not you. It's me."

I look at his relaxed smile and remember all of what we've shared in these past few months and I tell myself that once I tell him, he'll understand. He has a side to him that is so loving, so compassionate, so kind. I can't imagine he'd be anything less than wonderful. And not telling him makes me feel so lost, so lonely.

I look his way again and think if I want my loving him to grow deeper, I have to tell him. Because if I don't, I keep this wall between us. I turn towards him and nervously say, "John. There is something I have to tell you-it's about my father. It's about the way he died."

"What about it?"

"I told you my father died when I was eleven. But-but-but what I didn't tell you was how-how-how he died." I look towards the white front door of my home and in words I've gone over in my head at least a thousand times, I whisper, "My Dad killed himself. He took a knife, plunged it twice as close to his heart as possible, but missing it, he also swallowed DDT."

My hands and feet feel icy cold as I fearfully look to see if I can detect any sign of rejection; perhaps a stiff upper lip, a repulsed glance, or a rigid body stance. Maybe his calling an end to our evening by saying "I'll see you around." I know if I see anything like that I'll get out of this car, run into my house and never come out again as long as I live. But what I see is lots of confusion on John's face and then it's like he remembers I'm here, he looks over at me and once he sees my tearing eyes, tenderness fills his face. He reaches for me and pulls my reluctant body towards him. Giving in to my need to be comforted, I bury my face and quietly cry the tears of almost a decade into the hollow of his embrace.

Sobbing moments pass, then embracing moments and, as if in a dream I dreamt a million times, I hear John say, "How devastating it must have been for you to have your father die that way."

A new flood of tears wash out of my eyes and once I dry them, I moan, "It still hurts so bad."

He keeps his arms around me as he asks, "What drove him to it?"

In a shaking voice I whisper, "He had a nervous breakdown a few months before he did it and had to be hospitalized."

"Lots of people have breakdowns and they don't kill themselves. What does your mother say?"

"She can't talk about it. Sometimes Chris and I might have a sentence or two on it. But that's all. Nobody in the house really ever talks about it."

"Look, Roe, everybody in your family has opinions on everything and there isn't one of you that's shy about expressing what's on your minds. This doesn't make any sense. What the hell gives here?"

"It's too painful . . ."

"From what you've told me about your Dad, this doesn't make any sense," he cuts me off. "He doesn't sound like a man who would leave your mother with twelve children to raise. There's gaping holes in this story like a moth-eaten suit."

Feeling the pressure of needing to give John some kind of an explanation, I say, "It was because he was crazy. Don't you understand? He had a breakdown."

John's turned-up mouth and fiery eyes are telling me he's not buying what I'm saying and I know if I want to be completely honest with myself, I never in my whole life thought that my father was ever that crazy.

I look into his suspicious eyes and say, "Looking back on it all now, it was only a few months before he died when he started lying in bed during the day. But before he got into being sad, the thing he loved doing more than anything else was getting people all riled up. He'd argue about anything. It didn't even matter if he believed it or not. He'd argue with people cause it gave him great pleasure to get their goat."

"Just like Uncle Nick."

"Yeah, he really reminds me a lot of my Dad. And the way your Uncle's so bossy. Well, that's my Dad, too."

I start to laugh, but suddenly turn serious as John says, "There's something here that just doesn't make any sense. What the hell could have driven him to do such a thing? I wantta hear everything you remember about your father."

He gently wraps his arm around my shoulder, hands me his white handkerchief, and as I stare out the car window, I think about the things I've already told John about my father. I push my hair behind my good ear and tell myself there's really no point in repeating how my Dad worked seven days a week and how almost every morning he woke up before the crack of dawn. No point in repeating the stories about the birthday parties we had almost every month, sometimes two in one month. But after he died, those birthday parties stopped. No point in repeating the times my Dad and Uncle George took my three brothers and me in my father's truck filled with trash down to the dumps on Delaware Avenue. And whenever I looked out that truck window at those dumps that looked like hundreds of burning hells, I always shuddered inside. I was totally scared out of my mind even though I pretended to laugh whenever Pat wanted me to get out of the truck and help him look for rats. No point in repeating how in the Christmas season after supper, my father sat in the playroom, reading his newspaper, sipping his coffee, enjoying the large Christmas tree that my older sisters decorated and watched all us kids performing our made-up plays and singing our Christmas songs.

No point in repeating when I was really little how he held me on his lap and gave me bananas to eat and hugged me so tight that I thought he was going to squeeze the life out of me.

No point in repeating times when lightning and thunder were terrifying me, he picked me up and held me and said, "It's the angels bowling."

There's no point in repeating when he came into the house and whistled and all us kids all came running and he'd toss us in the air one at a time. Then he sat on the couch and while we all waited for Mom to finish supper, he let us brush his hair, shine his shoes, buff his nails and all the while, he'd have such a warm smile on his face. No point in repeating how his warm smile not only filled that warm spot in my heart, but even made my heart jump for joy.

And then there were those times, those very special times, when it was just my father and me. But I know I won't repeat telling John those times either cause I don't want to bore him. Times when my Dad and I went for walks together. Times we walked through the neighborhood on our way to his store, and even though I would love to, I won't repeat that one very special story about the time when we walked to the river and watched the ships from foreign lands going up and down the river. And how when my Dad heard the whistle blowing from the foreign ships, he sent my brothers to buy all kinds of breads, cheeses and cold beer. When the newly arriving immigrants passed his store, he welcomed them to America with a shake of hands and a warm smile, he pointed to his produce stand and the spread of food and drink to quench their thirst and satisfy their appetites.

John, he nudges me and I motion with my hand to give me a minute. The memories are rushing by too fast to stop now. I'm remembering how Dad sang love songs to the old ladies. How he teased some of the stingy customers, taunted the old men and sang, "When Irish Eyes Are Smiling." And since I know I've already told John at least a hundred times, I won't repeat how I especially loved listening to Dad whistling his soulful, made-up tunes.

I start to face John and as I rest my hands in his, excitement fills me cause I know I never told John about this one very special time:

A few months before my father died, I think it was the last time when it was just him and me. Life as far as I was concerned was very, very good. It was on an early Sunday morning in February. I remember it was the Sunday before my birthday. My Dad was getting ready to go to the seven o'clock Mass like he had been doing every Sunday since he came home from the hospital. So even though there's a cozy smell of hot coals coming up from the heating vent at the head of my bed, I still manage to pull myself from under those warm covers and jump feet-first out of bed. I reach down to the floor and put my heavy school socks on my cold feet. I put my maroon leggings over my bare legs. Then tie my laces on my brown shoes. Then, quietly, I put my head and arms through my cotton slip, pull my brown velvet dress over my head and quickly button those two buttons in the back.

I walk on my tippee toes into my sisters' bedroom, fly down the steps with one hand holding onto the railing and the other holding onto the wall so that my feet barely touch the steps. I run into the dark dining room and slowly, so the cellar door won't squeak, I open it just enough for me to pull my coat and scarf off the cellar door hook. That's when I hear my Dad limping down those steps, thump, bump, thump, bump, thump, bump, one at a time.

Once I hear the front door opening, I make a mad dash out the door and meet him on the bottom step.

"What do you think you're doing?" he asks.

Wrapping my gloved hand around his cigarette-stained fingers, I say, "I wantta go to Mass with you."

He keeps his unsure eyes on me as he pulls his blue wool hat over his ears and after he buttons the top of his navy peacoat, in a very firm voice, he states, "Aren't you supposed to go to the children's Mass?"

I lie by saying, "Sister said we could go to an earlier Mass if we want to. We just can't go to Masses that are after the children's Mass."

He looks at me with doubting eyes and asks, "Are you sure? You're not just making that up, are you?"

"No, Daddy. It's true. Sister said we could!"

He lets go of his suspicions and we walk down Hoffman Street. He grabs hold of my coat collar as I start slipping and sliding on the icy sidewalks. I start giggling, not only because I can't stand on my own two feet even with my father helping me, but I'm also laughing cause of how happy I am finally having some time alone with my Dad.

As we near the corner at Seventh Street, a howling wind whips around us, blowing me this way and that. I almost stumble again. It's impossible to catch my breathe. Dad motions me into his open peacoat, which swallows my head and protects me from the icy cold. I soon feel great relief cause I'm doing some heavy breathing. I take my head out of his coat when the wind starts dying down. Daddy takes a firm hold of my hand and as we push around the corner, another gust of bone-chilling wind blows and I lose my balance again. It's pretty funny cause Dad's sliding, too. Once I hold onto Mr. Rosenberg's gate, Dad lets go of my hand and starts sliding towards the stop sign. He harnesses his arms around the pole, and when he's standing on his crippled foot, too, he looks at me with a big grin on his face and we both burst out laughing.

Mr. Rosenberg's gate is so icy, I can't hold on long, and soon I'm sliding like an ice skater and yelling lots of "Uuuuuuhhhhh's" as I go zooming right toward the brightly lit bakery and land right on my rear end.

"Hurt?" Dad calls.

"Nope," I say. And we're laughing again, and the wind is blowing, and I hold onto the cellar door handle of the bakery as I pull myself off the ground.

The wind dies down and Daddy limps over to me and gives me a strong hand up.

"Between the wind and the icy ground, it's too dangerous to go to church this morning," he says. "Why don't we go into the bakery instead?"

I look into the bakery window, the one that has creme doughnuts, jelly doughnuts and pineapple cheesecake sitting next to a white cake that has a bride and groom on top. I breathe in the delicious aromas of pound cake, butter cake, chocolate chip cookies, butter cookies all coming at me at one time, and look over at the other window that has more creme doughnuts, cinnamon buns, hot tea biscuits, hot cross buns, and butter cookies. My head is filling with wonderful fantasies of eating everything in these windows even if I blow all the way up like the fat lady in the circus.

"Let's go and buy some doughnuts and cakes. We'll bring them home and your mother will make a pot of coffee for us and she'll make a big pot of hot cocoa for all of you."

Once inside the bakery, I stand next to my Dad and I tell myself I'm so glad Pat ain't here cause if he were, he'd be pushing me away from Daddy by standing in front of me. I put my nose against the glass case, the one that has creme doughnuts in it, and think I want twelve for breakfast, twenty for lunch and fifty for Sunday dinner. I pull on my father's coat sleeve and once I catch his sparkling eye, I point to the creme doughnut, the one that looks pregnant.

That's when he says, "Let her have that creme doughnut third from the front. The one that's filled to the brim with creme."

My eyes get really big when Dad hands it to me and, as I hold it between my gloved fingers, I bite that creme doughnut and as the creme oozes out, I lick it off my gloves. Powdered sugar looks like snow on my coat, and I don't stop eating that doughnut until it's all gone.

After Dad pays the lady in the white uniform, he hands me the smallest white bag, then tells me to open the door. We have to push home against the wind, but we hold on tight to each other's hand and neither of us slips. Not even once. Dad goes straight into the kitchen and I hear him say in a very loud voice to Mom, "Did you know that Rosemary's nun said they're allowed to go to Masses that are earlier than the children's Mass? Rosemary said that's why she could go to Mass with me this morning. We never did make it though. It's too dangerous to be out in that weather."

I hear Mom turning on the spigot and from the way the water sounds as it hits the pot, I know she's making coffee. "All the children must go to the children's Mass. They are not allowed to go to any other Mass," Mom says.

Oh boy, I think as I take off my coat, you're in a mess of trouble now.

"Rosemary! Get on in here!" It's Daddy calling me.

It's like I take forever to walk up those two steps and it's like it takes all day before I'm standing in the kitchen looking at my Dad, who's now looking at me. I look at my Mom, too; she's pouring milk into a very large pot and after she stirs in some Hershey cocoa, she sits next to Daddy and both of them look at me.

"Your mother says that you can only go to the children's Mass. Did you know that?"

I keep my eyes on the floor, and say, "I don't know?"

"Look at me when you speak."

227

I do and to my surprise, he winks. "Sometimes we can get a little mixed up about things we're supposed to do. But I don't think you'll ever get mixed up again about what Mass you're supposed to go to. Right, Rosemary?"

I nod and suddenly I got to pee so badly, I put my hands between my legs, run out of the kitchen. When I'm halfway into the dining room, I know no one's angry in the least cause I hear Dad and Mom laughing like two little kids.

"From all that you've ever told me about your father," John says, breaking my reverie, "I still don't see why he'd did what he did. There's something more here. You once told me that your father had card games at his store. I wonder if that had anything to do with it. Maybe somebody killed him."

It's such a relief to hear him say that. "Ya know, there's something that's haunted me all my life. It's not that I think somebody killed my Dad. But I believe there was some kind of crazy pressure put on him that made him take his own life."

"You know something, don't you?"

"I don't know. Maybe. But it's nothing anyone could prove. But the night he came home from the hospital, a stranger came to see him. I followed my Dad into the playroom and was holding onto his hand the whole time. This man was only there for a few minutes, but before he left, he whispered something into my father's ear. My father didn't wipe that frown off his face until that man showed himself out the door."

"Anything else?"

"I told you how my father had card games on weekends up in the apartment above his store. How us kids weren't allowed to stay at the store when those card games were going on. And we were never allowed to go upstairs to that empty apartment. But the last time I was in my father's store was when my Mom took us there and I went upstairs to see what was there. I saw half-empty wine bottles, empty beer bottles and the air had a stench of stale stogies mixed in with the alcohol smells, too. There were decks of cards, some on the table and some on the sink. But the big surprise came when I was leaving the apartment. That's when I was standing near the stairs in the hallway and I looked into the middle room. I saw phones, lots of black phones.

228

And thinking about it now, I wonder if my father had people up there taking horse bets or numbers or some such thing as that."

"It sure could be. Why else would he have all those phones?"

I put my head down and almost start crying cause it feels so wonderful to finally have somebody in my life who I can trust with my deep dark secret. Somebody who cares enough to want to know everything I know about my father's suicide.

I'm filled with love I have for John, and turning, I reach for him. We kiss passionately, my body melts into his. I softly call his name and our bodies intertwine. His arms caress me, his lips smother mine, and as I place my hand through his shirt touching the bareness of his broad chest, we lay together in each other's embrace and I know it's time to tell him about the day the two men came to see my father at his store. This haunting memory is one of the most painful of all.

Looking into his loving eyes, I whisper, "It was after my Dad was home from the hospital for a few months. I remember the weather was starting to change, maybe it was the end of March, beginning of April. I was standing on the steps of his store when I noticed my father and two men coming down from the upstairs apartment. The one dressed in the gray suit looked familiar to me and when I realized he was the man who came to see my father the night he came out of the hospital, I started to get scared. The other man was wearing a blue suit, but he didn't do anything, just kept looking around as he stood in front of the apartment steps.

"Once my father was in front of his produce stand, the man in the gray suit whispered in my father's ear just like he did that night my Dad came home from the hospital. Then the two men started walking towards center city and my Dad stared after them with this expression I had never seen on his face before. I don't know if it was fear or hate or despondency. Once they crossed Siegel Street, my father looked in the opposite direction and I saw utter terror in his eyes and his hands were shaking."

I cry, but this time, I don't cry for me or any living person. This time I cry for my Dad. I cry for his pain. I cry for his sorrow. I cry for his fear, for his anguish.

I clear my voice, and after I kiss John's cheek, I say, "Once my father realized I was standing on the store step, he got a mean look in his eyes and yelled, *'Get on home!'* Whenever I went to the store after that, he'd yell, *'Get on home!'* I stopped going to the store altogether.

The thing that haunts me the most about all that is how I never told anyone. Sometimes I think maybe if I did, he might still be alive today."

John kisses my eyes as he whispers, "You're not blaming yourself for what happened, are you?"

"I don't think so. I don't know, maybe I do. I have so many mixed feelings. Yeah, who am I kidding. I do blame myself. I just wish I could find a way to forgive myself for not having said anything to my mother."

"Roe, come off it. It wasn't your fault. You were just a little girl. And not only that, I can't imagine your father didn't talk to your mother about this. Don't do this to yourself. I won't allow it. I love you too much," he whispers as he cradles me in his arms. Then he adds, "Maybe you should talk to your mother about it one day."

"Knowing her, I'd have to pry it out of her."

"But from what you've told me, if anyone can do it, you can."

We hold onto each other as if wrapped together in a blanket. After a few moments, I say, "I've always felt very guilty about being so angry at him for his abandoning me. There are times I've even hated him for what he did. Times when I've seen daughters with their Dads and wishing I could love my Dad the way they do. It just feels so awful to be filled with so much rage for someone I love so completely."

"You got to stop being so hard on yourself. The thing is that you all stayed together as a family. Your poor mother. I have such respect for her. How in God's name did you all do it?"

Suddenly I feel more exposed than I've ever felt. I couldn't bear it if John is just pretending to be nice when what he's really feeling is sorry for me. Ignoring his question, I offer him way out. "I guess you want to get away from here as soon as possible. Don't you?"

"What? Why?"

"If this is all too much for you . . ."

His eyes moist, he says, "I can't believe you're saying this to me. You really know how to hurt a guy. If I stay or leave, what your father did has nothing to do with us. Another thing! Why didn't you tell me about this before?"

"You have to realize how horrible it was in South Philly when my father killed himself. We had to move because of it. I was afraid you'd turn away from me like Blind Man Joe did and my best friend, Carole."

His arms reach out to me and he says, "You really think I'm that shallow? Don't you realize there's nothing you could ever tell me that would make me stop loving you."

I look at John's pudgy nose and I remember how it was that my Dad had a pudgy nose. I look into his twinkling eyes and I remember how it was that my Dad had twinkling eyes, too. Warmth fills my being and I bury my cold nose in John's massive chest and breathe deeply into his sensuality. Silence falls again like warm raindrops and I am filled with a very deep sense of relief as I tell myself, "My secret is finally out. No more lies. No more half-truths."

We sit talking and holding and loving each other all night. It's only when the first rays of the morning sun peek over the old ladies' home that I pull myself out of John's embrace and whisper, "The sun's up. I better go in."

John walks me to the front door and once he unlocks it for me, he reaches for my hand and says, "I'm finding it more difficult leaving you at night."

I kiss him first on the forehead, then on his cheek; he wraps his arms around my waist, then kisses me in a most passionate embrace. Once he gently lets go of me, I whisper, "Me, too."

Chapter 28

WHEN THE PHONE on my vanity rings, I glance at my alarm clock. 6 A.M. I can't believe I've been up all night. As I reach for the phone my eyes linger on my white satin wedding gown hanging from the closet door and I am filled with the worries that haven't let me sleep. And it's not just last night. For the last few weeks I've been worrying on and off, questioning the love in my heart for John, and wondering if I really do want to spend my whole life with him. It got so bad I broke out with a rash all over my body. Until I tried to imagine my life without John. Which is when I realized just how empty and lonely my world would be if he wasn't in it.

The rash went away but another worry-more of a heartache-replaced my doubting getting married. And that's wishing my father were here to give me away.

The phone rings again and I pick up the receiver before Carmella, who's sleeping alongside me, wakes up. "Hello," I quietly whisper.

"Hi, honey."

It's John, the love of my life, and I sigh happily and lay my head against my pillow. In a sensual voice, I whisper, "John." The sound of his name echoes throughout my being and brings my worries of the sleepless night to a grinding halt. "I'm glad you called."

"Yeah, I am too."

"Were you able to sleep?"

"Only in between my thinking of you. And when I did sleep, I was dreaming sexy dreams about us."

I laugh and say, "What exactly were you dreaming?"

"I dreamt I was coming home from the printing shop and when I opened the front door, you were standing in the doorway naked. As you ripped my clothes off, I jumped your bones and we had wild passionate sex right on the living room floor."

"I hope you closed the front door."

John laughs, then in a lighthearted way, says, "Did you get much sleep?"

"Not much. The owl that lives in the big old oak tree at the old ladies' home kept hooting the whole night."

Silence follows and the only thing I hear is a faint buzzing from the phone. The silence grows and with it the hauntingly familiar void and heartache I've been fighting all night. Tears well up in my eyes and soon I'm sobbing.

"Roe, what's wrong?"

In between gasps of trying to stop crying, I whisper, "For the past few weeks all's I can think about is my father not being here . . ."

"Ahhhh. Roe, I wish I could be there. I'd hold you and never let go. What can I do to help you feel better?"

His concern makes me smile and I say, "Just listening helps me feel better."

With the wisdom of King Solomon, John says, "Roe, why don't you talk to your father? All's you really need to do is invite him in and I bet he'll come. I just know he will."

"Talk to him? The last time I spoke to my father was at his store, the night he tried to kill himself."

In a upbeat tone, he says, "What did he say?"

"He asked me to kiss him on the cheek and to be good to my Mom. Before I left the store, I looked back at him and with a big smile on his face he waved goodbye." I sob again.

"Roe, Roe, I'm so sorry . . ."

Deafening silence falls between us again and I know John's waiting for me to respond, but I can't. My mind is flooded with the sight of my Dad sitting on his counter next to the register. I can hear the sounds of the freezers' motors. I can smell the piercing odor of oranges sitting in wooden crates next to him. I'm transported back to a time and place never really forgotten, but just now remembered, and I cry for his death, my lonely years without him but mostly because he won't be here to give me away.

I come out of myself when John clears his throat and says, "Ya know, I'm really hurt."

I sit up and ask, "What's wrong? What did I do?"

"You never introduced me to him."

In a cocky tone, I say, "John! I hate to be the one to tell you, but he's dead."

In a firm voice, he says, "I want you to introduce me to him."

I get shocked when I feel eighteen-year-old Carmella kick the back of my leg and moan, "Can't a girl get some sleep around here? Can't you two wait a few more hours, then you can talk to each other for the rest of your lives."

I know John's hearing what Carmella said cause of how silent he is. I make big eyes at Carmella and say, "Sorry, didn't mean to wake you."

She tosses the covers on top of my head and says, "I may as well get up and take a bath before the bathroom traffic jam."

I take the blanket off my head and watch as she stands near the closet and says, "Lucky for you it's your wedding day. Otherwise I'd be furious with the two of you." In a much louder voice, she says, "That's right, John, even you!!"

I listen as John snickers and I wait, too, for Carmella to close the bedroom door. I talk into the phone. "Oh, this is idiotic. I'm not going to do that. Don't you know they'd put us both away if they heard us talking like this."

He laughs and says, "I'm not going to let you off the hook. I want you to introduce me to my future father-in-law."

I laugh. "Ya know, it would have been interesting to see the two of you bucking heads. Lord knows you would have."

With persistence in his voice, he says, "I want you to introduce me to him right now."

Feeling awkward as hell, I swallow hard, take a very deep breath, and say, "All right. You win." I look up at the ceiling and whisper, "Dad, I'd like you to meet my fiance, John. We're getting married today." A feeling of familiar contentment follows as I allow my words to slowly settle in the early-morning air. After a few more moments of quiet, I ask, "Aren't you going to say something?"

John says, "Are you talking to me?"

"Who else would I be talking to?"

"I thought you were still talking to your father."

"I don't believe what you're trying to pull here. You get me talking to my father and now, you won't talk to him."

With embarrassment hidden behind his words, he says, "That's not true. I was waiting for your father to say something first."

"John, just stop the crap and talk."

Swallowing with throaty sounds, he then laughs and says, "Hi, Dad."

The silence between us is strangely comforting as I imagine John and my father talking as they eyeball each other-with John losing the contest.

More silence, then in a voice as warm as a baby's breath, John says, "That was really nice."

My heart fills with feelings of tenderness and, not wanting this moment to end, I say, "Ya know, John, I think you should ask my father for my hand in marriage."

"Roe, let's not get carried away."

"Listen! You got me talking to my Dad. I think it's only fitting that you ask him if it's okay that you marry me."

"I don't believe this."

"What's the matter? Getting cold feet?"

"What if he doesn't like me?"

"He likes you. I can feel it in my bones."

"I don't know how you get me into these things."

"Me get you into these things. For God's sake, you're the one who has me talking to my dead father."

He sighs. "Okaaaaaay! I'll do it!"

I feel closer than ever before to John in this moment of waiting to hear the imagined words that are about to fall between him and my father. I close my eyes and invite love into the very fabric of my existence. A vision is borne as I hear echoing in the ears of my heart, "Dad, I love your daughter and I want to marry her."

I smile as I imagine my father, with squinting eyes and head tilted to one side, staring arrogantly at John. John's forehead is filled with beads of perspiration and anxiously, he wipes them away, then he wipes again. Dad, pleased with himself, laughingly looks my way and, only cause he sees the love I have for John, he clears his throat as he offers John his hand. Briskly, they keep shaking until Dad pulls John towards him and continues welcoming John into the family with a kiss on John's cheek.

I come out of my innermost heart and ask, "What are you thinking about?"

John clears his throat, pauses, then in a dreamy voice, says, "Oh, nothing."

I whisper, "I'm exhausted. I need to get some sleep."

"Oh please, just a few minutes more."

"Okay, but I wonder if it's bad luck to talk on the phone before we see each other at church."

"What in God's name are you talking about?"

"It's bad luck for the groom to see the bride before they marry."

"Do you really believe in that stupid crap?"

"I don't know; I just don't want to take any chances."

"I'll hang up only if you promise that I'll see you in six hours."

Laughing, I say, "A team of wild horses couldn't keep me away. I'll see you in church. The one with the white steeple bell."

"I love you."

"I love you, too, from the bottom of my heart."

I put the receiver down and pull the covers over my head. I feel wonderfully content as I listen to the church steeple chimes ringing "Ave Maria." I fall into a deep sleep like a child cuddled in loving arms.

The bed shakes with Carmella shrieking, "Roe! Roe! It's almost nine-thirty. You don't want to be late for your own wedding, do you?"

She pulls the covers off me, and that's when I grab her by her legs and yank her towards me. She falls on top of me and after a few moments of our play-fighting and giggling, she manages to break away and that's when I sit on the edge of the bed, and begin to sing,

"I'm getting married in the morning.

Ding, dong the bells are gonna chime."

Carmella yells, "Mom! She's up!"

Still singing, I burst out, "Today is November 6, 1965 and in a few hours, I'll be Mrs. Manes!" I fling open the top drawer of my vanity table and pull out my new silky white undergarments and, in the best humor I've been in weeks, I ask, "Do you know where this vanity comes from?"

Carmella rolls her eyes and says, "Oh brother!"

"This beauty of a vanity table comes from the bedroom set that Mommy and Daddy bought when they got married. Look at its carved mahogany wood. Look at its delicate handles! Why, I tell you, Carmella, it's a work of art."

She giggles, then puts both hands on her hips and says, "Yeah! Yeah! Yeah! All's I know is that after today, it becomes mine and for that I am eternally grateful."

I laugh, then sing, "For Pete's sake, get me to the church on . . ."

Carmella screeches, "Please! I can't take you singing this early in the morning."

I ignore her pleas and ask, "Do you know what movie that song is from? 'My Fair Lady.' John took me to see it for my twenty-first birthday just nine months ago."

She shakes her head like she can't believe me, and suddenly a sadness curtains her cockiness. It's as if our eyes are seeing each other for the first time this morning and I know she feels as sad as I do about my leaving. To her, I whisper, "We had some good times in this room, didn't we?"

She sits next to me, places her teary cheek on my shoulder and I gently massage her forearms and think how glad I am that I waited another year to marry. It gave Carmella a chance to graduate from high school. I couldn't bear her having to drop out of high school the way I did.

A few moments pass, then she pulls away and sighs, "Yeah, we sure did." As suddenly as the intimacy between us appeared, it vanishes as Carmella says, "Mom's making breakfast. You better hurry up." We both get up and I follow her downstairs. Once in the kitchen, I recklessly pull the chair out from under the table, sit and mouth off, "Mom, all's I want is a piece of dry toast and a glass of ice-cold milk."

She's standing by the sink washing dishes, and her sad eyes are making every effort not to look my way. In a flash I feel like I'm abandoning ship, but I can't let morbid thoughts like that ruin my wedding day. Especially not when I see standing next to the radiator an incredibly large brown box that has written across it, in big bold black letters, the word "KOTEX."

"Moooooomm! Why do you have this really large Kotex box in the kitchen?"

She turns from the sink and in her sweetest voice possible, she says, "After church some of the people will be here for hours before they go to the reception. I need it for the trash."

"Mom, you can't leave this huge Kotex box in here! It's as big as my bedroom."

Ignoring my pleading words, she begins to fold some new dish towels. "Do you realize my future in-laws will be here today," I plead. "This is so embarrassing. I know why you have that box in here. It's because you want to make sure everybody knows I'm not pregnant! That's what it is. I know it is!"

237

Once folded, she places the last dish towel on top of the others and passing by me like a whirlwind, says, "So what's wrong with that?"

I wait until her hand reaches for the banister and she takes her first step on the stairs before I yell, "Plenty!"

Carmella gestures with her hands. "Roe, you're getting yourself all worked up. Don't do this to yourself. Not on your wedding day."

The absolute absurdity of this large Kotex box standing in the kitchen fills my every crevice and I burst into uncontrollable laughter and scream, "Who brought the box home?"

Carmella smiles before she says, "Our brother John went with his car this morning to the Penn Fruit Supermarket."

"I'm shocked that he did it!"

Carmella's laughing a belly laugh and I see silly Antoinette and snickering Anna looking like two nosy old ladies as they stand in the doorway peering into the kitchen.

At the top of my lungs, I yell, "This has got to go!" I grab the box as I open the back door, then kick, push and shove until this monstrosity topples onto the back porch. With all my might, I slam the kitchen door shut.

A few seconds pass, then a light feeling comes over me and my sense of humor nudges at the dark corners of my heart. I smile and tell myself I can almost see my father sitting at the kitchen table drinking coffee from his beige coffee cup. It's as if he's here and he's making me realize just how foolish I am. I can almost hear his high-pitched laughter ringing in my ears, and I smile as I imagine him doubling over as he's pointing to the back door and the bashed-in Kotex box.

Shaking my head, I look at Carmella and say, smiling myself, "I have to get ready." Stifling a laugh, I walk out of the kitchen without another angry word being spoken.

Once in the sanctuary of my room, I lie across the bed, stare out the window, and allow myself to fall into a twilight of somewhere between here and there; I forget about time until my inner voice nudges me, saying, "You better get ready."

I sit up, give myself a really good body stretch, then stand and reach for my silky slip. That's when I notice a man's faded white handkerchief on the vanity. Leaning, I unfold its corners and my curious eyes get even bigger when I see in its center a pair of pearl earrings. My heart skips a beat. I know these are the earrings Daddy gave Mom. At the top of my lungs, I scream, "Mom, come here! Mom! Mom! I have something to show you! Hurry up."

I jump to my feet as I clip them onto my earlobes. "They look soooooooo beautiful," I croon as I look into the mirror over my vanity.

"What's up?" Mom asks as she comes in, a bit breathless from hurrying up the stairs.

I turn and whisper, "Look, Mom, these are the earrings Daddy gave you. I found them sitting in this old handkerchief next to my slip."

She sits at the edge of the bed and softly says, "Well, what do you know. I've been looking for them."

"You put them here, didn't you? Oh Mom, do you think it would be all right if I wear them today? Huh?"

She smiles, and says, "Yes."

I sit next to her, then run my fingers along the smooth surfaces of the pearl earrings and whisper, "I wish Daddy could be here."

After a few quiet seconds, Mom covers my hands with hers and says, "He is with us. Don't you feel him in this room right now?"

No matter that just a few hours earlier John and I were talking to my father like he was with us, I find myself impatient with my mother and snap, "Stop being silly. Even if he could be here today, why would he? He didn't want to be here ten years ago."

Her head, indeed her shoulders straighten like those of a soldier, and I watch as her hands grow stiff like claws. She stands and in a voice that slashes like a whip, she states, "Youth! You think you have all the answers. Life is black or white. Right or wrong. There is so much that you don't understand. What do you really know about life? You're still wet behind the ears."

With seething anger, I snap back, "I know all I need to know! Sometimes I think I hate him for what he's done to all of us!"

For the first time in my life, she slaps me hard across my face. But her words are far more stinging. "What do you know of your father's pain? You think that since your father was less than perfect, then all of what he was is bad or inadequate. Well, your father was neither perfect or inadequate. He was a man that I loved and still do. I won't have you say anything about him that's ugly."

I stare into her pained eyes and with tremendous guilt, I angrily think, You idiot! Why do you torture her? Hasn't she suffered enough? I'm so ashamed, I can't look at her, much less speak.

After a few moments, she sits beside me on the bed. Gently now, she says, "Why don't you stop hiding behind angry words and admit to yourself just how deeply hurt you are."

My hungry heart cries out, "I don't know how!"

Tenderness comes from her loving eyes as she caresses me and says, "I wish I could wave a magic wand and make everything all right for you. If I could, I'd take away all your suffering and in its place, I'd put only sweet remembrances of the love he has for you. The love he has for all of us. You have no idea how much he loved us. I believe he still does."

"Then why did he do it, Mom?" I ask, clinging to her.

My words hang like a dark cloud. I watch as glances from her suspicious eyes bounce off the four walls. It was the same suspicion that John gave voice to on that very special night when he and I talked till the sun came up. I know it's cause of the love that's between John and me that I have the strength to say, "There's more to the way Daddy died than meets the eye. I don't buy Daddy having a nervous breakdown as the reason why he killed himself. I don't buy Daddy would leave you with twelve children to raise on your own. And to be perfectly honest, I think you know more about this than you're letting on."

She looks at me in a way she's never looked at me before; it's as if I can read what's in them and I know that for the first time she's seeing me as a woman. Yet the silence stands between us until I plead, "Mom, I need to know. Whatever it is. No matter how horrible it is. I don't get why my father killed himself. I just don't get it."

"This is your wedding day. I only want happy talk today."

"Happy talk! That's a joke! I can't even really be happy on my wedding day, because I have this horrible thing that hangs over me. Daddy was the world to me, and I trusted him so completely. When he killed himself, it felt like my heart was ripped out from me."

Caressing my hand, she says, "He never meant to hurt you."

"I know. In my heart I know that but sometimes I can't help think he didn't care about me, not one iota. I hate that sometimes I think he didn't care about any of us. But I don't know what else to think. Because why in God's name would he bring twelve children into this world, then when living got rough for him, he threw all of us aside like a bunch of loose change and bowed out. There are times when I hate myself for feeling this way about him, but I can't help it. You know when Daddy died, I thought when I'd grow up, I'd have it all figured out and the heartache around it would end, but it hasn't. And now because it is my wedding day, the heartache is worse. He's not here to give me away. And I'm only left to think it's because he didn't really care about me."

"You have it all wrong," she says softly, sadly.

Tears stream down my cheeks as I plead, "Then tell me!"

"But . . . I-I-a . . . I real-really don't know . . . I have no proof . . ."

"Proof! Proof of what? That he killed himself?"

Her mouth forms words, but nothing comes out.

"You can't leave me hanging like this!"

She stands, starts pacing and talking more to herself than to me, she says, "I don't know what to do. Not a single one of them understands. Most of them are so angry at him that I can't even mention his name without one of them getting nuts. Why, I even think some of them hate him. And some, ha, they pretend he never even existed . . ."

My heart sinks as I listen to her. I know she's talking about my siblings and me, and I want to say that I don't hate him, but I can't. I want to say that I love him, but I don't say one word. Instead, I continue to watch her in her crazy frenzy, and once she calms down, she catches her breath, and reaches for my hands. I'm taken by surprise at how her embracing touch reveals a desire on her part to unburden herself. I stand, look into her eyes and will her out of her isolation.

"Ha, just think-all these years I guarded our secret as if I was guarding Fort Knox." She lets go of my hands, stands facing the vanity table and goes on to say, her voice softer now. "But I've been afraid that if I said something that your brother Ralph might do something crazy and get himself hurt or maybe even killed. I've been afraid that as the boys grew up they might want to do something, too."

"Do what? What would they do?" Then it's like my mind goes back in time, a time barely remembered, but never really forgotten. And my head fills with horrible memories of those men, those evil men, who came to see my Dad. I remember, too, what John said about my father talking about it to my mother. The truth seems so close, I can't let it vanish back into the silence, and I burst out, "There were these men, awful men! One of them came to see Daddy the night he came home from the hospital. He whispered something into Daddy's ear and whatever he whispered, it wiped the smile off Daddy's face. That same man came to see Daddy again at the store. But that time he was with another man and before he left, he whispered something into Daddy's ear again and I hated that man cause it was him that put the look of fear on Daddy's face."

She grabs at her chest and seeming to be thinking out loud, says, "I wondered if any of the other children might have seen things, too. I can't go on much longer like this. When I promised Browny I'd never tell, I had no idea it would hurt each of you in so many different ways. And God knows, I'm not going to live forever. I don't want this to die with me."

I jump in and say, "You know, Mom, Daddy's been a big part of John and my coming together. John's been the only person who's ever made any attempt to understand. He's the only one who's ever showed me any compassion around Daddy. And not only that, there are times when I look at John and I see Daddy. I hear Daddy in John's laughter. I see Daddy in his wit, in his tenderness, even in how thick-headed he can be. I see Daddy in John's love for me. Mom, I need to know and I need to know today! I need it for me. I need it for whatever life holds for us. I need . . ."

She interrupts me by saying, "I believe there were pressures brought onto your father that none of us knew anything about. I think he was in over his head."

"You mean the gambling?"

Her eyes lift to the ceiling and she says, "That night when I went looking for your father, I saw his bloody footprints on the store floor. When I found him, he was drenched in blood from the stab wounds. I asked him what happened. He said they were after him. He said he couldn't give them the money. He had all these kids to take care of."

My eyes are still looking into hers, but my mind is flooded with memories of the rooms in the apartment above my father's store. The one room with all those phones. The other room where they held weekend card games. The rooms in the empty apartment where we were forbidden to go.

I ask, "Was it ever looked into?"

She sighs. "Your father told the police he did it to himself. If there was anything more to it than that, he didn't want anyone to know. And when your father didn't want something known, that was that."

"But didn't Daddy tell you if he did it to himself or if somebody did it to him? Come on, Mom, you can tell me."

She shakes her head, then says, "You want to know, I'll tell you. The simple truth of the matter is, it doesn't matter how it actually happened, because it was your father's decision to end his life."

"What are you talking about?"

"Your father believed that the only way to protect his family was for him to die."

I scream, "What? Are you saying Daddy died protecting us? Is that what you're saying?"

"Finally, somebody's able to hear. Somebody finally gets it!" she says and, as her eyes fill with tears, she caresses my face. She grips my shoulders with firm hands, kisses both cheeks, then with indignation says, "It just breaks my heart the way some people think of him. All's they know is what they believe he's done wrong in his life. Who are they to judge him? What more could anyone possibly want from him?"

I bury my head in her arms and sob. "In all these years I never once imagined that he gave up his life for me, for all of us." I look into her eyes, eyes that are filled with so much love for him, and I plead, "I've never seen you angry at Daddy. How did you find a way to forgive him? Teach me. Teach me how to forgive him, too."

"There's nothing to forgive."

"I don't understand."

"When you can find it in your heart to forgive yourself for not honoring him as your father, then your heart will heal." She lifts my head and looks lovingly in my confused eyes and whispers, "The most important thing for you to ever remember about your father is how much he loved us, how much he loved you."

I am overwhelmed and confused, and I want to ask her why she never told anyone. But I don't ask because I remember what she promised him. I remember her words about her children's anger and about some who deny him. I remember what she said about her fears around my brothers seeking revenge. I kiss her soft cheek and she reaches for the man's handkerchief that held the earrings. Placing it into my hands she says, "This belonged to your father. Don't you remember how you used to iron his handkerchiefs on your little ironing board?"

I touch its frayed edges and my heart melts as my mind is overwhelmed with memories of his warmth and love. "Whenever I'd hand him his newly ironed handkerchief, he'd pick me up and give me a big bear hug and I'd feel so proud and so loved by him."

A loving silence passes between us and is only broken when I say, "You talk to Daddy all the time, don't you? Does he ever answer?"

She laughs and says, "Yeah, sometimes I think he does."

"Is he here now?"

Speaking more to herself than to me, she whispers, "He is. He is." Mom hastily releases her hold on me and says, "You better hurry. You don't want to be late for your own wedding." She stands and hurries across the room. But as if she suddenly can't walk another step, she leans her small body against the door frame and cries into her clenched hands.

"Mom, what's wrong?"

She doesn't answer.

You insensitive fool. Look what your words have done, I shout at myself. Hurrying to her, I call, "Oh Mom! I'm so sorry!"

But my words are no comfort to her, and as I near, her upright hand tells me to stay put. My temples pulsate as I see tears dropping from her drenched hands; with my nervous fingers, I reach for Daddy's handkerchief and offer it to her. Her fingers tremble as she presses the faded handkerchief against her eyes and years of ignored tears and hushed sobs pour from her.

I reach for her and with my heart filled with deepest respect I say, "Mom, I love you."

This time she doesn't push me away. She allows herself to relax in my arms and I feel the heat of her body penetrating mine. I am honored that she's allowing me to enter her world of suffering.

After a few moments she pulls away, straightens her dress and hands me Daddy's handkerchief. "Are you all right?" I question.

She brushes the front of her dress and staring at the floor, she says, "I'm fine."

I push the loose hairs from her eyes and again whisper, "I love you so much, Mom."

We embrace again, more gently now, less desperately and after a few moments, I laughingly say, "You know Mom, you've never said you loved me. I want you to tell me right now that you do."

She shakes her hands wildly and says, "Now you're being silly."

"I'm not going to let go of you until you tell me."

"Words can come up pretty empty. But actions, they speak louder than words ever could."

"I know you love me. I just need to hear you say it." I tickle her tummy, I tickle her throat and I tickle her back, and once my arms embrace her, I don't let go even though she's gently pushing me away, pretending she wants to be free of me.

After a few moments of giddiness, a quiet seriousness falls between us. With soft tears in her eyes and in a shaking voice, she whispers, "I love you, too."

Her words resonate in my heart, and I tell my questioning hearing not to doubt what I have just heard. I look at her glowing face, and I want to say thank you, Mom, but I can't. I want to teasingly say, that wasn't so hard, was it, Mom, but I don't say that either. Instead, I close my eyes and listen to my expanding heart.

After a few moments the mood changes as Mom anxiously says, "I don't know what's wrong with my mind the last few weeks. I can't remember a thing. I forgot to tell you. I called the florist and ordered one white rose. I asked them to attach it to your white muff. Before Mass begins, I'd like you to take the rose and place it on the altar in memory of your father. Would you do that for me?"

With newfound clarity in my heart, I say, "Yes." Feeling petty for my outburst in the kitchen, I whisper, "Mom, if you really want to put the Kotex box back into the kitchen, it's okay with me."

She blurts out, "It already is."

I shake my head and say, "When you get an idea in your head, there's no stopping you, is there?"

Smiling she leaves without another word.

I look again at the white rose and recall my mother saying that whenever I think of my father to call to mind his love for me. Now, a step away from the altar, I walk up the first of three steps and I find myself thinking back to my earliest memory of my father. I am sitting in the high chair waiting for my Daddy to come home, toss me in the air, then sit me on his lap as he fills the house whistling one of his made-up tunes. It's a memory I haven't thought of in years. And I'm not certain that it ever really happened or all that my father was to me has coalesced into this image that fills my heart to bursting. Once on the top step, I walk to the marble altar, remove the white rose from my muff, kiss its tender petals, then place it on the linen altar cloth. I keep my eyes on that beautiful white rose and Mom's words about me finding a way to forgive myself seep into the dark crevices of my heart. It seems both odd and wonderful that in order for this deep wound to heal, I do not need to find a way to forgive my father, but rather I need to ask for forgiveness. Forgiveness for holding onto all that anger, that hurt, that pain. Forgiveness for forgetting the love he had for me.

I look up at the darkened choir loft and for a split-second, I imagine I see a shadow of my father and I can almost see his loving wink. I can almost hear his whistling tune and see his warm smile. I touch the petals of the white rose and I say to the soul of my father, "I am truly sorry. Thanks for being my Dad."

I step away from the altar and as I walk towards John, I look into my mother's moist eyes and smiling face; her pleasure at my honoring my father on my wedding day feels like both a gift and freedom.

I take a few more steps and, once standing alongside of John, he gives me one of his loving glances, then asks, "What's with the white rose?"

"It's in memory of my Dad."

He smiles a broad smile, then says, "Nice. Really nice."

He proceeds to help me as he lifts my veiling away from my face and, with my eyes still on John, I watch as he lovingly brushes away a warm tear that's slowly running down my cheek. He places his arm around my waist and whispers, "Glad to see a team of wild horses couldn't keep you away."

I laugh as I place my muff onto the red leather chair that's behind me, and I look at John again, and with a silly grin I say, "I'm glad to see you were able to find the church with the white steeple."

Father Garagan says, "All rise."

John's finger touches the white rose and, once his eyes fall upon it, I turn towards the choir loft; what once was a darkened murky loft is filled with the sunshine of the day. I look at John again as Father says, "My dear brothers and sisters, we are gathered hear today to witness John and Rosemary becoming man and wife."

I kneel beside John and our hands intertwine like vines on a tree.

ABOUT THE AUTHOR

Rosemarie Manes holds a Master of Arts degree from LaSalle University. She received the prestigious Certificate of Recognition from Psi Chi's National Honor Society. She presented her research findings at Holy Family University and is considered published. Presently, she is applying for a Doctoral Degree at Eastern Baptist Seminary.

She is married to John and lives in Philadelphia, PA. Their children, Audrey and John, Jr. and their families live nearby.

She is a licensed marriage and family therapist and a certified addictions counselor. Her work with families in private practice taught her love is not always enough to ward off the horrors that can beset a family. She is qualified to write this memoir because she has lived it.

THE DEAFENING SILENCE
A memoir
By
Rosemarie Manes

www.ingramcontent.com/pod-product-compliance
Lightning Source LLC
Chambersburg PA
CBHW030301290526
45785CB00001B/176